I would like to dedicate this book to my family with the hope that they will always know how truly, deeply they are loved.

I wish to thank the following people for their help and support.

Terry Bandemer for giving his time to be interviewed for this book. I want to thank him for his relentless pursuit to find me and bring me home safely to my family.

Dan Ahlquist of the Bureau of Criminal Apprehension for his help in bringing me home.

Darrel Day for taking on this project and writing this book for me. I thank him for his encouragement and patience as we worked through the story together.

I also want to thank my family and friends for their love, support and understanding throughout this entire ordeal.

And to you, Mark, my husband; I thank you for loving me and supporting me and for accepting me as I am, baggage and all.

Last but most certainly not least, I thank God for giving me the strength to endure all that has been my life. I thank him for bringing me through it all and for allowing me to return to my loved ones safely.

Acknowledgements: Todd County Sheriff's Department

Bureau of Criminal Apprehension {BCA}

My family and my friends

Prologue

This is the story of **Connie {Sarff} Nelson**, a woman from Minnesota that was abducted by her estranged husband, James Sarff. She was taken from her apartment by this man and driven, naked and unconscious to Mexico, where she remained his prisoner for 15 days. This story of a lifetime of domestic violence will cover everything from Connie's own story to the trial that finally put this man behind bars.

Genesis 2:18

King James Version (KJV)

And the LORD God said it is not good that the man should be alone; I will make him a help meet for him. And the LORD God caused a deep sleep to fall upon Adam, and he slept: and he took one of his ribs, and closed up the flesh instead thereof; And the rib, which the LORD God had taken from man, made he a woman, and brought her unto the man. And Adam said this is now bone of my bones, and flesh of my flesh: she shall be called Woman, because she was taken out of Man. Therefore shall a man leave his father and his mother, and shall cleave unto his wife: and they shall be one flesh.

1st Corinthians 13:4-8

Love is patient, love is kind. It does not envy, it does not boast, it is not proud. It is not rude, it is not self-seeking, it is not easily angered, and it keeps no record of wrongs. Love does not delight in evil but rejoices with the truth. It always protects, always trusts, always hopes, and always perseveres. _Love never fails._

The Bible called her a help meet and Adam said she and he would be "one flesh." 1st Corinthians speaks of Love as patient and kind; slow to anger without ever keeping record of wrongs. It *always* protects and _never_... does love fail.

Never, it says? Sometimes, life takes turns that we simply do not see coming. We walk through this world in search of that love that we read about somewhere in our childhood. The Cinderella's and Belle's that always have that happy ending, dance through our dreams until one day, we wake and find that our Prince Charming and the Beast... were one and the same.

How does one begin to tell a story that is as old as time and as new as a moment ago? Where do you begin when speaking of a pain and a sorrow that goes beyond the realm of normal? We know that every day life isn't always perfect and that from time to time, bad things happen to good people. We accept that as simply, life. There are losses and times of sadness that touch every life now and then. We adjust our lives to them and then, we move on. Sadness turns to joy and scars of a past sorrow fade away, replaced with new happiness and new skin. Only the one that was hurt remembers where the scars were.

What happens then, when the scars do not heal? When new scars are put on top of old scars, they don't heal...

they simply hide the old. The fairytale becomes the nightmare and the Prince becomes the abuser. The "castle" is transformed in to a dark tower and a prison. The "Princess" is turned back in to "Cinder- Ella"; little more than a slave and a maid, held captive by a man bent on making her life as miserable and painful as his mind imagines.

Life itself becomes a place of horror and of fear, hidden by eyes that see but do not tell. Her heart and body surrender to the life she will now live for the next 30+ years. She will endure unimaginable pain and verbal abuse. She will wonder at times what it is she has done to cause the beatings. Her very life will depend on her ability to evolve from the "help meet" God created her to be; to the "obedient wife" that the man she calls her mate commands her to be. She will do whatever it takes to stay alive and survive his cruel ways. Why? Because she is still human, she is still a woman with dreams and she still wants to live.

If this reads like the synopsis of a suspense thriller; if it looks to be a fiction tale, spun from the mind of some writer of horror and mystery... it is *not*. The story you will read in this novel will take you on a journey into sin and pain that transcends even the most warped imagination.

Statistics and actual events will make you aware that this is much too common as they bring to life the reality that is our world. As you turn each page, you will feel exactly what this woman felt for what seemed like a forever. You will cry and want to reach out and give her comfort. You will find yourself relating and nodding and thinking that this could be you or that it in fact is a mirror of your life.

And in the end, you will see that you are not alone and that there is hope and there is a way to leave your tattered world. The strength and endurance of this woman far exceeds what should ever be asked of any human. Her faith is strong and her love for life, everlasting. She trusts in God and knows that he is with her always.

She is woman, hear her roar? Her roar was silenced many years ago but her fight to live was not! Remember as you read this story that all too often, *fact* is scarier than fiction. What you read is the true story of "the one that got away."

Perhaps we are getting ahead of ourselves here. How do you tell the story of a life that is lived by more than 6 million American females each year? You simply tell it exactly as it happened. From before 1968 to the present day 2013, Connie's story was created by a man she once called her husband. She painfully recalls the fears and pain and the horror that was and is today, a part of her very existence.

She is a survivor and hopes that her words will allow others like her to be survivors also. A story of endurance, love, faith and hope that I was privileged to be allowed to write.

Chapter 1

{Facts and statistics concerning the abused and the abuser}

If it were a simple thing, like pushing a button or turning a key, that told us who is or would be a Domestic Abuser, it would perhaps lower the number of women that are hurt or killed each year by their spouse or partner. Unfortunately, there isn't a manual or cheat sheet to know these things. There are however, sites that are dedicated to helping woman see a little better, some of the traits of an abuser.

Abuse, in nearly every form that it presents itself, is most generally about control. There are things in the abusers life that give off warning signs that they may indeed harm a woman. A simple search for the profile of an abuser will bring you too many great sites that open windows into the personalities of the abuser. Are they always seen by the spouse/partner? Most times, it is the partner that sees it only once the violence begins. In Connie's own words, she tells the same story of not seeing things until it was too late for her.

~~~~~~~~~~

"My best friend had pointed out to me that even while Jim and I were first dating, he always wanted us to do exactly what he wanted to do! It was the start of power and control that I didn't see at all. Perhaps, I was so blinded by our love and wanting to be in love. I can't say that I ever really saw it as him trying to control me back then. In the late sixties, male and female roles were very different from what they are today. Though I do still believe that we live in a very male dominate society, women are doing more untraditional things. Though this may be true, for those that live in and deal with a relationship of power and control... sadly, little has changed."

~~~~~~~~~~

Abuse is often a word we find ourselves whispering or hushing completely. The word all by itself causes our God given senses to somehow suddenly go dormant. Seeing eyes seem to become totally blind. Ears that have heard whispers and secrets being told didn't hear the cries of a woman in pain. Or perhaps, they were not so blind and maybe their ears heard just fine. If that is true, what causes a person to see and hear but not speak out? What hidden fear allows us to know that domestic violence happens far too often, but not reach out a hand to help?

Violence turned on a person that tries to help is common. Sometimes, it turns deadly or the person stepping in to help is hurt in some way. This may be one reason why people can see the hurt and still look away. What is not understood is feared and domestic abuse, for many, is *not* understood and therefore, it is feared and shunned. Because of this very fear, the victims are often left alone to their life as an abused person. Alone, I think, being the opportune word.

. How many women see and feel what Connie did? The numbers are staggering and may seem almost un-real but sadly... they are probably *lower* in actuality than what you will see here. Statistics, gathered from numerous sources, can only reflect the victims of domestic violence that have reported it. Much like a rape victim, the victims of domestic violence often fear retaliation or embarrassment and therefore choose to remain silent. The belief that there is no "safe place" for them, they stay with the abuser for lack of knowing where to turn for help.

Even in coming forward, there is the fear that they will not be believed or that they have somehow brought the abuse on themselves. Alone, for them is sometimes thought to be worse than the abuse. The abused endure the pain and fear at times, because of their children. They, as mothers, want to protect their children from abuse and so again, they stay. A mother's love and instinct places their own safety far below that of their children.

The protection of the children in an abusive home also carries with it merit. Though her reasoning may be more maternal than looking to the future, the mother will do most anything to shield her children from the abuse. The witnessing of violent acts leaves the child, more in males than females, two times more likely to abuse their own children. This alone is reason enough to protect the children from the anguish that is the victim's life.

According to the NCADV, the National Coalition Against Domestic Violence, www.ncadv.org/files/DomesticViolenceFactSheet%28National%29, 1.3 million women are victims of physical abuse by an intimate partner each year. 85 percent of domestic violence victims are women. Nearly one third of female homicides are at the hands of an intimate partner. In 70 to

80 percent of intimate partner homicides, no matter which partner was killed, the man did physically abuse the women before the murder.

The cost of treatment for abused women, both physical and mental is nearly 5.8 billion dollars a year. 4.1 billion dollars of the cost is for direct medical or mental health services. One woman is beaten by her partner every 15 seconds in the United States. One in three will be assaulted by her partner in her lifetime, and an average of three women is killed by their partner everyday in the United States.

About 20 percent of the 1.3 million women abused obtain a civil protection order. About half of those orders were violated by the abuser. Still, they are there to give some sort of comfort and protection for the woman. There are more statistics and you will read about them as this story progresses. The statistics already shown here speak in loud volume as to the number of women that are victimized and yet...

Though the numbers are extremely high and the knowledge that the violence does happen each and every day, they carry the most weight when it is someone you know or it is *you that* is one of those numbers. Connie {Sarff} Nelson is very much one of those numbers. Her story, the life of a woman, who for who 30 + years of her life learned to hide scars, lie to friends and family and simply try to survive, is more than a statistic. The reality of the pain and torture she endured is at times, hard to imagine. A kidney lost and muscles and bones torn and broken; bloodied clothing, a stroke caused by pressure and fear that she might die every time she woke in the morning, were just some of the things this woman faced.

You will read more about statistics and the life of those affected by domestic violence as her story is told. Questions that were asked of Connie, common in their own way, were almost blaming and at times presented to her callously. She had survived a lifetime of beatings only to have her reasoning for staying brought in to question.

The only way to understand why she allowed herself to be the victim of such heinous crimes is to first know the woman. She is a woman, not at all unlike the millions of other women that fill out the population of our planet. She laughs and cries and dreams and she has wants and desires, the same as any other woman. She would not stand out in a crowd but would blend in with any group of women. She walks and talks no differently than her friends and family and no one would look at her and say… "She was a victim of violent abuse."

But, she is also different than other women. There are things that separate her from the "rest" of the crowd. Elements from her past and feelings as she walked through her childhood and teen years that helped to form the person she became. Self-esteem or more honestly, the lack there-of, is most definitely an inward personality trait that brings a wall of separation between one woman and another.

She is not the same as others because her world has been molded by the thoughts and words and actions of those most important to her. Her will to survive and to simply "get along" made her the perfect target for abuse. Whether her abuse has come from physical or mental actions; if it was purposely or totally un-intentional, the effects are still the same. She has become a giver and believes that by doing so, she can avoid confrontations.

Connie Sarff {Nelson}, giver, victim, survivor… is both like and very un-like the millions of women we see every day. She is the daughter and mother and sister and lover that we pass every day. She is un-lucky in the fact that she had to live through all that she did. She is lucky to have ever survived. You need to know her, from her younger days to the present to understand how she could wear so many hats. This is her story of the world she lived in for more years than you might want to believe. Thirty years for Connie, transferred into a lifetime.

Though told in its most accurate form, names of many have been changed or omitted to give those that do not want to be mentioned their privacy and their anonymity. This is her story and life. The words here will take you from meeting the man that would nearly kill her many times over to the trial that finally put him behind bars for far too few years. But first, you need to meet the woman who endured what was a lifetime of beatings and severe pain. She lived through hospital stays and verbal abuse that was as sharp as a knife and as dangerous to her as the man wielding that horrible "weapon." It was a "virtual" knife; one that Connie could not always see but always knew it was near-by. She feared the blade that with the help of the man she loved would through-out their thirty plus years together, slash through her self-esteem until it no longer existed.

This is the story, as real as it gets, about one woman's struggle to stay alive, while being swallowed whole by a violence that changed her life and who she was, forever. Pain, beyond anyone's greatest imagination was her constant companion. She lived a life that too many have lived and that some have died from. She hopes that in reading of her fight to live, others will know they do not need to be alone. It is but one story, a story that women across the globe could insert their name in to and understand her sorrows and fears.

Chapter 2

Who is Connie {Sarff} Nelson?

Connie Jane Oftedahl was born December 19th, 1950. She was a C-section baby and thought to be a hefty baby. She was born into a family of farmers and enjoyed a nice country type life. She was one of two children, her sibling also a girl, born and raised in Minnesota.

"I always thought I had a relatively normal childhood but I guess everyone thinks that. We often have little to base it on and the way we live is what we know. My parents taught me to be nice to people because if you were nice to people, people would be nice to you. In some instances, that statement is probably true. There was one thing that I did not learn, at least not soon enough to save me from a life of torture and pain. I didn't learn that it was alright to stand up for your own self.

I was mom's favorite and enjoyed the time spent in the kitchen with mother. My sister spent most of her time with my dad while I was inside with Mom. I learned from watching my mom and sister, that making mom happy was important to my life and my relationship with her. Punishment was less often and less severe if I just "got along" and did as I was told. That was not anything that any other child didn't learn. Mother was a powerful influence on me, helping to form the woman I grew into. Mother was very vocal and I was very shy. I learned quickly that if you wanted to stay out of trouble, you simply went along with everything that was happening. It was best not to "rock the boat" as some might say.

Life was always much better if I was obedient and it seemed to be easy and completely normal to me. It was the way I approached the relationship I had with Jim. I failed to see the things that he did as the controlling need that he had inside. I viewed his words as normal and was used to a lifestyle of pleasing and making those you loved happy. It came to me seemingly very naturally. No blame or accusations, I just know now that my mother had influenced my future and some of who I would be.

As a teen, I was involved in my school choir, the FHA {Future Homemakers of America}, and I was a cheer leader in my seventh grade year. Like all teenage girls, I had crushes on boys, most of who never knew I liked them. It wasn't alright to be a girl and make the first move. I dreamed of being a hairdresser or a nurse but I also always loved kids. I did a lot of babysitting and worked at one job or another throughout my high school years. I took my driver's training at age 15 and then took the actually driving test at age 16 and passed. That was huge for me and at the same time; it didn't really do much for me. I very rarely got to drive the car as Mom was a worrier. And so once again, the please those you love mind-set came out in me.

I always felt that I couldn't really do anything and somewhere along the road, I lost my courage to even try. I was a people pleaser who never said no. I always put others wants and needs ahead of my own desires. I missed out on so much in life because of not feeling that I had any right to be an individual. I felt like I could never do what I liked or wanted or desired. I felt the loss of my own self-esteem and that was instrumental in how I grew up.

I hated when people were angry, yelling or just pissed off. I took it on myself to just do what was asked of me and maybe, even just a little bit more. Whatever it took to keep the peace at home that is what I had disciplined myself to do. Everyone seemed kinder and my world appeared to be a better place to be.

When defining myself, I would call myself a little shy, friendly, but not one that ever let anyone get too close to me. I always had a best friend and a few that were considered close friends. I was a private person that kept quiet to avoid confrontations. I wasn't Miss popular but at the same time, I was not un-liked. That suited me just fine.

As I moved upwards into Senior high, I noticed boys more, as most girls did at that age. I had my first boyfriend, who was a good person and a great friend. We went out a couple of times, one time that my parents weren't aware of. They caught me and this resulted in my getting grounded from most of the school activities for the rest of the year. Only the activities that my parents decided were pertinent were allowed.

I think my self-esteem was lowered even more at that time. I was escorted to and from my basketball games which left me totally embarrassed and feeling very devastated. My dad wasn't prone to anger very often but I knew that if he was taking me to and from the games, I was in pretty big trouble. I learned then that the consequences for making him mad would be serious.

When it rains it pours they tell me and pour, it did. Shortly after my grounding, I found that my boyfriend had begun to see my best friend. Once again, the devastation caused another setback for me. I had lost a boyfriend and my best friend, all in one single night. Any confidence that I may have gained by having a boyfriend was stripped from me now. The hope of being accepted and to feel a part of something real was gone from me. Once again, it was nothing that had never happened to any other girl, or boy for that matter but it kicked me hard. The name "wallflower" was whispered and that may have been truer than I would have wanted to believe.

After the grounding ended, my life returned to what was somewhat normal. I went into my sophomore year and found school not easy for me at all. It seemed to me that I spent a lot of time on my homework. I struggled to maintain a C average though I did do a bit better in one or two classes.

It was in my 10th grade year that I began to notice a boy that was a junior. He was tall, good looking and he had a cool car. In the sixties, those things seemed not only important but exciting. The boy already had a girlfriend and I found myself envious of her. My low self-esteem kicked in and I remember saying to myself, "What are you thinking, Connie… he is way out of your league and he has a girlfriend." I gave up on thinking about him until I heard he was no longer dating the other girl. Once again, I had some hopes and began to dream again.

I was not fancy dresser but I was always clean and in the sixties, girls always wore skirts and dresses for school. Jeans were not allowed to be worn unless they were worn under the skirt. This was mainly a thing we did because of the cold winters in Minnesota. {My grand-daughters are in awe of such rules against wearing jeans to school}. I had long brown hair which I spent long nights wrapping in soup cans in the hope of getting more curl. The days before curling irons, we did what we had to do to look nice. I remember sprucing myself up in an attempt to attract this young man.

My best friend had eyes on my cousin and that worked out well for me. My cousin was Jim's classmate and they shared some common interests such as farming and basketball. Both of them appeared to be 'girl shy' to me. About the middle of my Jr. Year, we began dating. I had to wait until I was 16 to date and for me that was not until December. It seemed like a lifetime for me then. Our relationship started out very slowly and months went by before he would even hold my hand. I was sure that forever had passed before he kissed me for the first time.

My best friend and I had sleepovers a lot and most of our time was spent talking about our boyfriends. It was in May of '67 that Jim actually asked me to go to the Senior Prom. I was extremely excited to be going to the prom. He was a perfect gentleman and appeared to have good values, leaving me dazzled, to say the least. Prom dress shopping was to be spent looking for a second hand dress. This was my Jr. Prom and therefore I did not need a new dress. I would be allowed to spend more money and pick out my own"new" dress next year for my Sr. prom.

My parents weren't what I would ever call poor. Looking back today, I would say that financially, we were fairly average for our area. We may have even been a little bit above average, though I don't believe my parents saw it that way. We lived about 120 miles from the Twin Cities and I can remember the kids that came from the southern part of the state for school events. We would over hear kids saying things like we either lived on a reservation or for certain had no indoor plumbing, because we lived in the far north of the state. Actually, we were very centrally located but we were still thought of us "northern rednecks." We are a mix of Scandinavian and German decent with just a touch of Polish and Irish tossed in.

But, now we go back to the prom. The day of the prom was exciting because my hair was long and the hair dresser wrapped it and pulled it up from my neck. We didn't go to a tanning booth in those days. Instead, we primped and lotioned and strived to look our very best for the prom and our date. We had a nice sit down dinner and then we coaxed our dates out on to the floor. When a slow dance or romantic song played, the floor was full of couples.

As I mentioned earlier, we lived in central Minnesota in a community of between five and six hundred people. Everyone knew everyone and the jobs mostly consisted of farming of some type. Many milked cows and a usual herd was between twenty and thirty cows. If you are familiar with milk cows, you know they expect to be and have to be milked two times a day. It is a very demanding life and leaves a person feeling very confined. I felt privileged to have been allowed to go and not worry about coming home to any work for a night. When the prom ended, everyone jumped in to cars and we all went to the Drive-In movie. I slept through most of it and my date, Jim, was a perfect gentleman. There was no way that you could have convinced me then that he would be the man I know now. I truly felt like Cinderella at the Ball, especially when he pinned the corsage on my dress.

The next morning, my best friend and my cousin and Jim returned to my house. I don't even remember if we ate breakfast or not. We were all sitting on the couch, dozing in and out of sleep. It was another couple of hours before everyone dispensed.

We dated all summer between my Jr. and Sr. year and in December of 1967, half way through my senior year, Jim asked me to marry him and I said yes. I, myself had still not seen the side of Jim that so many others did. Perhaps I simply didn't want to admit or see what my best friend saw in him. I loved him and wanted to be with him, that is what I knew back then. As far as I could tell, all was well for Jim and me. By this time, my best friend had already been pointing out to me how we always did what Jim wanted to do. I did not see this at all, nor did I view his insistence that we do what he decided as a sign of control. The beginning of that power and control was right in front of me and I failed to see the red flags going up. Love all too often seems to put blinders on us and they block the things that we should see.

By the time we were engaged, he was already half way through his first year of tech school. We dated often but his life was very busy with school and helping on the family farm. I was working for a teacher as well as waitressing, so my life too was busy. In 1968, I graduated from high school. Jim had already been living with me at home since he and his father had argued and had a falling out.

After graduation, like many of my classmates, I ventured to the twin cities. Minneapolis was where I found a job and though my plans were to come back home, that didn't work out. I wanted to return home and start classes at a Tech school myself. I believe that Jim moved back home during this time. I found a job at Gambles, a department store much like our Target today. I worked in the shoe department which wasn't overly exciting but it did pay and I earned money for my schooling. I stayed with a friend and her Aunt while working there. A co-worker of mine invited me to go to a Minnesota Twins game one night, which I of course turned down. I already knew then that Jim would never have accepted that we were simply co-worker friends. Being engaged meant no more fraternizing with male friends. I was right as too how Jim would have reacted to the invite. I told him about the invite I had turned down. He was extremely upset with me and made me feel horrible and guilty for even having considered the invitation. It was not my fault of course as my friend was the one that approached me, not the other way around. Once again, I had missed a warning sign of things to come.

The day after I started my job at Gambles I received a call from the firm of Piper and Jaffery informing me that they had a position for me. That job would have been so much more lucrative for me. I wonder sometimes what my life would have been like if I had accepted the position that day. Perhaps I would not have even been telling you this story. Mother always wanted me to be a beautician and so instead, I went back home and I started at a tech school to be a beautician. Jim visited me a couple of times that summer and I did go home a time or two. He looked for employment while I was away but could never seem to find anything.

On my weekend's home, I found a ride back and forth to the metro with one of Jim's good friends. Even it being his friend, Jim indicated that he really didn't like me riding home with his friend, even though there were always others with us. His lack of trust confused me because I never looked at another man in a wanting way and certainly not his friend. Just another red flag that passed by me, un-noticed.

When autumn came, Jim went to work his second year as a farm mechanic and I went to beauty school. I lived in student housing and Jim lived on the family farm. He was helping his father even though he told me there were a lot of abusive situations there. He said it was family and that is what family did.

I remember back when I was a senior, that I got a call from his mother one Sunday night. She told me that Jim had been kicked by a cow and that he was in the hospital in St. Cloud, Minnesota. My heart truly hurt for him and the buzz around the school was all about his broken leg. My friends and I tried to make arrangements to go see him at the hospital. I remember that I had seen him at school one day with a black eye. I asked him how he had gotten it and he said he had stepped on a broom handle. The handle came up and hit him in the eye. It seemed like a clumsy act and Jim was not clumsy in any way. I believed what he told me though and let it pass. After the leg incident, he did later tell a friend that his leg had been broken in an abusive incident between his father and him. He also admitted that the black eye was from his father.

After these two attacks, I remembered overhearing my grandma and Jim's aunt talking about a lady that was being abused in her home. The lady they were talking about was Jim's mother. Many years later in my life, when I was the abused spouse, I thought to myself, "Why would you not want a life that was different from the abusive life you had grown up in?"

Beauty school had started in September of 1968, a time that today seems like forever ago. I enjoyed being back in school and managed to find a part time job as a waitress at a truck stop. I enjoyed that as it gave me a little spending money. I found that having a job, school and the homework that came with it was extremely demanding on me.

There was to be a formal dance in September and I was very excited about it. I loved dressing up and I loved dancing. I invited Jim of course and he said yes as I was hoping that he would. When the night finally came, a friend and I got ready. We did the hair thing and the make-up and all the prissiness that goes with getting ready for a big date. Her date arrived and they left for the dance. I sat alone and waited and waited for Jim to show up. I was so anxious to go and so I waited for him still. I realized he was not going to show up and I was devastated all over again. Around 10:30 that night, I put my head on my pillow and I cried myself to sleep. How many times was I going to allow this man to do this to me? Cell phones didn't exist in the sixties but I did try to call him. There was no answer of course and that was the end of my formal dance.

A few days after the dance, Jim showed up at my apartment. I wonder now, if I had seen the significance of things that were happening, if I could have avoided another night that he would show up at an apartment I was living in. That was a night that would be the beginning of my horrifying days of being abducted and taken to Mexico.

The night he showed up at my apartment, after the dance, he had to stay outside as it was a 'girls only' housing unit. I went outside and asked why he had not shown up for the dance. His only response was that he had forgotten. He had forgotten? I was so angry and hurt but he was already a master at excuses. I am not really remembering now if I believed him or not but I forgave him and we continued to date. We were after all engaged, I told myself. I felt a responsibility to being engaged and to Jim.

By this point in our relationship, we were very intimate; sexually intimate mostly. I have since learned that there is so much more than just sex in an intimate relationship. It was supposed to be a give and take in a relationship. For Jim and me, it was simply him taking and me giving. School was also beginning to over-whelm me and I was having doubts that being a beautician was really 'my calling.'

Chapter 3

Married... With Children

{Evolving from Verbal to Physical abuse}

Mid October, 1968, was to be another huge turning point in both mine and Jim's life. I was not feeling well nearly every morning and soon, it was bad enough that I began missing school. I was making up excuses as to why I could not attend classes. I can't say that my mother ever sat me down and told me about the birds and the bees. Most of what I had learned about sex and a man and a woman came from my best friend's mother.

She and I sat together one night just to talk. I told her what I had been experiencing in the morning and she said "I think you are pregnant." Just the word alone scared the hell out of me. Oh My God, what was I supposed to do now? I knew I could not tell my parents, for sure. I knew they would be furious with me. Pregnancy before marriage only happened to "bad" girls. That's what I was taught as I grew up and I knew how my "condition" would be viewed by others.

I knew I loved children and caring for them and had even been a Sunday school teacher. I also knew that this was probably not a great time to become a mother. I was eighteen years old, in school and had only a part-time job. I was afraid of what Jim was going to think of it all. Would he tell me to get out of his life? Even if he didn't, how were we or I myself going to take care of a new born baby? The next time he and I were together, I shared the news with him. I waited with fear and anticipation for him to respond to what I had told him. To my delight, he was thrilled that we were going to have a baby. The problem was that we were not married. We needed to be married and neither of us wanted to tell our parents about the baby. We were definitely bonded in so many ways now, including sharing a fear about our future. Carrying, literally, our secret and planning our future was now priority one for us.

Telling our parents was not an option for us. We both agreed on that for sure. We decided to sneak off to South Dakota, thinking the laws concerning age were better than Minnesota. We would simply have to elope and come back as Mr. and Mrs. James Sarff, a name that no longer holds the excitement for me that it did at eighteen. We would tell people that the baby was conceived on our first night as newlyweds. Obviously the math would not have added up but we didn't think about that then.

I remember feeling very alone, even with Jim at my side. I had hoped for a totally different scenario for the beginning of our life together. That hope was diminished the moment I conceived. I was not sad that I was pregnant at all; simply wishing that things had been different for us at the time.

I could already hear my mother's voice, speaking to me when she would learn of the pregnancy. That too, I wished could have been different. My mother and I had been close as I grew up. We seemed to have drifted apart when I had gone off to school. As for my relationship with my father, I think we simply loved each other.

My younger sister, Beverly, had always been "daddy's girl" and I was my mother's girl. Beverly was always the outside kind of girl and spent most of her time with my dad. She was willing to do more things that Dad was interested in and was definitely more of an outdoors person than I was. He never had a son, just two daughters and Beverly was for him, his helper.

I think that part of the reason that mother and I got along well was that I was always the people pleaser, to a fault. I did what I was told, most often without questioning why. Beverly was not that type of person and she and I had totally different personalities. She did question and she did not do what mother told her to do without questioning. This personality conflict caused a non-compliance situation in the home and so it worked out best for all that I was indoors and she was outdoors. I felt that mom and I had grown apart and that I had gone my own separate way. Now, I was left with trying to explain a pregnancy that would not be well received. Once again, I opted for the "don't ask and I won't tell" motto.

All of that aside, here we were; Jim and I were on our way home from South Dakota, pregnant and un-married. My mother's words rang in my ear. "If you play with fire, you are going to get burned" she would say to me." I was not looking forward to the confrontation that was sure to come. We were hoping to get their blessings on our wedding before we told them of the baby. Our original plan was to get married as soon as I turned eighteen. Jim's age was a problem for us also as he had not turned twenty- one yet. Jim figured he could make it happen anyways. After trying to find a way to hide our secret to no avail, we went to our parents. We convinced them that we could live cheaper together than we could apart and that we were both ready to be married. Our parents consented and the planning process for our wedding was under way.

Jim and I were as poor as a church mouse, didn't want people to suspect the pregnancy and opted for a family wedding. Our two best friends would be our witnesses and we would be married in his church. That was a point of contention but of course, to help keep the peace, I once again gave in. The next issue that came up was the fact that Jim did not want our aunts and uncles to come to the wedding. I argued that they were my family and his but he was absolutely adamant that they were not to be invited. We argued one more time and when he turned to leave I told him that if he walked out the door, not to bother coming back again. Testing me, he shrugged, said fine and kept walking.

I wonder now, what would life have been for me. It would have been 100% different but I also know that I would not have had the beautiful children that I have. That would have been a huge loss. Then again, thinking about my relationship with my children today, perhaps all of the children would have been with me today. Thinking about it all really changes nothing today.

The blatant ways he slapped me in the face without ever touching me should have told me all I needed to know about our future. I continually fell for his ways and now, with a child on the way, I was even more easily blinded. I was in love and pregnant and when he continued to walk away, I found myself running after him. I apologized for my words and in an instant, all was good and we were back on track. How many times, I cannot even count, have I thought about how different, how much less painful, my life would have been if I had let him keep walking.

With all that was happening, the wedding day was still set for November 29, 1968. I borrowed a wedding dress from a family member. My best friend wore a royal blue velvet dress as my maid of honor. There were very few flowers and only our very immediate family present, just as Jim wanted. His control over me and everything that touched my life was alive and thriving. I, on the other hand, was totally oblivious to it all.

Just a few days before the wedding, my mother put her thoughts in, as was normal. "You know his father is a mean man to him and his mother. The same could easily happen to you." I, in all of my divine, eighteen years of wisdom responded to her comments with "I am not his mother, he is not his father and that will not happen to me."

I truly had no way of imaging the horror that was waiting for me not very far down the road. I was exactly like a million other women that believed that their partner was incapable of hurting them. He loved me and that was all that needed said. There wasn't a shed of fear within me that I would one day be abused by the man I was going to marry. Even if it were possible, I would never allow that to happen to me. Funny, looking back today, I was already taking responsibility for the happiness in our relationship.

The very belief that I could stop the abusive behavior that was to become my constant companion said so.

In spite of my mother's warning, the wedding went on as planned. On November 29, 1968, in a time era that abuse was still a hushed word, I married the man I loved. Surrounded by brothers and sisters and our parents, the only "outside" people being our best friends Dan and Sherry, I never took the time to realize that Jim had controlled the wedding from the beginning. After the wedding, we went to my parent's house for an informal reception. We had cake and coffee and this was absolutely not the wedding day I had dreamed of but, it was our wedding.

Later that evening, we left my parents house to return to our home in Wadena. We had rented the house earlier in '68. During the drive to the house, it was lightly snowing. It was one of those snows that you see in the movies. The snow was falling gently and the sky was perfectly lit so that the scene was as romantic as one would ever dream of. Wedded bliss was all around us as we drove. The beautiful scenario was disturbed only once when a train showed up out of no-where. We were nearly struck by the train on our way home. Though it rattled us a little, the wedding happiness and the wonderful feelings that come with it had not been disrupted. We spent that first night doing what every newlywed does on their wedding night. This man was gentle and he was never going to hurt me. I could not have been more wrong.

I left school shortly after we were married. Morning sickness was taking its toll on me, filling nearly all of my day. My mother was very unhappy with my decision to leave school. The truth was that I was married, pregnant and working. I could work the afternoon and the evening shifts at the truck stop if I quit school. I continued to work as a waitress and we began preparing for our first child. We needed the income to help pay for rent and gas and food. Even at a dollar a gallon, wages were lower and therefore the gas was just as much a burden on a budget as it is today. I was thankful for the tips I was getting from work.

The idea of marriage, being on my own, or at least independent from my mother and father, was so very exciting. Both Jim and I were anxiously awaiting the arrival of our first born. Life was good then and we were a typical, struggling to make ends meet young couple, trying to get our lives started. We rarely argued and as I am even today, I was easy to please and respectful of other's right to be their own person. The man that I saw in the very early moments of our marriage was not the monster that beat and tortured and locked me inside of grain bins. At that place in my life, I would have told anyone that was worried for me that their fears were totally unfounded.

Were there signs of abuse that should have been seen? Was the need for Jim to control everything about me and our life evident in those first dawning hours of our life together? It was, without a doubt. The problem was that I either passed it off as "no big deal" or I was still wearing the blinders that often come with being in love. Looking back does little good and it certainly does not, nor will it ever take away the pain and memory of all that Jim did to me.

Still, I do look back and I do remember and I tell you this story in hopes that someone else will not have to suffer the way that I suffered. The want to reach out, perhaps even more, the need to do so, serves a dual purpose. To finally tell my story and find even a small measure of relief in doing so, may be something inside of me that has needed to be found for a very long time. Skeletons that have hung in the family closet, demons that have haunted my dreams, need to be released. Secondly, this story will show others that you *can survive* and that there is hope and even life after an abusive relationship. If it rescues even one partner from a life of fear, hatred and scars, then I have accomplished what I have set out to do.

~~~~~~~~~~

{In the years that Connie and Jim were together, there was only a brief time, shortly into their marriage that he was not abusive to her. The physical abuse did not come until they had been married for a few years. The verbal abuse and the rage came very early in their marriage. This is her recollection of the incident.}

~~~~~~~~~~

The first time I noticed any true aggressiveness from Jim was shortly after we had been married. It was in December of '68. It was the first time I had felt insecure or unsafe with Jim. We were driving to our home in Wadena, Minnesota. Jim had picked me up from work and we were going up our quarter mile driveway. Our car slipped off of the driveway and went in to a ditch. He tried to back it out and then tried going forward. Nothing was working for him. He opened the car door and told me to slide over in to the driver's seat. He was going to try and push the car while I was steering. The car was a stick-shift and at that time, I was unfamiliar with how to operate a car like that. I was only familiar with automatic transmissions. I was worried because I had never had any experience at all with the stick-shift. This of course goes back to the fact that I was very much a house girl and had not been taught to drive the different types of cars that were out there. I was very uncomfortable with the position I had just been placed in.

As we worked to get the vehicle free of the snow, I could see that Jim was visibly becoming more and more frustrated. When he first asked me to move to the driver's side I said "no, I can't do this." The fear of doing something wrong and making matters worse was so strong inside of me. I suggested that we walk up to the building site to find something that might help us get the vehicle free. The house that we rented was a second house on a farmstead. The people in the other house were our landlords and were very kind people. I knew that they had a tractor and would be able to pull us out of the ditch. Jim refused and I am not even sure how we did get out of the ditch that day.

What I do remember is that for the very first time since I had been with Jim, I found myself afraid of more than just the Minnesota winters we were facing together. The straight stick driving and the things that I had always perceived as dangerous predicaments had taken a back seat to the fear I now carried with me. I felt myself fearing my new husband as he got in my face and hollered and screamed and swore at me. His demanding that I do exactly what had been asked of me scared the hell out of me. I was unaccustomed to such verbal abuse and his body language caused me to wonder who this man was. He showed no regard and could have cared less about my fears or my feelings, inside or outside. Outwardly I cried but inside, where Jim could not see, I felt afraid and very threatened. This was something that I had never experienced in my life. The intensity of his rage was like nothing I had seen from anyone. I wasn't sure how to respond or how I was supposed to feel. Fighting back and arguing was never a way that I dealt with anything. My gut instinct was telling me this was not a good time to decide to be aggressive.

We lived at the house where the first incident took place for about four months before moving to his family's farm. Finances had become stressed for us and we were left no choice but to stay with his family. We lived in an upstairs room where our privacy was very limited. Jim was still going to school and I was getting bigger and bigger with my pregnancy progressing along. We had only one vehicle and so it became necessary for me to quit my job completely. I helped out at the house and around the farm. We were only there for a short time and after a family argument ensued, we left.

We had to move in with my family and stayed with them for about six weeks. I was still expecting our first son in June. Jim had gone to mechanics school and he had graduated and got a job as a mechanic at Green Giant in Glencoe, Minnesota. I stayed behind at my parent's house as my Doctor was nearby. Jim continued to work in Glencoe, staying there during the week and coming home on his days off. By the end of May, I was very uncomfortable and ready for the baby to come.

Our best friends from high school were getting married and asked Jim and I to be their maid of honor and Best man. Their wedding was on the fourteenth of June and we asked them to have standby's as I was due only days from that date. I missed Jim terribly while he worked away but I knew that it was the best way for us at the time. I didn't want to move to him in Glencoe because the due date was so close and my doctor was where I was.

Finally the day came and our first son was born on the 14th of June. We contacted Jim to let him know we were going to the hospital and that he should come home. Jim was excited and came home right away. He arrived in the very wee hours of the morning but I didn't mind. I wanted him to be there for the arrival of our son. We were exhausted and thrilled with our first child. Jim was very happy and he was proud to have a son to carry on the family name. Our best friend's wedding went on without us obviously and after 40 years, they remain together. Their lives definitely took a different avenue than did Jim and mine.

Five days after our son was born, we made our first trip as a family to Glencoe. I was excited to start our life together, in one home with Jim, me and our precious baby. I would join Jim to stay and live in Glencoe only a month after our son was born. How very exciting it was for us to have our own home and to be making our own plans for our future. I was very happy at that time in my life. We purchased a mobile home there and I had a couple of part time jobs and also worked at Green Giant for a short period of time. In the '60's, a lot of young couples lived in mobile homes as they were affordable. We had a two bedroom which was perfect for us. We were comfortable and content even with some financial issues. We struggled to make a living and though prices were less than today, the wages also were low, making life a challenge for us.

Jim's job kept him busy most of the time in the spring and summer months. His job was to keep all of the machinery running to plant and harvest the crops. It was, for the most part, corn and peas that was planted. He seemed at first to really enjoy his job. He made some friendships with his co-workers and was given a company truck to drive. While Jim worked long hours at the plant, I kept active doing chores and being a mom. I loved the life and spent my days mowing and cleaning and taking care of our baby boy. I was completely enjoying and loving being a mom.

I recall after leaving Jim's parents farm, how I would wonder why we were so estranged from his family. It wasn't just his parents that we didn't see. We stopped seeing his entire family, totally. I questioned Jim about why his family had virtually nothing to do with us at all. I knew that there was bad blood between Jim and his parents, which was just a fact. His siblings however were adults and could decide on their own who they saw and who they did not see. They were away from Jim's parents and all had their own homes and lives. There was absolutely no communication between Jim and his siblings at all. It hurt me that none of them had taken the time to come see our new home or our baby boy. In my family, it was almost a tradition to visit after someone had a new baby in their home. It was just odd to me that only my parents and sister had come to visit us. I was grateful for that as it was the only family connection that we had. I was never given an answer to my question.

Only a few months after our move to Glencoe, I found that I was pregnant again. Our relationship was having some minor ups and downs at that time but I felt that was normal for any couple just getting started in the lives. For the most part, Jim and I were doing well. Eleven months after our first child was born, in May of 1970, I gave birth to our first daughter. She was beautiful and our son was fascinated with the new addition to the home. We were very fortunate to have good natured and happy babies. It was fun for me to look at the little girl dresses and I even sewed some of their clothes myself. I loved the kids and I loved being a mother.

I can remember growing up and teaching Sunday school and I did a lot of babysitting. I really wanted to be a something special, but mostly, I just wanted to be a mom. At one point I thought about being a nurse and of course, there was the hairdresser that my mother wanted me to be. I didn't know how to say "I just want to be a mom." The teens in school and people I knew thought it strange that my one desire was to have children. Perhaps it was different but it was where I had always been.

When our daughter was only a few months old, I took our car to the store one morning. This was not just any car; it was a nice 1969 GTO. We had car seats then but they were much different from the car seats today. They were a new concept then and not everyone had them. I strapped the kids in to their seats and headed down the road. To get to town, I had to turn on to a State highway that went through our town. I pulled up to the stop sign, looked both ways and proceeded onto the highway. I had just gotten in to the lane and felt a startling jolt. Our daughter's seat flipped to the floor and I had to struggle to maintain control of the vehicle. I eased the car off to the side of the road to check my daughter. She was unharmed, other than being scared and crying.

As I shut the car off and got out, I realized I had been rear ended hard. A young man had come around a curve at a high rate of speed and couldn't stop in time to avoid hitting me. I was concerned for him but saw him get out of his car and ask me if the kids and I were alright. I asked the same question and he said he was fine. The police arrived and questions were asked. A tow truck was called as were accident reconstruction materials. It wasn't until everything was handled and I knew that both kids were alright that I began to think about Jim. I wondered what his reaction was going to be when he found out about the accident. Not only had the accident itself worried me but the fact that the GTO was smashed up badly bothered me terribly. Jim had always been a car man and he loved to race them and work on them any time he could. He especially loved Chevy's but this GTO was his baby.

I knew he wasn't going to be very happy when he saw what had happened to the car. I was most certainly no more happy about the accident than he was going to be; or at least that is what I thought. Accident or not, he was absolutely livid when he heard and saw what had happened. He did have a few moments of worry that we were all alright but that quickly passed for him. His main focus and concern was really all about that GTO. For the first time since the car in the ditch incident, I felt very uncomfortable and weary of what was going to come after he started yelling. That fear that I had felt before crept up on me and I was waiting for the slap or kick to come. I realized that I was actually fearful of my own husband.

He started out by yelling at me as his anger rose, telling me I should not have driven the car because I did not know what I was doing. He told me I was unsafe and that I could have killed the children. I already felt like shit for what had happened and yet, he found a way to make me feel even worse. I was terribly hurt but not because of the accident nor because of the fact that I might have hurt the kids. Those things were important to me and I knew he was right but there was something more to my pain. Suddenly, I was back to being stupid and careless and not intelligent enough to even drive a car.

When your self-esteem is already a wreck, it doesn't take much to kick you further in to that feeling of not being worthy of anything. To feel as if you have nothing to give or as if anything you try will end in failure is a horrible feeling. It leaves you afraid to even put one foot in front of the other for fear that you are going to trip. Here I was, married with a house of my own and babies to love and somehow, at that moment, it didn't mean a lot. I was waiting for Jim to ground me like my parents would have when I was in high school. I felt like his child instead of his wife. There was no "equal" about him and me. The yelling finally stopped and we went on again, as if nothing had happened. Deep inside of me, no matter how he was, I knew he had not forgotten the accident; and nor were we finished with it.

After a few days of walking on eggshells around the house, things seemed to be getting back to normal. I was relieved that there was no violence after the incident. I received a ticket in the mail charging me with careless driving. This meant that I would have to go to a court appearance and would be fined. I knew that this was not going to make Jim happy in any way. As soon as he saw the ticket, he became instantly pissed at me. He informed me that I was on my own and that I had better find a way to pay the fine. As if I were a child, he told me; more accurately screamed at me that he was not going to pay the fine. I needed to learn how to be more responsible for my actions. I needed to be accountable for the stupid things I did in life.

I look back on that moment and so many more and it almost makes me cry again. Where was my supportive husband when I needed him the most? Where was the man that swore to love me and stand by me for the rest of our lives? I had no issues paying the fine, although I would need to find some work and pay for daycare also. I simply wondered why he could not have shown me just a tiny amount of compassion. What would have been so damned difficult about acting as if he loved me and wanted to support me as a husband should.

The car incident moved me in to a different place inside. It was a place where I felt very alone and scared. There was a new awareness of my husband and the father of our children. I knew now that there was no safety net for me. Mistakes were not going to be acceptable and Jim would tolerate nothing but perfection from me. I felt I had always taken responsibility for my action. I was mature sometimes beyond my years. Life had taught me to grow up quicker than I should have needed to. Why then, was I sitting there feeling worthless and stupid? Why couldn't my husband offer me some sort of touch or words that would make me feel confident and capable? A marriage was supposed to be both people working together and walking with one another through life's ups and downs. That was certainly not true of Jim and my relationship.

I did find a job at Green Giant as it was harvest season then. They needed line workers in the factory and that gave me an easy in for a job. Other than babysitting and housework, I had absolutely zero experience out in the real world. The hours were very long and the work was less than pleasant for me but I did my best to get through each and every day. I did find a high school girl to watch the kids while I was working. The job wasn't a bad one, it was just very messy. I came home every day covered in corn juice and sticky from my head to my toes. I left work every day, went to pick the kids up and then drove home to prepare supper.

More demands were being put on me all the time. Supper time was an absolute for me. Jim wanted his supper hot and ready when he walked through the door at night. He did not want his dinner to be late, ever. The job only lasted for two weeks as the constant moving of the conveyor belt made me sick and dizzy. The money I earned working there did not cover the cost of the ticket. Paying the babysitter and other expenses left me with little to no money at all. Jim still refused to help me with the cost and so I found another job. I got lucky and found a waitressing job at a café. It was a twenty-four hour restaurant/truck stop in town. To save money and not have to pay for daycare, I took the night shift that was eleven at night until seven in the morning. Jim was with the children most of the time while I worked and that did help me. I did finally earn enough to pay off my fine.

That Fall, on one of my days off, I was home taking care of the kids and there was a knock on the door. As I went to see who was knocking on the door, I looked out to the street to see if there was a car and to see who might be stopping by our house. I was completely surprised when I opened the door and saw who it was. This was during the time between us moving again, while Jim was still working at Green Giant.

Jim's sisters, who I had not seen in a forever, had decided to come visit me. I invited them in but as I made the invitation, I felt a terrible sense of panic come over me. The family was not connected in any way anymore but they knew we had a new baby in the house. As we made small talk, the sisters played with the babies as any aunt would.

We talked about the family separation and all decided that it was crazy and un-needed. They wanted to take some pictures of the children that they could take back with them and show other family members. For a moment, I didn't answer them. I was afraid and was telling myself that this was not a good idea. I wanted some say and some control in the house and so I told them yes.

The family I was raised in was so completely opposite of Jim's family. We, referring to my own family, were always together and shared our lives with one another. We didn't always spend a lot of family time together but the knowledge that they were always there if we needed them, was a comfort to me. It bothered me that my children didn't know their own aunts and that their aunts did not know them. There just seemed to be something wrong with that whole picture. Jim's sisters didn't stay very long and I thought it strange that they did not want to see Jim. It seemed like a long ways to come and then miss seeing your own brother. They took pictures of the kids and left.

That night, Jim came home and I told him about the visit from his sisters. I also told him that it might be time to make amends with his family and start associating with them again. He instantly became furious with me that I had allowed them to take pictures. He tossed his dinner into the sink, scaring the kids and then turned back to look at me. The look in his eyes told me exactly how huge a mistake I had made. He told me that I was going to walk to Minneapolis and get the pictures back. He said he did not care how long it took me to get there and he didn't really care if I made it back home. That was his remedy to the situation. He told me he did not want them to have the pictures and he did not want his parents to see the pictures. He said that I had no right to allow them into his home... not "our" home, and that allowing them to take pictures was not my call to make. I told him that I could not walk to Minneapolis and that I had children to care for. Now, for the first time in our marriage, which was only two and a half years old, the arguing escalated to the point of physical abuse.

He told me to go to our bedroom and once again I was little more than some child to him. I was so scared that my entire body was trembling. I was back to the feeling of the movie, when the girl walks in to a room and some creature or madman jumps out and begins to beat her. This was my world, minus the director and cameras. He followed me in to the room and began to physically attack me. He punched me in the face and gave me a black eye. That was the first time I had experienced the physical side of abuse. Our children were out in the other room listening to Jim scream and beat me. They could hear my cries and hear their father viciously attacking their mother.

Looking back, I can see the abuse and the controlling features of our relationship. He dictated to me exactly what his expectations were. He insisted that his dinner was to always be ready and on the table when he walked through the door. That was only a very minuet part of his controlling demons. I was to have the kids cleaned up before he got home. We had no social life at all so everything revolved around the home and what Jim wanted.

It was fairly quiet in the home after that first beating. The only real words spoken between us were in regards to caring for the children. He did not make me walk to Minneapolis but in hind sight, that may have been the safest and smartest walk I could have taken. I often wonder if I had taken that walk, would I have come back at all. Had I left then and sent for the kids, would my life have been filled with more smiles and less bruises and broken bones. That is a question that I can never answer but it still exists inside my soul.

I had developed a friendship with the young mom across the street from us. I went to meet her for coffee the morning after the attack. I was hoping that I would not have to explain the marks on me. I trusted her and she and I were good friends but I was way wrong as far as the bruises and the black eye. She immediately asked me what had happened and I told her the truth. I didn't make up an excuse or tell her a lie and that felt great. Her response to me was "did you call the cops on him?" My eyes must have gotten huge when she said that if you can have huge eyes when they are swollen and black and blue. My response was of course, "No, no way!" I would never have even thought of calling the police on Jim. She disagreed with my decision not to call the cops but respected my wishes and left it at that.

I went back to questioning Jim's love for me. Though the eye did heal, I don't think that my heart ever did again. Asking myself over and over how a man that claimed to love me so much, could ever do these things to me and not feel any remorse. Never did Jim walk over to me and say he was sorry for inflicting the kind of pain that he did on my body. I was terrified inside and wasn't even sure how to go on with life.

In a short time, maybe a few weeks, the healing was done and all was back to normal for a little while. We were speaking and laughing again. I quit my job and went back to being a full time mom. That was exactly all I really wanted from my life. I loved taking the kids for walks or rides in the stroller up our road. We went to church and I loved dressing the kids up for that. We were a church going family and loved God even if the things that were happening in our home were not very God like. Perhaps I didn't realize it then, but I believe that I truly treasured my relationship with God. I don't think that I knew how vital that relationship was going to be to my survival in the future.

Like all couples, we had our fun times. I will not say that at no time in our marriage did I smile and laugh. That would be telling you a lie. Occasionally, we would take a couple of days off and we would go to my parent's house to visit. This was before I was forbidden to see my family, of course. The children loved Grandma and Grandpa and they were the apple of my parent's eyes. The kids were well behaved and I am sure that sense I had of being good and pleasing and avoiding discipline was a part of them.

Because they heard the fighting and the violence that was part of my life and theirs, they were more well behaved then other kids of that age. As the years passed and the kids got older, they knew when to talk and when they should be quiet. They could sense the tension and I am certain that from time to time, they felt insecure and unsafe, just as I did. We all knew to keep fears and our secrets to our selves. I think of the words that have been spoken since the Abduction and it makes me cry. The denial that is ever a part of my children's lives astonishes me as much as it hurts me deep inside. They will, I am sure, never know how torn up my heart really is.

Chapter 4

{Physical abuse, hospitals and more physical abuse}

In the early '70's, Green Giant mechanic workers began talking about forming a Union in the shop. Jim became very involved with the plan. It was also the start of more abuse that would escalate into injuries I had not ever imagined. Life was taking so many turns for us and I found that I was still very afraid of my own husband.

After our second child was born, I was done working. We lived in Glencoe for about five years. We then moved to Eagle Bend where in 1971, our third child was born. We were both happy about the pregnancy but our plate was already so full. Jim was buying farm equipment and showing an ever increasing interest in becoming a farmer. In '71, we had rented a farm site in the country, just a few miles from Glencoe and moved our growing family to the country. Jim rented some land a few miles from our home and began farming it. His plan was to do well enough to be able to leave Green Giant and become his own boss. Jim wanted to answer to no one and do what he wanted to do, when he wanted to do it. I went along with his ideas because they seem to make him happy.

We began dreaming about owning our own farm someday, perhaps we thought, back in Eagle Bend. Land prices were much lower there than the $1200.00 dollars an acre in Glencoe. Our third child, a daughter, was born in September of '71 and we were now the proud parents of three great kids. At that time, we were still estranged from Jim's family.

During this same time frame, we had bought some Holstein cows for milking. Taking care of the cows and anything to do with the animals, including the milking was now, for the most part, left up to me to take care of. That responsibility, along with caring for the children and anything he deemed "my job", fell on me. I was about half afraid of the milk cows at first as I had never lived on a dairy farm in my life. My dad had a few cows when my sister and I were growing up but they were only for our own use for milk. My father had a full time job with the road maintenance department in the county that we lived in.

In those days, we had seven to ten cows to milk and all of the milk was stored. We put the milk in large cans which it was up to me to move. They were ten gallon cans and the cans were quite heavy no matter when they needed to be moved. I would do the milking, load the cans and the kids into the vehicle and then drive to town. The milk cans were delivered to the local creamery. We were very busy between the kids, the job, milking and farming the land. We did enjoy the country life as the kids had room to run and play and Jim and I had some privacy too. We were after-all, country people and loved that kind of living. These times were moments I at least could look back on and not shudder in fear.

There was nothing easy about a farmer's life and there were a lot of demands of our time. It was extremely physical and time consuming and we were seldom able to just pick up and go anywhere. My family was very good about coming to see us at the farm, including my sister. They came to visit us as often as they could find time to do so. I did find myself very isolated except for my trips to the creamery each day. At that time, I think I was mostly alright with the seclusion as we had a great deal to keep us busy. Jim seemed to be very content with where we were at in life. That was a good thing for me and the children. As long as life was moving along smoothly and Jim didn't have any interruptions in what "he" felt was important, my life, the children's lives and our home, were a better place to be.

As hard as I tried, I simply wasn't able to keep our life that way for very long. Life, Mother Nature and just the air that I breathed seemed to be conspiring against me at every corner. The "bound to happen" elements of farming would be waiting to come along. Jim would be in the fields about four miles from our home and run out of gas, break down or get stuck. He would have to walk back to the farm from the fields. This was never a good thing for me. Many times I would be present when the fuel ran out. I was expected to run back to the farm and bring five gallon jugs out to him. He would fill the tractor and then fling the empties across the field. He would watch as I ran to gather them and take them back to the barn. It was as if he were playing a game of fetch with a dog. On occasion, something incredibly heavy was needed like a battery. I would have to carry that heavy thing across the field to him. Never did he get off the tractor to help and he, not one time ever said thank you to me. It was my job and that was it. Somebody always had to be at his beck and call.

Somehow, mechanical failures or fuel shortages were always my fault, though to this day, I can't figure out how. I should have been in the field with him, watching and waiting for him to "need" me, I guess. If I had brought him his lunch on time or seen that he was going to get stuck, he would not have been forced to walk to the farm. When I did bring him his lunch, he would see me waiting for him. He would continue to drive the tractor past me time after time. When he was ready to stop, he would do so, but only when he was ready. It did not matter how long I stood there waiting for him. Heaven forbid that I ever set his food down and walk away. He had no regards whatsoever for my time or anything that I might have to do back at the farm. They were all family or farm related as I had no friends at all. It was always all about him. These things that I did for him were always things that I should have just done, without him having to tell me... or at least that is how he saw things.

It took time for me to come to terms with our life or maybe, I never actually did. Whatever the dilemma, where ever it came from, the end was always going to be the same. It was going to be my fault and I was going to face more abuse from Jim. There would be the verbal abuse and the name calling that he seemed to thrive on. He would be certain to remind me that I was worthless and incompetent. I was to be at his beck and call and if I wasn't, there would be "Hell" to pay. I was damned if I did something and damned if I did not do something.

I will be the first to admit that I was not perfect and I did make mistakes now and then. That is just life and it happens. The issue that I had was that I was not treated as a wife. To Jim, I was little more than a slave to be worked and used in whatever way he decided. That wasn't acceptable then and it certainly is not alright today. I felt that there was never going to be a chance for me to make life better or to change the nightmare I was living in. I realized I was in a total "no win" situation and we had not yet seen a full four years of marriage.

Through the early '70's, I tried to stay focused on making our lives as good as I could make them. We stayed focused on our farming, Jim's job, my milk cows and our children. Even with such a full platter in front of us, we still managed to make it to church most Sundays. There were times of calm, though they were few, and I truly was happy during those few and far moments.

In May of '72, my sister graduated from high school. My parents hosted a very nice reception for her and it was nice that we were able to get back to see family. I missed them so much and was able to visit with them for a while. My parents had moved from the house I had grown up in and they bought my Grandma and Grandpa's home. My Aunt and Uncle lived in the house prior to mom and dad buying it.

I smile as I think about my father at that time. I think that it was a dream of my fathers to own that farm because his mom and dad, my grandparents, had owned it. Dad loved being there and seeing a dream of his realized was so good for him and us. Dad could now crop farm as he had wanted too and have some pigs and a few head of cattle. Mother now had her chickens and it was a little bit like what

I imagined the "Old McDonalds" farm from the song would have looked liked. I also felt warm and happy inside as I thought about visits to my Grandma's home and the smell of her cookies baking in the oven. Those are the memories and thoughts that often kept me going. They were beautiful and pain free and gave me the strength to survive..

In 1973, I miscarried what would have been our fourth child. Both Jim and I were saddened by this. My sister and my parents came to visit for Christmas that year. We had a dangerous ice storm just prior to their visit and I was so thankful they were still able to come. My sister had graduated and was living in our mobile home while working in Hutchinson. That was only about fifteen miles from us and she was able to visit often. She was a huge help to us with the kids and that gave me more peace and brought me more joy than she probably ever knew.

We still had no affiliation with Jim's family and that was entirely by his own choice. His family would have visited us if he had allowed it. I guess when you don't agree with someone and how they do things, you simply eliminate them from your life completely. That is how Jim dealt with pretty much everything. To make an offer of the "olive branch", acceptance that the whole world did not have to agree with your life, was not something Jim was ever going to do. God forbid that sometimes he may have actually been in the wrong about anything. He had his mind set on how life was going to be and there was no allowance for anything else.

Still in 1973, Jim appeared to be more agitated and a lot more often. Things were not going well for him at his work.

The issue with trying to start a Union was coming back on the entire plant. There were people being fired and meetings and hard feelings between co-workers and with the management. We had, by this time acquired twenty head of milk cows and we were renting a barn from the neighbor's farm. We used only their barn as they were still living in the house. When we went over there to do the chores, the kids would stay at the house and play.

On one of the nights that we were milking, I must have done something that set Jim off. Thinking back, it might not have even been me that triggered his rage. He was suddenly, without any warning, furious with me. While he yelled and cursed and told me what a worthless woman I was, I continued doing my chores. He yelled for me to look at him while he was scolding me. As I did what he had asked of me, I turned to face the end of a metal pipe. This was not plastic and light in any way. It was pure metal, four feet long and Jim was determined to use it on my body. I raised my hand to protect myself but it didn't slow down the hit. I felt the blow to my head from the pipe and suddenly I felt dazed and confused and could not understand why he was hitting me. The top of my skull hurt so terribly bad and yet still, he continued to beat me. I reached out to grab a pole in the barn so I didn't fall down. I felt something warm running down my forehead and reached up to touch it. The pain was almost unbearable and I nearly passed out. There was so much blood and I was scared I would bleed to death.

Jim was, as he always was when something happened to me; calm. As if it was nothing, he found a wet cloth and held it on my head. The gash was deep and the blood flowed heavily for a time. I was still dazed and the pain wasn't subsiding at all. He held the cloth on my head, oblivious or perhaps uncaring of the pain it was causing me. The bleeding slowed to a stop finally, leaving only a huge gash in my skull. The remark that he made both devastated and hurt me inside. He looked at me with anger still burning in his eyes.

"Now look what you have gone and done! You are going to have a scar from that cut!" He never said to me "can I help you?" or "are you going to be alright?" He never said that he was sorry or indicated that he felt anything what-so ever concerning what had just happened to me. The only thing that he cared about was that there would be a scar and that someone might see it. He didn't want people to ask questions about what happened or how it happened.

Funny, but when I think back on that incident, there were no calls to the police and no trip to the hospital for stitches. To Jim, the incident was done and finished and never to be mentioned again. We finished chores and then left to pick up the kids. This was to be the first, though for certain not the last time that Jim had used a weapon, other than his hands or feet to hurt me.

I think back to his abusive ways and shudder at times. We had a car while living in Glencoe. It was a 1966 Chevy Impala SS hardtop and it was a "cool" car in its day. We were having issues with the car and it would not start. We were out on the highway that ran in front of our house. We were trying to get it running better but it was backfiring on us. We were trying everything to get the car going, including ether, but it wasn't working. I still hadn't learned how to drive a car like the Impala and we were on a busy road. I was extremely nervous doing this. The test drive was almost finished so we were only yards away from our driveway. Suddenly, the car caught fire under the hood, so we pulled it off in to our driveway. We tried to put water on it to douse the flames. We were having no luck at all. The car was burned too badly by the time the flames were subsiding. Jim was not going to call the fire department and he left the car burning.

Jim had become extremely angry and began yelling and cursing, all directed at me. I didn't understand why he refused to call the fire department. I knew it was going to cost us for them to come out but we now had the cost of getting another car. This incident of course became my fault and though I far too often did not know what made it my fault; it was always my fault. The fact that we now only had Jim's pick-up for a car angered him also. This was to be the second time that I had come face to face with Jim's real physical abuse. He came in to the house and began hitting me and knocking me around the house. I don't recall all the injuries that time or whether he gave me another black eye; I just remember that the car burning was my fault and I got beat for it.

My only real saving grace that day was that my sister showed up for a visit. He would not hit me in front of her. He would however point out my stupidity and my inadequacy. I could handle that and the fact the hitting was done for a time was a good thing also. Back then, I could handle most anything he threw at me but the beatings left me weary and afraid. I felt ashamed in front of Bev but I prayed silently that she would stay for a while. She did seem to see that I was upset and afraid and graciously stayed with me for a time. Jim ranted and screamed and went on and on but he did not dare hit me as long as Bev was there.

Bev had to leave and the fear welled up inside of me as I watched her drive away. My body shook with the knowing of what was coming. This was to be the second time that I had come face to face with Jim's real physical abuse. He came in to the house and began hitting me and knocking me around the house. I felt like a rag doll as he threw me around the kitchen. I don't recall all the injuries that time or whether he gave me another black eye; I just remember that the car burning was my fault and I got beat for it. When his "tantrum" was over, I tiptoed through the house trying my best not to set him off again. At least this time, the little ones were in bed. That was not always the situation.

In the spring of '74, Jim lost his job at Green Giant because he pushed hard to form the Union in the plant. The company did not want a union and so, as companies did a lot back then, they fired Jim and that was the end of that job. It turned out to be an illegal firing but we had already discussed moving and getting our own farm. At that time, we decided to move back to Eagle Bend, which is where we had both grown up and graduated high school. Land prices were much cheaper there and I thought that this was a good thing for us. This was Jim's big dream, to farm and live on a farm as it was what he knew best. I was excited about the move because I thought it might help Jim and it also brought us closer to where my parents lived again.

The summer had gone by quickly with only a few incidents of violent behavior. I say violent because there was always some kind of abuse. It wasn't always vicious but it was always there. It no longer seemed to matter what it was that brought it on, be it a tractor stuck or a field breakdown; even an unfortunate encounter with a neighbor. I was the one held responsible and accountable for his fits of anger.

After some bargaining and securing a loan, we bought our farm. We moved back to Eagle Bend to a 240 acre dairy farm. The sale included forty-five head of dairy cows. Shortly before we were to move on to our new farm, we were informed that we could not move in to the farm house on the set closing date. The family that was in there had nowhere to go and would need a while longer to get out. We had to find a place to stay until we could move in to the house. With three kids and one on the way, this was not going to be easy. We had a herd of about twenty cattle that we also needed to find a place for. We did find a barn about a half mile from my cousins who had offered his home to us for a short time and we accepted. We milked the cows from that barn for a time.

We lived with my cousin and his wife for only a few months. For the most part, our relationship seemed a little better. Jim was busy and that was always good for me. As the weeks passed and still no word on our home, Jim began to show signs of frustration. He was more aggressive and much quicker to anger. He argued with the realtor and the seller, neither of which seemed to help at all. My cousin's wife and I were both pregnant at that time. We weren't a lot of help at all but we both did whatever we could do to help the men out.

We moved onto our farm on December fifteenth of '74 and between the times we had moved around, there had been moments of what I considered "normal" abuse. I am not sure how my mind decided any of it was normal, but that was my thought process at that point in my life. I think I called it normal abuse because it had become just that. It was normal for Jim to verbally and/or physically abuse me and I just lived with it. He would become angry with me and yell and scream and hit me. I could never truly understand why and sometimes, not even know what my fault was. I didn't seem to know one hundred percent of the time what I had done that had angered him so much that he felt the need to beat me. I felt completely overwhelmed by his anger and his actions.

I remember that when he would yell at me or hit me, my thought was that I needed to get my crap together. I felt as if it were me that was broken and needed to be fixed. I felt as if I needed to do better and that I needed to make our marriage work somehow. I did feel that the responsibility of keeping our marriage together was mine. It was never even a thought in my mind that perhaps some of the issues were his or that any of our problems were his fault. I didn't feel that he needed to make an effort to make things work for us. In any argument we had, the end result was always the same. Jim was always going to be right and I was always going to be wrong. I didn't really question it and felt that this was simply the way that things were. He had broken me down so far that I truly believed that something I myself had done made him hit me. I told myself that Jim would never strike me if I hadn't been so stupid. His control and his constant degradation had done exactly what he wanted it to do. He had me where he wanted me and my life was no longer mine.

We bought a tractor and some other machinery and suddenly, we were farming. I began to feel good about what we were doing as it seemed to calm Jim. This move would hopefully allow me some family time. I was looking forward to having some real time to spend with my mom and dad and Bev. As long as Jim stayed pleased with what he was doing, I was allowed some privileges. Seeing my family was the best of all.

In December of '74, just a few days after moving into our house, our fourth child, a son, was born. I went into labor pains on the night of my 24th birthday. I was feeling the hard pains but knew I needed to finish with the chores first. I did manage to get through all of them before going to the hospital. I went to the hospital instead of having him at home as Jim and I had planned to do. I was home in 3 days. I didn't want to be there any longer than I had to be. The bills would add up and that would anger Jim. I did anything I could to avoid situations that would give him cause to hit me.

The fourth day home, which would have been Christmas Eve, I was back in the barn milking the cows. Life always seemed to be a little better right after one of the babies were born. It wasn't long however before Jim would begin to feel jealousy and he felt like he wasn't getting enough attention. I had four babies running around and cows to milk and mouths to feed. There are only so many hours in a day and I only had two hands, though at times I wished I had ten of them. The only thing I ever wondered about then was how I was going to keep up. I needed to do that in order to keep Jim happy but I really had no idea how I was going to pull it off. The very thought that I was neglecting Jim on purpose or for any reason, now seems so absurd. I don't know why I couldn't see these things back then.

When I was lacking in my ability to keep the house running smoothly, Jim became upset and irritated. I would force myself to try harder to make Jim happy any way that I could. A great deal of physical abuse had resurfaced in my life at that time. He didn't always hit me during his angry moments but I knew that he could at any given moment. I was ready for the assault any time Jim was agitated or angry.

Though the abuse escalated and our lives were filled with good and bad times, we remained on the farm from 1974 until 1998. I learned, or at the very least, I thought I was learning, how to keep Jim calmer. As long as he was happy and content, life was good for us. We did have moments of peace from time to time, but they seemed to be much fewer and less far in between. Abuse, whether it was verbal or physical; often times, one bringing on the other, had become a way of life for me. It wasn't about the loving and laughter and "happily ever after" anymore. Life for me was about survival, rolling with the blows and trying to keep Jim happy.

As we got further in to the middle of the '70's, the physical abuse had escalated to a new high. No longer did I simply have to endure Jim's constant degradation of my very being. Wearing me down with his negative words, stripping me of any self-esteem I may have possibly still possessed; though I doubt there was any left by this point, was no longer enough for him anymore. There was a cruel, violent side of him that was showing itself more every time I upset him. When I think back, finally I realize that the truth is, it didn't need to be me that upset him. I was simply the one that was blamed for all of his faults or failures. It was my mind and my body that he tore apart when life didn't go according to his plans.

There were times during our years together that I thought I maybe should leave. It wasn't really an option for me though; more of a thought. I had children that needed to be raised and I wanted so badly to make our marriage work somehow. Life was set for me and I simply had to learn to live Jim's way or no way. I would milk the cows and work with Jim in the fields in the day. When it was supper time, I had to be sure that supper was exactly on time. Not some set time that might have made my life easier. That was never one of Jim's priorities. If dinner was not done when he thought it should be, there was going to be Hell to pay. I swear that at times, he sat out on the tractor and thought of ways to humiliate me.

Jim's actions often reminded me of my own children. He threw tantrums and yelled and screamed at me. If the meal I made wasn't up to his standards, he would toss the plate across the room, shattering it and everything on it against a wall. Sometimes he would get up from the table and slam his dish in the sink so hard it broke. He would tell me to get it cleaned up and walk outside. I never knew from day to day what our meals were going to be like. The kids all sat and watched their father as he went into a rage over something as simple as buttered bread. It was not only me that walked around on eggshells in that house. The kids saw and were scared of the same things that scared me. I hated even sitting down to dinner because I didn't know what was going to happen.

If we were outdoors and I angered him, the rage was more intense. He would grab me and shake me and yell as loud as he could at me. His foul mouth could be heard all across the fields. There was no way that the children did not hear it, though today, some say they heard nothing from their father. That, I think hurts me more than the physical abuse itself did. He tossed tools at me and if I was too slow to move, the tool would hit me hard. Jim's reaction to my crying out or falling as I was attempting to get out of the way was that I was a klutz. He would call me a "fat bitch" or "cow." I weighed in at 130 pounds in those days and his words would cut through me like a knife. I couldn't understand where his hateful words came from. I only knew that to argue or respond to his bashing would just bring on more words and more hitting.

As the mid-seventies were rolling forward, the anger became more than just words; more than just a slap or punch. Jim often sat me down in a chair or on the couch and even sometimes while we were in bed and he would become verbally abusive. He would be calling me horrible names and he would become angrier while talking. He would make the discussion go on all night long. I was not allowed to sleep at anytime during his fits of rage. The following morning, I was still expected to get up and do the chores. I also had to make sure that everyone got up and the kids were fed and off to school, as if I had slept all night.

When our oldest son was in school, I believe it was first grade; he missed the bus one morning. At that time, the woman that lived across the road from us was a school teacher. Jim was angry because our son had missed the bus. He decided to make that little boy of six years old start walking to school. We lived twelve and a half miles from school at the time. Fortunately for him, the teacher had not left for school yet. As she was driving to school, she stopped and picked our son up and took him to school. This was a six year old child, walking twelve miles to school, alone, and yet, never was there a report about this nor was anyone of authority ever contacted concerning this incident.

I didn't believe that at that time in our lives Jim's reputation had really made its way in to the community's eyes. That was my thought until people began to come forward and tell me stories of what they had heard and had seen. Adults had already been telling their families to try and avoid our place or at the very least, try to avoid having contact with Jim. His means of control and of influencing the people of our town were still in the hushed stages then. Any talk that might have been spoken was kept indoors. Perhaps many had not seen the things that were truly happening in the fields and at our home as of yet. If they had, no one had said anything to me about it, yet.

We were well known in the community. We went to church there at a Lutheran church every Sunday; the same church that Jim and I had been married in. That was Jim's choice, as always and I simply went where I was told. I think back to the wedding and it makes me sad. We had a small wedding with just immediate family and there wasn't even an option to be married where I grew up and went to church. It was all about what Jim wanted and how he wanted things and who he would allow to attend the wedding. He insisted we would have a small wedding at the church and told me that my aunts and uncles would *not be invited to the wedding.* One of my uncles was devastated by Jim's decision and could not imagine why he had not been invited to our wedding or to the reception. I didn't even have a good answer for him.

It was in 1976 that the really horrifying physical abuse began. The list of violent attacks that Jim did to me went on and on in '76 and '77. The things that happened to me were noted in the complaints that I brought against Jim. He assaulted me on January 29th and the 30th of '76. The abuse began with a fight that I never really knew what had prompted these attacks. He used his fists for much of the assaults on both days. He then struck me with a 2 X 4 that was about four feet long.

We had been sawing 8 X 12 foot long logs which we would later sell in town. We sold firewood to help pay the bills on the farm. It was hard work and the logs were very heavy for me. I was tired and could not find the strength to lift my end of the log we were cutting. Jim became violently angry with me. He picked me up and tossed me across the yard. He then jumped up in the air and landed on my stomach. I got away from him and ran to the barn for safety. Jim followed me and shoved me, causing me to cut myself. Having furniture thrown at me, being kicked in the head and the stomach; having my head bashed into a wall and having my ribs cracked, had become just things to expect. They were the prices I had to pay for loving this monster. Sadly, I did still love him through all of the torture.

The fear that had welled up inside of me is hard to even convey to anyone that reads this story. In the moments of Jim's violent rages, I believe I knew exactly how a helpless animal must have felt when they were being pursued by a predator. My heart was racing and all I could think about was getting away from Jim. In those moments, you don't have time to think or to figure out what your next move should be. There is only panic and a terrible sense that you could die if you don't escape. Just like that poor animal, tired from running, yet to afraid to stop, you simply make yourself keep going.

The predator has one thing in mind and that is to hurt its prey or to kill it. There is no sadness or thought about what its prey is feeling. The creature simply does not care at that time. It cares only about the end result. That is how I believe that Jim felt and as for the prey, I *do know* what it is feeling just before the creature chasing it catches up to it. His intention was very clear to me and that was to hurt me in any way that he could. He hit me and hurt me that day and it was just the start of what was to be the most horrifying attacks of my life with Jim.

I did finally seek help from a shelter and that didn't last very long. In January of '77, while I was at the shelter, Jim went to see his Father. It was the first time in eight years that he had made any attempt to contact his father. He was seeking advice from a man he hated but still respected his opinion. It wasn't strange to ask his father the question Jim needed answered. After-all, his father had done the same to his own wife that Jim was doing to me.

"How do I get my wife to come home to me?" was his question to his father. All of the years that had passed without any relationship with his parents or siblings were lost. They could not ever be recovered and would remain wasted years forever. It was not just a loss for Jim and his family, though. We, ourselves… the kids and I had also lost those years. My kids spent their childhood not even knowing they had a second set of grandparents. There were aunts and uncles and cousins that the kids had never met. Jim's home life and family life were marred with domestic violence and now he needed the advice of the man that beat them and their mother in an attempt to find a way to bring me back again. He wanted to know how his father "fixed" things with his mother. I am not sure what the advice was that Jim was given. Perhaps he gave him nothing for an answer. I only know that the conversation between them opened up a new door for family relations for all of us. That relationship was not going to be a "cake walk" for any of us either.

Jim and his dad were both very angry people who needed to be in control. The problem was that, as in any relationship like theirs, there can only be one boss. Jim's dad hired us to do his field work but like father, like son, he was never pleased with anything we did. Doing the best that we could, it just was never enough for his dad. Never had I seen two men that were more alike than Jim and his father. The statement I had made to my mother crept back into my mind. "Jim is not his father and I am not his mother." Those words had now come back to haunt me and I realized how very wrong I had been in speaking them. The renewed relationship was not good and it certainly did not make my life any easier. There were so many disagreements concerning us helping his father. There were some between us but most of them were Jim and his father arguing and disagreeing. Both of them had to be right all of the time.

When you put two head strong, controlling people together, you get nitro-glycerin. Volatile and so very easy to set off, the "explosions" always came back on me. I was the place he released all of his anger on in one way or in another. The pain was going to be the same no matter what the outcome was. Frustration does not even begin to relay to you the feelings I had over all that was going on. Nothing and I do mean nothing that I did was ever going to be right with either one of them. Now, I had Jim and his father to contend with. How could I not feel trapped and totally unsafe?

Chapter 5

{Of Life Changing Injuries and Jail-time}

One of the most horrendous and frightening attacks came on January 14th of 1977. We were sawing firewood again. Jim once again became angry with me. By this point in my life, it no longer mattered to me why he was angry with me. The very fact that something… anything, had angered him was all that really mattered. The reason behind the anger was extremely secondary to the assaults, now. The pain would not be less if I knew what had angered him. That much I was certain of and nothing was going to change that fact.

Jim continued his attack on me and lifted me up so that he could toss me down onto the stock watering tank. I hit the tank hard on my side, causing internal damages. I raced to the barn to avoid more pain. I don't recall being really winded but I do remember the pain I felt suddenly. Jim followed me in to the barn, cussing and calling my terrible names. He told me to get back outside and do some work. He pushed me down and I cut my knee open on the gutter in the barn. I had to go in to the house because my pants were cut. It was cold outside because of it being in January. We had a load of wood ready to go and to be sold. He was going to leave that afternoon with the load of wood to be sold in the cities. I knew that there were still cows to milk and chores to finish and so I did all that needed to be done. Jim decided not to go in to the cities that night.

When the day was done and I was ready to bathe, Jim never mentioned anything about the incident outside. I went in to the bathroom to take my bath. When I went to the bathroom, I realized that there was a lot of blood in my urine. Jim came into the bathroom and asked what was wrong with me. He was still angry at me and asked if I had my period again. I told him that I did not have my period, which seemed to anger him more. He wanted to know why I was peeing blood and I told him I didn't know. I carefully lowered myself in to the tub. My knee was hurting so terribly and the water in the tub was hot. I was hoping that the bath would soothe some of the pain I was experiencing after being thrown down onto the water tank. I finished my bath and wrapped my knee without any more interruptions from Jim. I went to bed at that time.

I was kept awake all night because my stomach was hurting me so badly. I could feel something wrong inside of my body. The area around my kidney began to hurt as I lay in the bed. My back began to hurt also and later I would find that all of the things I was feeling were related to the injury I had sustained earlier in the day. The following morning, Jim left for the cities with the load of wood. I did as I had done every day for as long as we had lived on the farm. I went out to the barn to milk the cows and before I could do my chores, I nearly passed out. I walked back to the house, where at that time we still had a house phone. It was just one of the many out-reaches that we had that Jim would eventually remove.

It was not clear to me yet the depth of his obsession with separating me from the outside world. He was intent on shutting me off from contact with anyone or anything that was precious to my life. The less I had contact with my family or his family, the better he liked it. He did not want me to have someone to call or to talk to if he did something to me. How it is that I was so blinded to his evil intentions, even after all I had already endured, I cannot tell you. I guess I simply did not want to see it.

I went into the house and I called Jim's mom and my brother-in-law. I told them I needed some help with the chores because I was not feeling well. They did come to help me and in fact did the chores for me. I was inside lying on the couch when they came back inside. They left and I remember sending one of the kids across the street to the neighbor's house. I asked them to tell the neighbor that their mommy did not feel good. They came in to the house and though I could still talk, I was in an extremely weakened state. They called the ambulance in Parkers Prairie to come and take me to the hospital. The doctors spent only a moment examining me and decided that they were not going to even attempt to do anything further there. They sent me to Alexandria and by the time we arrived, I was already semi-comatose. I vaguely remember the doctor handing me a paper and telling me that I needed to sign it. It was a paper giving the doctor permission to do surgery. I didn't fully understand what was happening and no longer can recall if I signed my name or scratched an X where I was supposed to sign.

They took me into surgery almost immediately after I had arrived at the hospital. The doctors originally thought they would find a shattered spleen but soon found out that my kidney had been smashed. They removed my kidney that day and placed me in a room. The doctors sent word out to the highway patrol to try to locate Jim. They needed to inform him that I had been admitted to the hospital. They had not wrapped my knee at all because they said it had too many germs in the wound. The doctors were very concerned at the time with infections, especially just following surgery. Jim was found and came to the hospital. He was angry and looked at me as if to accuse me of faking my injuries. He didn't think my injuries could be as bad as he was being told they were. The following day, they cleaned out my knee and told me I needed to go into the whirlpool to help the wound heal faster.

I don't recall exactly how many days I was in the hospital for that injury. I believe I was only in the hospital about four or five days. The doctors were not convinced that I had simply injured myself. They questioned me over and over and I did finally tell them what had happened to me. I asked the doctor I was speaking to not to tell anyone or report Jim. I was already afraid enough of being hurt again and did not want to upset or anger Jim any more. I didn't trust enough in the court systems to actually protect me and I knew what would happen if Jim was arrested. Nothing was said about the incident at that time and no arrest was made.

It was not until later that I learned that my doctor was not convinced in any way of how I had injured my kidney. He was a good man and wanted to know the truth. My injuries were not something he had seen from a fall. He knew that something more was happening to me. I had lied so often about the beatings that it became second nature to me. I think sometimes I almost believed the stories I told myself.

I returned home and things were good for a very short time. It had only been three days since I had been released from the hospital following the removal of one of my kidney. The bills arrived at the house for my hospital stay and surgery. Jim became extremely angry and began to attack me, physically, once again. I was still recovering from my surgery but he didn't care about that. He began to hit me and then tossed me around in a chair and then threw me to the floor in the living room. His violence was becoming more frequent and it did not seem to matter what the reason was for him hitting me anymore. In fact, Jim seemed to no longer need a reason to abuse me other than being irritated by life itself.

Two months after I had come home from the hospital, we received a bill and judgment against us from a Creamery. This was enough to anger Jim and of course, it was my fault entirely. Once again, he beat me and kicked me and even threatened to kill me. He kicked me on my good side until I could hardly move. He picked up a highchair that was nearby and smashed me with it over and over again. The pain that ran through my body was almost unbearable. I just kept telling myself that I had babies to take care of and cows to milk. My mind was so deeply set on those priorities that I seemed to block out the reality of what Jim was doing to my body.

When Jim left that day I got to the phone and I called his mom again for help. She took me to the hospital where a doctor convinced me to report the attack and file charges against him. I did that and Jim was arrested that day. The doctor that had seen me testified against Jim. He was very involved and told the court that he felt I was high risk for more abuse. He recanted the story of me arriving at the hospital that day.

"She, Connie Sarff, came in to the E.R. complaining of pain in her side and other extremities. After examining her, I found that she had sustained a broken rib, severe bruising and other injuries. Her story of falling off of a tractor at the family farm, not believable the first time, held even less truth to me now. After a second time of seeing her, I was convinced that he {Jim Sarff} was kicking her. I pushed for charges to be filed against her husband because I believed that her life was in danger of more violence." Now retired, the doctor still recalled how difficult it was to convince me to press charges against Jim. "It took a very long time for me to gain Connie's confidence enough to talk her into having Jim arrested."

. The doctor that had convinced me to have Jim arrested was angry and disgusted at the court's decision. He was quoted as saying "I called the attorney general's office and asked them what the Hell was going on? It is a perfect example of our failed system. We have let this woman down in the worst way. Jim Sarff is a very bad man." His words fell on deaf ears and the attacks went on.

Jim was charged with aggravated assault and was sentenced to time in jail but was allowed to work during the day and serve his jail time at night. That still left him free to hurt me anytime he wanted to. His anger seemed to have no ending and the fire of rage that burned constantly inside of him never got full. It ate at him and devoured his thoughts. He didn't tire of hurting me nor did he feel any type of remorse for the nearly crippling beatings he inflicted on me.

The police and doctors viewed me as the sadly typical profile of an abused spouse. I fit perfectly into the patterns they had seen over and over. I suffered through the beatings and anything else he decided to do to me. I played with the idea of turning him in to the authorities and then I would forgive him and let it all go. I really am not certain that forgive would always be the best word to use. I think that mostly, I was scared and didn't want to antagonize him any more than needed. He didn't really need reason to hurt me so I did all I could to tip-toe in his presence.

It was March of '77 when I finally decided to get out of harm's way. I knew that the only way I could accomplish that was to leave the farm. Like a scared child, trying to run away from home, I waited until nightfall to leave. Jim was in jail when I left him. The fact that he would not be in jail for long was one of the reasons I did not trust the judicial system. The very thought that this man was given daily outs to farm was beyond my comprehension. Why did I bother to call on him? What gain was there for me if he was still able to leave the jail and come home daily? It made absolutely no sense to me, leaving me afraid and distrusting the courts in every way.

My fears finally bringing me to my senses, some relatives found me shelter at the Women's Advocates, a battered women's shelter in St. Paul, Minnesota. I grabbed whatever I could for the kids and left Jim. It was not long before Jim found out where I was. He came to visit me and the kids and tried very hard to talk me in to coming back to the farm. I felt very much out of my element but still managed to find the courage to tell him no; at least for a little while. I remained in the shelter for nearly six months. I had surprised myself that I had not gone back to the farm. With my two oldest children ready to start school, I had decisions that needed to be made. These were hard decisions for me because part of me wanted to go back home. I did love the farm and I still loved Jim, as impossible as that might be to believe.

I had a cousin that taught school in Wabasso and the house beside her was open to be rented. I rented the house and moved in with my kids. I wanted to start fresh and begin living. I don't consider what I did with Jim living at all. That was just staying alive; going through the motions without really experiencing life. Hiding or walking around, just waiting for the hand or the boot or whatever was convenient to throw at me to come my way was almost less than living. It felt wonderful to have a place of my own. After living in the shelter for so long, I wanted the privacy that the house would offer to me.

The kids were not as receptive to the move because they missed their father. They did not like being so far away from him. They truly had no idea what it meant to me to be away from their father. I think that this bothered me some but perhaps not for the reasons you may think. It upset me because I could not believe that after all that had happened to me. They were there and heard it and saw some of it. Were they so deeply closed off that they truly did not see what was happening to me? The mind has a way of protecting itself from things it cannot either understand or process. For whatever reason, the kids wanted to be home again, on the farm, with their father.

Jim had been sent to St. Peter for a psych evaluation. I took the kids there to visit with him. They loved their father and wanted to see him. I could not deny them that no matter where Jim and I were in our relationship. He was very pleasant to me, almost doting over me at times. He was doing anything and everything that he could do to get me to come home. Again, I did not return to the farm with him. I was still very afraid of him and the kids were in school. I had a job as a café waitress and I think I was actually beginning to gain some self-esteem again. I did not want to lose that feeling and feared that returning home would steal that away from me again. I had seen this side of Jim before and knew he was merely showing m e his best behavior. It was not enough to bring me home.

After only thirty days, Jim was released. I was only half shocked by what the report had to say. Jim had an incredible way of making people see a totally different man than the one that had nearly killed me. He could be as normal as anyone and could turn on a charm that left people convinced that he was a good man. He was very persuasive also and somehow, he convinced these doctors that he was fine. Not only did they say he was fine; they also said they found that he did not suffer from any mental issues or illnesses. This man, who had struck me hard more times than I could count and beat me so bad I lost a kidney and broke my ribs, had no issues?!? Were they kidding me? I wondered, if Jim was getting released and had to live next to the doctor himself, if the decision would have been the same. In the end, none of it really mattered. No matter what I thought, it wasn't going to change a single thing for me or where I had been in my past.

In August of the same year, I saw, or perhaps better stated, heard about Jim's anger aimed at another of God's creation. How sad that I think back and hang my head. The fact that he took his anger out on something other than me meant exactly that. It was *not me* that he was beating at the time. A cow had kicked him and injured him. He was, of course angry and his anger turned to violence that scared the hell out of me. I knew that it could have just as easily have been me that had set him off. His fierce attack on the animal that had hurt him was more sickening than scary. Jim went out the following day and literally beat the cow to death. The sheer mentality of a man that could do such a thing is overwhelming. The magnitude of his intense, raging brutality, even after all he had done to me, still at times leaves me speechless. Investigators came to our farm to follow up on the complaint that Jim had killed one of our cows. I do not know to this day who filed the complaint. Jim had asked some of our neighbors to watch the cows but he was turned down by all of them. The police report stated that Jim appeared to not be very popular."

Though Jim's abusive nature towards animals may have been new and horrendous to the investigators, it was not new to me. Perhaps people hearing about the death of a cow, cruelly and nearly unbelievably beat to death thought it was an isolated incident. I knew first hand that they were terribly wrong. Many times in our cattle raising years, I saw Jim and his anger in full swing. It was not at all unheard of for me to see him chase them down with the truck. He would crash the truck into their bodies and knock them to the ground. Once they were tired or knocked down, he would beat them with a pipe or boards. He would beat them until his anger was burnt out or the cow was dead. The reasons for the cruel torture ranged from a cow kicking to a cow simply getting out of the fence.

During one particular attack, Jim began beating one of the milk cows because she had got out of the fence. This cow was our best milk cow and I didn't want to see her dead. I watched as he beat her over and over again, feeling her pain and knowing exactly what she was experiencing. During those times of violence, I think some of my fear was that when he finished with her, it would be my turn. After-all, it was going to be my fault she got out and my fault that he was forced to kill her. I pleaded with him to stop beating her but my words fell on deaf ears. He didn't stop and he did beat her to death, right before my eyes. When he was finished, he simply strung her up and hung her from a tree so that we could butcher her.

The sight of someone beating an animal, any animal to death is not something that ever leaves your memory. I can still see it so vividly to this day and my heart breaks over and over again for that poor animal. Like me, she was only guilty of being the one chosen by Jim to feed his rage and his need to cause harm to something or someone. She had defied him in some way and that was something he would not ever tolerate. Her escaping from where he had placed her was more than just "getting out" to Jim. It was a lack of respect for his authority and she paid the price as I had so many times. I cried for that cow and I cried for my own self that day.

I know about the evolution of life, especially in farm animals. I understand that cows eat the grass and other foods that we feed to them. I understand that from that, we derive our milk and meat to sustain us. The lesser are consumed by the greater and so goes the life cycle of farm animals. All of this is true and I know that it is the way of survival for mankind. This… the beating to death of an animal and then butchering it so that we could eat was not evolution. This was not ever how God intended for life to be; not for the animals or for humans. What Jim did was completely uncalled for. The actions that he displayed were absolute anger and violence at its very worst. What he did that day and so many other days scared me to death. I think sometimes I simply waited as much as expected for the day that he would do the same to me.

I wonder sometimes if the words you are reading will ever transfer the fear and reality of what Jim subjected me to for 30+ years. I tremble at the thoughts; the memories that are at times, as real today as they were when they were happening. There is little more that I could do to cause you to absorb and process what life had been like while I was with Jim. It wasn't living as much as it was making it through each and every day and being thankful every morning that I woke. It meant that I had lived through the night and for me… that was a bonus. Jim tore my body apart, leaving me scarred inside and outside for the rest of my life. The images and the pain that I still see and feel every day of my life are constant reminders of Jim. A person may in fact "move on" but they never forget. There is always something to remind me of what I lived through no matter how hard I try to block it all out. That is something that will probably never leave me.

In October of '77, I was taken to another Shelter for battered women and remained there for ninety days. I thought I was safe and would not have to deal with Jim but, he found me and asked me to come home with him. I told him I would not go back with him and he left. During my time in the shelter, a cousin of mine told me about a house that was available. There was the chance for a job also and so I took the house and tried to settle down for a while. It was a tough time for me as I had four little kids with me. I was not receiving any child support from Jim and trying to work and raise four children alone was extremely taxing. It was certainly better than being assaulted and having the kids watch it as it happened.

I made acquaintances and became friends with one of the advocates from the shelter. We had become closer than the boundaries actually should have allowed us to do. Her husband was a lawyer and he agreed to by my legal counsel. I was making plans to start divorce proceedings and needed an attorney to do that. Sometime during this time, Jim threatened to kill both me and my attorney. Jim was evaluated by the county and it was decided that he was definitely capable of carrying out his threats. At that time, the Todd County Attorney's office asked that a Bench Warrant be issued for Jim and was granted the request.

It was not until December that he was brought back in to court to be sentenced for the abuse he had been found guilty of. The court found him guilty of aggravated assault with the use of a dangerous weapon. That is a felony charge and yet, the lawyers and the judge talked back and forth about the situation. The fact that it was a domestic issue seemed to matter to them. It was in truth, assault that could have ended my life. Some of what Jim had done to me over the years was nothing short, at times, of attempted murder. I could have died for certain from my injuries or been crippled in some way for the rest of my life. The sentencing should have reflected better the reality and the severity of my injuries. The sentence that was given to Jim was almost a slap in the face for me. Jim was given a stay of execution and the final decision handed down by the judge was five years on probation.

I had gone to visit Jim once while he was at St. Peter's State Hospital. He was still the kids' father and I wanted them to see him and him to be able to see them. I loved my job at the little café and I was enjoying the freedom I was experiencing. I had met a wonderfully sweet elderly lady who would watch my kids whenever I needed to work. Everything seemed to be going well for me, and life, although hard at times, was good for me and the kids. I can remember to this day, during one of the calls to my mother,

her telling me what a friend had said to her. "If she can get through the Christmas holiday away from Jim, she will be on her way to a new and safe life." I wished I had listened more closely to those words of wisdom.

After his release from St. Peter's, he came to my house to visit me. He talked all of the right talk that night and his sweet talk and manipulating words still had the effect on me that he wanted them to. Jim promised he was going to change and that he would do anything "I" needed him to do if I would just come home and be a family again. He told me to just name it and he would do it, as long as I came home with him. What he wanted, I also still desperately wanted too. I wanted that marriage and family and togetherness that Jim was speaking of.

Some things, at that time in my life had changed. I didn't want to be brutalized anymore. I didn't want to live in fear every single day of my life. The feelings, which over the years become so second nature that you nearly forget they are there, are the very feelings that will hide themselves when you want to be loved and have a family. The remembrance of a slap or punch; the feeling of being kicked in the head or the face would seem like enough to never be forgotten. That pain and the fear that you might be breathing your last breath should be enough to cause you to say "No way!" They most assuredly should be… but they are not always. The strong want and desire to see what you started come full circle is powerful. No, I did not want to feel that pain again but I did want so completely to have my family back together again that I fell for his words again. I took them in as if he were actually going to keep his promises to me. While he was there at my house that night, we made love. It was something we both wanted and shared that night. Not only did we make love that night but I also conceived our daughter that night.

Whatever was to come of my decision to return home, it was still yet to be seen. Somewhere in the back of my mind, I am sure there were fears. There was no way that there could not have been, given the violence I had already experienced from Jim. I think that sometimes, we want something to be true or real. I married Jim with the belief that our life together was going to be everything I had ever dreamed married life would be. Fixing him, fixing *us,* was something I was certain I could do. I was determined to show those that doubted we could ever survive this marriage just how very wrong they were. The words I had said to my family about how I was *not* Jim's mother and Jim was *not* his father were going to come back to haunt me again and again. The words echoed through my head and yet, I was determined to have a marriage with this man.

Although I did not return home with Jim immediately, I did eventually give in to his promises and returned home to the farm. I had things I needed to finish up first. I had to prepare the kids for the move back home with their father and me together again. Not only was my life going to change again… their lives were too.

After the first time he came and asked me to come home, we had contact several more times. Before my return to the farm we continued to see one another again. The kids were in school already and I did not want to pull them out in the middle of the school season. I waited until the end of May of 1978 to return to the farm with Jim. The things we had agreed on lasted about one month. I told him that I also wanted a job so that I could help out with finances. It was also to be a chance for me to get away from the farm for a little while each day. He agreed to the job for me.

Chapter 6

{Returning Home, for Better or Worse?}

Thinking back now, my memory sometimes releasing thoughts once buried, it was in '77 that I had angered Jim because I had called my Dad. Jim came in and ripped the phone off of the wall. I had called him after one of the times that Jim had abused me. Jim was very violent and wanted to make sure that I did not call my family after the call to my Dad. There was no phone in the house for a very long time after that. By removing the means for me to contact anyone, especially our immediate family, Jim gained more power of control over my life. We were twelve miles from town and by this time, the neighbor across the road from us had moved away. There was nobody anywhere close to us that could help me if I needed anything. I could have run up and down the road for miles and there would have been no safe place or a single person to reach out to. Jim preferred it that way and I had no say in the matter.

Jim stuck firmly to the isolation part of his control over me. He was free to abuse me and work me and to do whatever else he decided fit the moment. The mailman and the school bus were pretty much the only vehicles I saw out our way. In 1977, he told me I was not to have any contact with my family, at all. One of the promises he had made to me in our "get back together" conversation was that I could have contact anytime I wanted with my family again. I was foolish and dreamed of a better life with Jim. It was just one of too many to count promises that he would break again and again.

During my time away from Jim, people had begun to talk. I suspect now that they always had but that it was private and shushed in the town. I had heard later the fact that people told one another that they had seen Jim beating me in the fields. I cannot help but wonder in my mind if they saw it, why didn't anyone step forward and tell the authorities. One family member, we will call him "Fred" for the protecting of the innocent, spoke out publicly concerning things they knew about. When Jim had cut off all connections for me and my family, the man was quoted as saying "We all knew it wasn't right. How can someone say that you cannot see your family nor have contact with them? Connie was told so many times that her parents were the problem that she began to believe it herself. That is a sad thing."

Words such as "we knew" or "we were concerned for her safety" still leave me a little empty at times. Somewhere in there should have been a call to the local police or DHS. What a different life I might have known if just one person would have taken the initiative to speak out in my defense. In knowing and yet saying nothing, it left me alone and at the mercy of Jim's rage. I had no idea that people were aware and I took drastic measures to try and keep things that way. I truly wish that someone would have come forward and reached out to me during those times.

The issues with Jim; the abuse and the fear were no longer exclusive to the farm. I knew the moment that my dad went after Jim that everyone was aware of what was happening. I guess I wondered; if everyone was so aware of all, or at least some of the things that were happening to me... where were they. It was almost better when I believed that no-one really knew what Jim was putting me through. If they did know, it was left unspoken to me and life simply went on. I was truly alone at the farm. Perhaps 30+ years of my life could have been less painful. I supposed it matters very little now but I would be lying if I told you it never crossed my mind.

Friends visited me from time to time before I moved home. I shared with them the fact that I was pregnant and that I would be going back to Jim. They were shocked and extremely concerned about my decision. They reminded me of the very reasons I had left Jim and that I was placing myself right back on the "front line." They were certain that he was not going to change and that the abuse would start over again with my return. I appreciated their caring but they failed to understand that I was struggling each and every day. I was not "making it" and I was not financially fixed in any way. There was not enough money to pay the bills. I could not even afford the car insurance any longer. What little assistance I was receiving from the government was not enough. We lived on hand-me-downs and gifts and I was thankful for everything I was getting. Thankful wasn't going to pay the rent or feed my children.

My parents were devastated at learning I was going back. They remembered the cutting of all ties to them when I was trying to break free of Jim's hold on me. They too feared the very worst for me. They knew that Jim was going to hurt me again and that life would go back to exactly the way it was before I left. They were afraid of losing the rekindled relationship that I had found with them and my friends. I told them of Jim's promises and that we would be able to stay close. They doubted his words and told me they were afraid for me and the kids. The main difference between me and everyone else was that I believed Jim's words. I believed everything that man told me. Why? Because he was my husband and he said he loved me. I still lived in a very "Cinderella" dream world.

I started working in a town called Miltona and worked at my job for a very short time. I think I was there for about three weeks. Jim would drive me to work and always picked me up after work to drive me home. We were on our way home one night and he brought up the farm. He was angry because there were things that were going wrong at the farm. He told me it was my fault because I was working instead of home taking care of the kids and the farm with him. That is what a good wife did and I was falling short of my duties. The kids were not with us because he always left them home alone when he came to pick me up. Coming around a corner to turn onto our road, he hit some loose gravel and almost rolled the car. He was mad and wasn't paying attention to the road. I could feel the tension in the car and remember fear creeping up on me again. I wanted nothing more at that moment than to push my door open and jump from the car. The gravel would hurt far worse than Jim's fists. The truth is, Jim was not incapable of helping me fulfill that thought. Shoving me out of a moving vehicle was right up his alley.

Jim informed me that I was done working and that I would be quitting my job. He told me I needed to take responsibility for the kids and helping out at the farm. Jim told me that it was my place to be home and not out working somewhere. I really wasn't left with any choice and so the next day, I found myself no longer working off the farm. The promises he had made to me in order to get me back were falling apart in a very big way. All that he had said had been nothing but lies and I had been so ignorant that I believed every word this man had said to me.

About a week before our daughter was born, the probation officer had come out to the farm. He informed Jim that he had been taken off probation early because he was displaying the qualities of a good and reformed man. He had served only about one and a half to two years because he had been such a good boy and a model citizen. He was not allowed to have any firearms because his arrest was a felony charge. Jim was absolutely furious about the law. Our son had received a BB gun for his birthday and Jim became enraged. He took the gun from our son and broke it right in front of him. Even though the law said he couldn't possess any guns, we had one right in the living room. Laws, to Jim, had been made for criminals and someone other than himself.

Shortly after the probation officer left, something upset Jim and off on a raging tantrum he went. Jim made the kids sit on the couch, one of the older kids holding the baby and proceeded to chew me out in front of them. Jim told me to go to the basement, which I did. I was never sure what the abuse would be but I knew it was coming. There was a small pile of gravel on the basement floor as we were doing some work downstairs. He shoved me down on top of the gravel pile. Jim then pulled out his shotgun, a gun that should *not* have been in his possession. He told me it was time for me to be killed. He said that he could take care of the farm and the kids and that I was no longer wanted or needed in his life. Just by his look, I had no doubt in my mind that he was very serious. I did not know if the gun was loaded or not. I did totally believe in my heart that I was going to die that day. The fear inside of me is a fear that I have no words to describe it. My entire body shook as I waited for the sound of the blast from the shotgun. What stopped him from killing me, to this day, I will never know.

Another time, with kids on the couch as always, he told me I was going to die. He got the gun and he put it against my head and he told me he was going to kill me right then and there. I, once again have no idea why he didn't shoot me that day. The look in his eyes told me that he would kill me without a question and yet, he did not that day. I am sure now that it was just another way for Jim to control me and to scare me into submission. It was without a doubt, working.

~~~~~~~~~~

{Note :} I am aware of the fact that at times I jump back and forth here. My memory and the thoughts that have been buried away for so long find their way to the surface without warning. Remembering and allowing these thoughts to resurface is a very scary thing for me. I hope that you will bear with me as I continue to tell you my story.

~~~~~~~~~~

Before our daughter was born, I can remember the kids sitting on the couch. The couch was huge and seemed to swallow them up. There was a grate in the floor; one of the big metal vents that all the old farmhouses used to have in them. The room that Jim and I were in was directly below the kids. They could hear every word that was being said. There I was, sitting on the bed, a gun pressed against my head with Jim telling me he was going to shoot me. I don't really know if there was a bullet in the gun that day either. What I do know is that I was scared that he would actually pull the trigger. We heard the kids crying upstairs so Jim let me go. We went upstairs and it was like the incident had never happened.

This incident took my mind to another level of fear of the man I called my husband. I now wondered what day would be the one that he would decide to really pull the trigger. What moment would mark the last time that I would see my children or kiss them or hold them to me. Every time that I said goodbye to my family or told my baby's goodnight, I now had to fear that I might not ever tell them I loved them again. That level of fear is something that eats at you like a cancer. You try to push it to the back of your thoughts but it emerges at every hello or goodbye. Those words seemed almost hollow and I wondered if goodbye was to become a four letter word for me. I could not image never seeing those that I loved again. What would become of my children? How would my parents and my sister handle the news that their daughter/sister had been killed? There could not have been a more horrifying thought to carry around with me than that.

Jim continued the abuse and I spent night after night, sitting on that very same bed, Jim yelling at me and verbally abusing me in whatever way that he could. His words were harsh and accusing and he knew exactly what to say and how to say it so that his words cut me as deeply as possible. He would reprimand me for things I had not done and when I denied his accusations, it only served to anger him further. There was no end to the days and weeks and sometimes months of sleepless nights, listening to the man I loved strip me of my self-esteem and of any dignities I might have had left in me. I sat and waited for the barrage of his fists and fury to explode directly at my face and my body.

He often went into a fit of rage and screaming about how worthless and awful my family was. He would degrade my family and even their heritage to make him-self seem superior. He was always proud of the German descent that was his although he was also English and Scandinavian. Quite often, he took it on himself to remind me that he was German and that the Germans were always the "elite" race. He told me that the strong would one day inherit all of the earth. He scared me a bit and reminded me a lot of another man that believed that the Germans were the superior race and all others should be destroyed.

I could not let my sadness or any other emotion show. I think I finally decided to simply not show feelings as it protected me from horrible beatings. I was never really trying for strength; I had simply learned early on that it was better not to let Jim see an emotional side to me. Sad or lonely emotions were the worst. Jim would ridicule me if I cried during a sad movie. He would ask me what I was crying about. There always seemed to be something that he could pull out of the air and toss at me. He would tell me I had more important things to cry about then a movie. The really terrible truth was... he was right. I did have so much more to cry about, like my own sad life.

Sometime after 1977, I do not recall all of the dates; Jim was getting ready to go in to town. He was always thinking that I was going to leave him again. I wonder today, why it was that I waited so long to do exactly that. Most of the time, I was forced to go where-ever Jim was going. His distrust was enormous, more-so after I had left him the first time. It was in the middle of summer and the heat was fierce at that time. He called me over to the grain bin one hot day. This was an enormous steel grain bin that was sealed to hold small grains. To make certain that I did not try to leave, he told me to get inside and then he proceeded to lock me inside of the grain bin. He left me inside of the bin for what seemed like a forever. The reality of it is that it was probably only two or three hours. When you are locked inside something with the hot of the sun burning down on you, time takes on an entirely new meaning. He did not let me out until after he returned home that day. He left me with no water and nothing to eat and I had no place to go to the bathroom. Those things were unimportant to Jim and I think he enjoyed knowing that he had locked me inside the bin. He owned me and had 100% control over everything about my life. When he did finally let me out he said "Now I know how to keep you from leaving."

In July of 1978, our daughter was to be born. I was going to have her at the farm as we wanted a child born at home. The doctor was already set up to come to the farm and deliver her. We didn't have health insurance because he had sold the cows prior to me coming home and had used the money. The sale of the cows had also been one of the stipulations for me coming back to the farm. I wanted the dairy herd gone because I was tired of being the "chore girl" and refused to go back to milking the cows. Our only real income at that time was the sale of firewood. Because of the absence of health insurance, the doctor had made the agreement to deliver our daughter in our home

The morning I woke up not feeling well, I was certain it was time for the baby to come. I told Jim and he went to a neighbor's house and used their phone to call the doctor. Our daughter started coming before the doctor was able to get to us. The contractions were very close by the time that Jim had returned. We prepared for her birth as best we could. It was a little bit like a scene out of Little House on the Prairie. Our daughter didn't wait for the doctor to arrive. She came before he could make it out to our farm. Jim actually had to deliver her himself. He cut the cord and cleaned her up and laid her beside me. Shortly after the delivery, I started to hemorrhage. The doctor had arrived by then and informed us that I needed to go to the hospital. An ambulance was called and while I went to the hospital, our new baby girl stayed home with her dad. I needed to be given some blood for the hemorrhaging. All of this happened only two months after I had returned to the farm and our marriage.

The promises he had made and the life he had assured me of were all gone. I was forbidden once again from any type of life outside of the farm. I was exactly where I had been when I left the first time. I wondered how I could have been fooled by his sweet words. I was trapped again in Jim's world and there seemed to be no way out. This mistake, even I had to say I was to blame for. I chose to come back home. When he had been charged with aggravated assault with a deadly weapon and given five years supervised probation the year before, he was extremely angry and told me so. He held me 100% responsible for that arrest and penalty. He was making me pay for it in any way that he could.

Somehow, my father had heard about the ambulance being sent out to the farm. At the hospital, they gave me a couple of pints of blood and the following day, they released me to go home. Jim came to get me that day and as we were walking out of the hospital, I saw my dad and a co-worker standing in the parking lot. Dad and Jim got into a physical fight in the parking lot. My dad hit him so hard that it knocked Jim out. When Jim recovered from the hit, he immediately called the police. Jim pressed assault charges against my dad. Dad was in fact charged with 5th degree assault, arrested and had to go to court over the incident. Needless almost too even say but things just got worse after that. Jim now despised my father and his anger was fierce.

Although today I understand why my dad felt he needed to assault Jim, I was very angry with him for hitting Jim then. I knew without question that there was going to be a price-tag placed on the assault and I was going to be the one that had to pay the bill, with interest. Jim was not ever going to let me forget that my father had struck him. He could do the most unspeakable things to me; beatings and what amounted to rape and sodomy but to have someone come against him, especially physically, was taboo. To seek revenge or to try and avenge his daughters hurt was something Jim would not tolerate from my father or anyone else. I am certain that if my dad's co-workers had not been there that dad, the assault would have been far worse. I think that one of the hardest things about that day for me was knowing my dad had stepped totally out of his character in hitting Jim. He is a gentle man and seldom did I ever see him angry. He was never prone to violence and the fact that he attacked Jim told me that dad had seen and heard enough. He was not going to stand around and allow Jim to do the things to me he was doing. Dad's forwardness against Jim told me he wanted it to end for me. He simply didn't understand the repercussions that would follow his actions. That was the last time I saw my dad for more months than I can recall.

The seclusion was clear and my family now knew that to see me and stop and talk would only bring on another beating from Jim. If I saw them in the store and those times were often, I could not acknowledge them in any way. I had to look away from my own family because if Jim saw me talking to them, he would become instantly enraged. That was my life and I could not have anything to do with my family at all. Jim controlled every aspect of my life. My grandfather on my dad's side passed away and both of my mom's parents passed away and I was not allowed to even go to their funerals. I had to read about their deaths in the newspaper. By this time in my life, my own family knew not to contact me for any reason or I would pay the price. It seemed to me that the price was getting higher and higher with each incident. I wondered sometimes when the price was going to be my life.

Jim's actions remained violent and his words, cruel. No matter what we were doing, he found a reason to yell at me or hit me. We were building a corn crib and it was snowing outside. It was cold and the wood we were using was heavy and slippery. We were sweeping the snow from the floor so that we could put boards down. I once again did something to anger him and as was usual, I had no idea what it was that I had done to provoke his rage. If things weren't done exactly the way he wanted them done, I suffered for the mistakes. I think that there was always rage inside of him that simply needed released. My presence was apparently all that was needed to bring it to life.

This particular time, Jim reached for a snow shovel that was lying on the floor. He used it to strike my legs, right through my pants, as hard as he could. He hit me over and over with the shovel until I could no longer stand. When he was enraged in the way he was that day, he didn't stop hitting me until his anger was satisfied. The pain and suffering I endured meant nothing to him. My knees are still numb from that beating, even after 30+ years have gone by. The violent beatings I received from all the years we were together have left scars and pain that will never go away. They are a constant reminder of the frightening abuse that Jim inflicted upon my body and my mind. When they hurt or I see the scars, sometimes my stomach will still knot up and the fear returns. I lived in a constant state of anticipation; waiting and wondering when the next barrage of his fists and fury was going to explode in my face.

Prior to Jim selling our herd, we had about twenty cows to milk twice daily. We were down in the barn one night, milking, when something went wrong. A cow kicked Jim or I breathed the wrong way and Jim became angry *again.* Jim picked up a metal water pipe that was lying in the barn. He turned towards me and struck me in the head with the pipe. He split my head wide open and the scar still remains. The scar is two inches long and Jim would always scream at me if I didn't wear my hair so that it covered the ugly scar. He didn't want anyone to see the scar he had put there. That was the only thing about that attack that ever bothered him. The fact he had given me the scar was of little or no relevance to him.

Beating with straps from the barn was not uncommon. He always told me he did not trust me and why, I never knew. I had never done anything to betray his trust or to give him a reason to think I would ever be unfaithful to him. If he was beating me and he did not think I was hurting enough, he would grab a milking hose and use it as a belt. His weapon of choice was anything that was within reach when he was angered. Belts, boards, shovels, straps and any other thing he could get his hands on were used to reprimand me or to hurt me for reasons unknown to this day. Perhaps, when I really look back, he didn't need a reason to hurt me. Breathing life and the memories of Jim's own childhood and abuse were enough. I was just the means to an end for him. He was always extremely quick to anger and there was no moment of thought for him before he would assault me. I returned to the house after milking with welts and bruises and blood oozing from the wounds he had inflicted on me. I walked through that door in excruciating pain more times than my mind really wants to remember.

   We had a representative from the Federal Land Bank stopped at the farm one day. Jim hated to talk to people and so he would always send me out to talk to whoever stopped. He would tell me to go outside, find out what they wanted and then to get right back inside. The conversation took longer than Jim thought it should have. When I came back in, he had gone upstairs. When I went to tell him what the man wanted, he kicked his foot through the side of an antique trunk that my parent's had given me. He then proceeded to destroy the trunk. He was beyond reasoning and when I tried to tell him the conversation, he became even angrier. He informed me that I was to go outside, say "what do you want" and get back inside the house.

   It didn't seem to matter really who came to the farm. There were times when the mailman would need a package signed for or a special letter would come and I needed to talk to him about it. Jim would listen to every word that was spoken but never come out and join in. For me to laugh with the mailman or have any type of interaction was absolutely forbidden. Sometimes, it was completely impossible for me not to speak to him. When I would come back inside, he would be waiting for me. The quick slap in the face or the kick to knock me off my feet was followed by him accusing me of "wanting" the mail man. Not then, nor ever, did I "want" anyone accept for Jim. His issues and his anger never let him see or believe that was true.

  I wish that somehow I could truly convey in words the horror that was my life with Jim. The words you read here will never be or seem as alive and real as our life was. Living with Jim was often like watching a horror flick at the movies. The movies always kept you in suspense and though you knew in your mind that something bad was getting ready to happen, you sat waiting for it. Out in some very dark part of the forest or a closet with no lights, the creature would hide until he was ready to devour you. Your heart racing and the feeling of unbelievable fear totally engulfed your being. Somebody touching your shoulder or leaning forward to speak was enough to cause you to jump nearly out of your skin. You would close your eyes or you held your hands over your face, terrified of what the monster or madman was about to do. You would ask yourself why they didn't run or what would ever have possessed the victim to stay in the house. Knowing that something so cruel and so abominable was lurking in the shadows was almost too frightening to watch; yet, you stayed to see the ending.

  Though the words written here speak of a movie I was never in, I could have starred in the movie. The only things different about the movie and my life were that there wasn't always a forest for the creature to hide in and it wasn't always something crouching in a closet. Sometimes the monster you feared the most was standing right in front of or directly behind you. It was a Jeckle and Hyde and I never knew when the bad side of Jim would emerge. He attacked without any warning and struck with the fierceness of a Bengal tiger. My own words do not do justice to the never ending attacks and scars that Jim tattooed forever on my body and inside of my mind. I did want to stay and see how "our" movie ended but it didn't end like the movies. The creature wasn't killed and the police didn't show up just in the nick of time to save me from the man that was hurting me. I stood alone, with no family and no friends to help me or to save me from Jim. I suppose there was one more huge difference between the movie and my life. I didn't have the option to walk away at anytime as I could have the movie. No one yelled "cut" and I am very glad that there was no director to call out for a "re-take" of the scene we had just finished. I could not walk away from my children and our farm to escape the monster that Jim had become.

Again, I say, my words can only tell you the story of a life of domestic violence that I somehow managed lived through. I can tell you that the feeling of cuts and bruises and of the unimaginable pain that even Jim's bare hands caused me, are as real as life gets. My body reminds me each and every day, with each flinch or jerk that the pain causes me, that it happened to me.

Chapter 7

{A Change in Venue}

Going back for a moment to 1976, Jim and I both had joined the National Farm Organization. The NFO worked to bring farmers together in an effort to manifest a "collective bargaining" for farm products. For the first several years we went to all of the meetings. We went to the functions that the organization put on and began to get involved in their matters. It was in the '80's that Jim himself became very involved. He started on the county level, holding different offices. He quickly moved up the ladder and in no time, he was at the State and national level of issues. He had then and perhaps still has today, a true passion for his fellow farmers. Their welfare and the way they were treated or mistreated was extremely important to Jim.

Jim was somehow elected to the National board of directors which of course placed more work and farm related chores on me and the kids. What it really meant to us was that we could work in peace. As long as Jim was gone, we could work at our own pace without the fear of feeling his rage. I found myself actually looking forward to Jim's board meeting times as he was gone for at least a couple of days at a time. That meant a break for me and an opportunity to sleep at night without being so afraid that I would be woken in the middle of the night. No nights of sitting up for the entire night, listening to Jim rave. No waiting for his fury to reach its boiling point, as it always did, and feeling his fists all over my body.

He always took me to the main convention with him as Jim was the director. It was my job to be the navigator on our road trips. If I got us lost or didn't direct him exactly to where we needed to be, he would become angry at me. As long as I was near him he remained angry but when I walked out of the room, he was fine. When we were around people, we were like the ideal couple. No one would have ever sensed that there were any issues between Jim and I. Even at home, if we had an argument or there was a physical encounter, whatever happened outside, he expected me to forget the incident. It was to be treated as if it had never happened and I was not to speak of it, ever.

By the 80's, we were deep into the cattle business as a beef seller and we were farming over five hundred acres of land. Also in 1980, another child was born and he too was born at our home. He was to be our last child. We had a Nurse Practitioner come to the farm. The morning he was born I was stacking hay bales. Life was what it was and that is all there was to it.

Most of our income came from bailing alfalfa and selling it. We bailed small bales, loaded them on hayracks and then later loaded them on to a conveyor belt to stack in the hayloft or a large shed we had on the property. The entire family helped except for the two youngest, of course. They were playing while we worked in the fields. Our eleven year old son was on the tractor while my oldest son and I stayed on the rack and stacked bales. We also pulled the silage from the box and placed it on a conveyor to blow it up 60 feet into the silo. In the winter, we would load them from the shed or barn on to a fifth wheel trailer and haul them to the buyers farm. There, they were unloaded and we would go back to get another load. It was very intense labor and the bales each weighed about 50 to 65 pounds.

Most of the time we were bailing hay, the kids were on the rack with me, loading more bales of hay. It was not unusual for kids to help out on the family farms. Wives had their place in the fields also and I spent a great amount of my time there when it was hay season. It was seldom a pleasant experience because there was always something that broke and I, of course, was the responsible party. Whether it was a string that broke, spilling hay back onto the field or a string that didn't tie, I was expected to run along the side of the bailer and feed the hay back into the bailer. We were always in a huge rush and Jim would scream at us because we were not moving fast enough. There was never a concern from him about our well being or whether or not the work we were doing was safe. To slow down a little and make our job less intense was never a thought of Jims. He did not care how hard we worked and considered it just part of farming.

In 1985, we were busy chopping corn to feed to the cattle during the winter months. We cut it and then blew it up into a large silo on the farm. We worked mostly every day of the week, including Sunday. It was not a day of worship for us as it had once been. Sunday was simply another day of the week now. My faith was always there with me but at times, I found it harder to hold on to. Life had changed so much for me and there were times that I wondered if God was too busy for me. A terrible thing to think, I know, but given the life I was living, not really so strange of a question.

October of 1985, we were still very busy with the corn chopping. The entire family helped except for the two youngest children. They again played while we loaded and worked. Our 11 year old was on the tractor and I and my oldest were behind the wagon of corn. It was our job to pull the silage from the box on to a conveyor and let it dump into the 60 foot high silo. Jim was busy fixing a part by the shop, a couple of hundred feet from where we were. Our youngest had come over to see what we were doing. The wind was blowing hard as he walked past the power take off shaft on the tractor. The wind blew under his jacket and a part of his jacket got caught up in the PTO gears. The jacket was nylon and did not break, but rather stretched and drew him closer to the turning gear. I don't remember which of us actually saw him first but we shut the tractor down as quickly as we could.

Nothing can match the feelings of dread and fear that swallowed me up as I ran towards our son. I saw my 5 year old son's body wrapped around the steel shaft of the PTO. Jim was beside me now and may have been the one that actually saw it happening first. He reached around him and my heart felt overwhelmed. Our baby boy was still breathing. We unhooked the shaft from the tractor and working together, we turned it backwards. Slowly, painfully, we un-wrapped his tiny body from around the steel shaft that held him. We were both very scared because we knew that many farm accidents resulted in the death of the person injured. If they do live through the ordeal, they end up with lifelong effects from the injuries their bodies have sustained. When he was completely free of the shaft, we raced to the truck.

The next twenty-five miles was going to be one of the longest rides of my life. Holding him in my lap, exactly as Jim had placed him there, I cried. His body was limp and I chastised myself for thinking the worst. We had grabbed some wet towels and wrapped them around his arms to try and slow the bleeding. I talked to our son the entire way to the hospital, trying desperately to keep him awake. Still not having a phone because Jim had ripped it off the wall so many months before, we needed to find a way to let the hospital know that we were coming. Jim pulled off the road into the parking lot of a convenience store and notified the hospital. By the time we got nearly to the hospital, they were waiting for us. They immediately transferred him to the ambulance and began administering care. Jim went with the ambulance and I followed in the truck.

Alone, in the truck, I prayed to God. I prayed that he would spare my little baby and allow him to live. I don't know that I could have endured the loss of one of my children. They were my life and the only reason that I endured all that Jim had done to me. I could and would take all of the pain that Jim inflicted on me and still go on. To lose one of my kids would have been one mountain to high for me to climb. I wonder if they ever really knew and understood that. I can only hope that if they do not know, that one day they will open their hearts to see it.

At the E.R., we were told that both of his legs had been broken, his one arm was broken up near his forearm and that his hand had been very severely severed on three sides. The only side that had not been cut was the inside of his arm where all of the vital veins were. I hung my head and thanked God. He had answered my prayers and watched over that precious baby. Though his injuries were terrible, he was going to live. That is what mattered most to me.

While waiting to see the doctor again, the minister from our church came by. He came to console us and to offer his and the church's support. He was a kind gentleman and it gave me a peace to see him there. The kids and I had been going to his little country church and had become members of the flock. I don't know if I would have made it through that first day had it not been for the minister stopping by. He was a blessing. I remember feeling scared inside for another reason, other than for our son. I knew already, before it ever happened, that I would for certain, be blamed for the accident. That I am afraid... was just a given now.

If my memory serves me correctly, Jim stayed with our son through the night. I went home as there were still chores to do and five other children to care for. Our children were home alone and because we had no phone, I could not even tell them their brother was alive. When I returned home, they were all crying and terrified. I hugged them all and assured them that their brother was going to be alright. One daughter had taken off running when the accident first happened. She was crying so hard and as I hugged her, she began to stop crying and settled herself some.

When I returned to the hospital the next day, our son was going in to a full body cast. They had reattached his hand and though he would recover, he would have issues for a very long time. The best news was the fact that he had sustained no internal injuries and that all of his broken body would eventually heal. I give the thanks for all of his healings to God. Our son was to stay in the hospital for nearly a week, mending and being closely watched by Doctors and nurses until he was well enough to return home.

Jim and I went back and forth to the hospital every day. I could sense his anxiety rising every day. I held my body tense, waiting and knowing with all too much certainty that I was going to have to suffer for the accident. On the third night's drive home from the hospital, shortly after pulling onto the main road, Jim pulled the car over to the side of the road. I knew exactly what was coming my way and I tried to brace myself for the first punch. He began screaming at me and telling me what garbage I was. He told me he could not believe that I was so incapable of watching our kids. He told me he should have known that I was not able to do anything right. He also cursed at me and told me that our other two sons were also responsible for the accident happening. I could not believe the words I was hearing from him.

Jim reached out suddenly and grabbed my hair in his hand. My hair was very long and he managed to get as much of it as he could in his hand, wrapping it around his fingers to hold on tighter. I could not escape the onslaught of his anger. There was nowhere for me to run, even if I could have. He began to shake my head and then slammed it as hard as he could in to the window. I truly do not know why the window did not shatter from the impact. That is how hard he was slamming it into the window. He punched at my face and my body over and over, striking me with such force that it shook my entire body. I tried, between the punches, to tell him it was no one's fault. I told him that accidents happen and that is why they call them accidents. He did not want to hear anything I said to him. My words only served to infuriate him more and feed the fire that was already ablaze inside of him. The angrier he became, the harder the punches came to me.

As with all things that happened with Jim, someone had to be blamed... someone was at fault except for him. After what seemed like an eternity, he stopped hitting me and began to drive again. He told me to pull myself together and straighten myself up before we got home. He did not want the kids to see me looking so terrible. He was insistent that the kids not know what he had done to me on our drive home. While he thought about someone seeing his handi-work on my face, all I could think of was what a horrifying experience the accident had been for us all. I couldn't help but think that we should all be supporting one another and gathering together as a family, loving one another. Wasn't that the way it was meant to be? Wasn't that exactly the way a family was supposed to react to such a frightening experience? Jim had apparently never received that teaching.

After our son's stay in the hospital, he was sent home. He came home in a full body cast and we did the nursing at home. A week before Thanksgiving, he was able to come out of the cast. His healing was remarkable but the doctors told us he would need to learn to walk all over again. He was five years old and we had not sent him to school that fall. To see our little boy have to resort to crawling like an infant to get where he needed to go absolutely broke my heart. We watched him and waited, thinking about the six month time frame that the doctors had given him to walk again.

On Thanksgiving morning, we were blessed with yet another miracle. I walked out into the kitchen and our son came walking across the floor to me. The entire family cheered for him and it gave us such reason for celebrating Thanksgiving Day that year. Life began to move forward again for us. I was thankful to God and very blessed to have had the pastor become such as very deep part of our family. Our son had surgery on his arm that December because the bones were so twisted that the ends of the nerves were dead. Bone marrow was scraped from his hip and grafted into his arm. It was all held together by plates and screws until the new bone began to grow and heal.

His abuse never seemed to cease for me. He always had another reason to beat me I always left a winter jacket hanging in the barn. I had learned from past actions to always try and be as prepared as possible. Often times, Jim would be angry at me and throw me outside and lock the door. This would be after the kids had been put to bed so that he did not have to put them to bed. This little game he played may not have happened a tremendous amount of times but once was too many. It was freezing cold outside and he didn't really care how cold I got. Outside, in a cold barn in the middle of a Minnesota winter was for certain not a place to spend the night. Some of the times he would unlock the door and other times he would come out to get me. I preferred the door unlocked because if he came to get me, there would be a beating. I would, at times, slip into the house before it was time for the kids to get up and ready for school. They didn't need to know that their father had locked me out or that their mother had spent the entire night sleeping in the frigid barn.

When I read or hear about the kids stating that they "grew up in a normal home" or that they saw no abuse, I shake my head in wonder. I know that a great many incidents happened while they were at school; as a matter of fact, most of them happened when they were away. Still, the bruises were very often in plain sight so I would have to tell the kids a lie as to where the marks came from. I truly felt I was doing this in the best interest of my children. The verbal abuse was witnessed by the kids more times than I can count. Jim took every opportunity to tell them exactly how worthless I was. I will say that Jim was not in the least bit shy of telling any of us how stupid we were if we made a mistake. No one, not I or the kids were safe from his terrible ranting and accusations.

There were things I taught myself to do well in order to save myself. I became the world's most perfect liar. I could conjure up reasons for marks that he left on me in an instant. I could create stories about why we couldn't visit or why we could not have visitors to the farm. The lies became a learned necessity in order for me to avoid at least a few beatings. The pain had become so much that being honest or seeing my family and friends became almost secondary to me. When there was a black eye, I either ran in to a silo or stepped on a broom in the barn. I used any excuse that I could think of to explain what had happened to me. To be honest or tell someone what was really happening to me was like signing my own death warrant. What would have followed would never have made the truth worth it to me.

Throughout the years to come, there was always some sort of abuse happening to me. The abuse would sometimes subside for a time and we would actually live what was to me, a normal life. There were words that he would call me that he knew I hated so badly. They were foul words that served absolutely no other purpose than to degrade a woman. Jim knew those words far too well and he would toss them at me when we fought. Sometimes I think he used them to get me angry so that he had more reason to beat me harder.

The eighties brought with them some new dynamics for our family. We now had teenagers in the house and that changes a home even at its best. Good kids or the not so good kids, they are going to change your household for a time. Our children were always hard workers. They had learned right along side of me that the harder you worked and the more Jim liked what you were doing, the better for everyone. A great deal of the time that we all worked together, the kids and me, things would go fairly smooth for us. There were even moments that we shared laughter and smiles while working. Even when we were working around the cattle, which can be very challenging all by its self, we still managed to enjoy ourselves. I found it to be a very pleasant working atmosphere for the kids and me. It was different when Jim was there working with us. The animals themselves seemed to sense something in Jim that made them nervous. They would become almost immediately unruly and nearly impossible to handle. I am sure that they could sense the evil and abusiveness that was Jim.

I loved the farm in every way. I loved my home and my family with everything that I was. I remember waiting until everyone had gone to bed and then I would slip outside by myself. I walked from our house to the corner of the road and back in the darkness. The peace and solace there was indescribable. I have never been afraid of the dark or of animals or anything else that the night might offer me. I feared more the light and what waited inside the place that should have been my sanctuary. It is a strange feeling to think that I was more comfortable and felt safer outside in the darkness than inside in the comfort of my own home.

In the dark, you cannot see what is coming towards you. You may only hear the sounds of an approaching animal. You at least know that whatever is in the darkness might be more afraid of you than you are of it. If it does attack you, you at least have a chance to defend yourself. You even have a reason for the attack. The animal feels threatened or you are in its territory. When you are in an abusive relationship, the creature that stalks you is not defending its territory. It does not feel threatened by you in any way. It does not need a reason to attack you. It simply needs you and that is all the reason it needs. There is for certain more to fear from an abusive partner than anything that hides in the darkness.

As the kids got older, he used them to humiliate me as much as he could. He would tell them what a stupid mother they had and that I was nothing more than a stupid bitch. He had no issues with telling them that if something went wrong, it was my fault. He would tell them I couldn't do anything right or that I had screwed something up. "I feel like I have another child besides you kids" was one of his favorite things to say to the kids. He told me many times that I was useless unless I was picking up rocks or in the kitchen. The kids were told over and over that I was unteachable. Jim told me that the farm was the best place for me because that way, no one saw my ignorance. "There is no one that would ever hire someone that was as stupid you." Those were his words to me. "Your incompetence would get you fired anyways."

When I became almost immune to the words he said to me, he would find another way to hurt me. He would call my father a "fucking old man" and say he was worthless. "You got your stupid worthlessness from your father." He would refer to my mother as "the witch" and say terrible things about her. He knew that I loved my family and that I wanted badly to just be able to see them. Tearing them down was just another way of him pulling me further into his very own world? His words were bitter and cruel and their cut was worse than any knife a person could weld.

There came a point in which Jim decided that people might be seeing what he was doing to me. The water man or the meter-man that came out to our farm might see something that Jim did not want them to talk about or tell anyone. Even the mailman became a threat to Jim and so he did a change-up on me. People had started asking questions about the bruising on me and some of the marks he left on me. His new venue was going to be even crueler than what I had endured in the past. I had no idea that things could actually get worse than what they already were. It didn't take me very long to figure out just how wrong I had been in thinking that way.

In the 80's, most of the abuse was now of the sexual nature. This was a part of the violence and sickness of our relationship that I didn't know if I would ever share. Knowing without a doubt that I do not stand alone in this type of abuse, I feel it is a part of the atrocities that take domestic abuse to a far different level of horror. Being slapped or kicked or beaten with a steel pipe are terribly frightening. The pain is unforgettable and is the makings of some unimaginable nightmares. His newly thought up avenue of destroying me was horrifying.

This new found way to humiliate me was sexually violent abuse. Verbal, emotional and economical abuse was always a part of whatever game it was he was playing. It was a daily happening for me and I had grown used to being abused. That doesn't ever mean that I was o.k. with it. I had simply reserved myself to the fact that it was going to happen. To think otherwise would have left me open and vulnerable to the worst things that he could think of.

Sexual abuse from the partner you trusted to protect you from someone violating you in that way has no way of truly being conveyed. The beating will take from you many things inside of your mind and soul. Sexual abuse, rape, if it was by anyone else besides your partner, takes away your… everything. You have no pride, no dignity and your soul dies a little every time it happens. It leaves you feeling as if you are no more than a whore to be toyed with and hurt.

  Even with all of the abuse, I never denied him sex. I used it as much as he did but for different reasons. For me, it was a means of protecting myself from some of the more violent physical abuse. It took away some of the more painful destruction that Jim was doing to my body. It had become almost a safe haven for me and I welcomed the sex in placement of the beatings. Even that place, he simply could not leave alone.

 The only thing that I knew I had become a pro at was covering scars and telling lies to hide the shame. I knew how to hide my feelings, if I even knew any longer what they were. I wasn't supposed to show emotions and I became very good at not doing that. He used my lack of emotions to call me a cold hearted bitch or to tell me I was made of ice. I had learned that it was simply not safe to show sadness, compassion or concern for anything other than Jim. Anything outside of him would only bring me pain and I was growing weary of that hurt.

 Up until his choice of degradation changed, he had not been what I would call sexually abusive to me. I was able to use the sex to my advantage. Somewhere along the road, Jim apparently decided that the sexual side of our relationship was also open to abuse. He read Pornography a lot and was always looking at other women in a sexual way. He left one's mind to think that he believed that was what a female's purpose was on the earth. They were to be eyed and ogled and used for man's any desire. That was his mindset and now it seemed that I was to become one of those "toys."

He began to turn our sex in to a sick method of abuse. I do not remember him and me kissing very much. I would even go as far as to say that it was not ever part of our intimacy, especially during sex. Sex for us was nearly always a "Wam, bam and thank you maam." I don't know for sure, except in the very beginning, if there was ever any love or passion in our relationship. Never do I look back and refer to our sexual relationship as "making love." It was completely sex and though it was very often… it was just sex. And now, even the sex was no longer a safety net for me. He would do horrible things to me. He played them off at first as "trying something new" but I knew this was far more than "playing house."

There are things about that time in our life that even after counseling and support groups and a little therapy tossed in; I still find it very difficult to share with you. I do want other women to know that their abuse is not secluded and that others, including myself, suffered through it. I know the importance of finding a connection with someone that says "hey, I understand and I will hold your hand." Knowing these things does not make it any easier for me to tell you all of the things that he did to me.

Sexual abuse from any one is a horrible experience that leaves the victim stripped of their dignity and self worth. It demoralizes them and leaves within them a feeling of uncertainty, guilt and shame. Although physical abuse by itself is a shredding thing, there is something different about sexual abuse. Your teachings and your morals and your personal and very private places are violated in ways that can only be felt and known by a victim of this abuse. The humiliation and demeaning that comes with the abuse has no ending. His violent actions were in no way alright. The pain that came with everything he did to me was perhaps the most extreme pain I had dealt with. I would rather have had him beat me with whatever he could find than to have suffered through this abuse.

Dignity becomes a word that no longer can be found in your minds dictionary. The sheer terror of what Jim might be planning to do to me next was enough to render me helpless. I think back now and tell myself I should have said no. I curse myself for not fighting back when he was sexually abusing me. The beatings that would have come from denying him would have been less painful, less degrading than what he did to me. When it was done… I was left just a shell that huddled in a corner and wished I was somewhere else.

He also had begun accusing me more and more of having an affair. How in the world I could have had an affair was beyond my comprehension. I was a prisoner and the fact that he might think or believe that I was cheating on him was absurd. It wasn't even remotely a thought in my mind.

He was simply looking for more reasons to abuse me in every possible way.

Jim's youngest brother got married and we went to the reception and dance. I loved dancing and so I danced. As the evening went on, Jim disappeared and was gone for a long time. As was normal, I never knew where he went or who he went with. A gentleman at the reception asked me to dance with him and since Jim had abandoned me, I said yes to the man's request. We danced and talked and then danced again. I was very much enjoying the dancing as that was something Jim and I did not do. The man's friends were ready to leave and so he left with them. I don't know that I even knew his name. We simply danced and enjoyed a few laughs.

Jim returned from where ever he had been and as usual, had no explanation as to where he had gone. That was his way and he fully believed that he did not owe me an explanation. Where he went and what he did was none of my business and he made that very clear to me. It was not the same for me, of course. If I was five minutes late for church, I had better have a damn good reason why I was late. Jim's thinking was always about him and never was there a care or an interest in my thoughts.

We drove home that night and all the way home Jim continued to accuse me of having sex with a man in the parking lot. Thinking back now, that was probably exactly what *he* was doing while he was absent from the reception. His badgering and accusations were relentless. I kept trying to tell him that I did not have sex with anyone but the more I pleaded my case, the angrier he became. I was once again extremely fearful of what was to come from his torrent insanity. I knew that a beating, at the very least, was coming my way.

On our property was a large gravel pit. Jim pulled the car right next to it and parked. For a moment, he tried to be nice to me. I guess he thought if he changed his tactics I might own up to what he swore I had done. In a flash, he grabbed hold of my hair, wrapping his fingers in it to get a tight hold. He began jerking my head all around, insisting that I had sex with a man. He called me a liar and continued to smash my head in the car. I was crying and my head hurt and I was scared, so very terribly scared. What should have been a great night had quickly turned in to another nightmare. The hair pulling and shaking of my entire body seemed to go on forever. He just kept calling me a liar and telling me that he knew I had sex.

At this point, I was trying desperately to figure a way to decelerate his madness. I decided that if that is what he wanted to hear and believe, I was going to give it to him. It was the only thing that I could think of in the midst of Jim's brutal assault. I had hopes that my choice would lessen the beating. I finally yelled out "You are right… I did have sex with him in the parking lot!" I did not but I had to do something to stop him. The car suddenly went still and quiet. I wasn't sure what to expect in the wake of my lying confession. Hell, I had told so many lies to others for so long, what was one more lie going to hurt. I figured that lying to Jim was the very least of my sins. It was time I lied to the man that started all of this shit.

What a shock for me when Jim smiled at me. It was as if he enjoyed the thought of me having sex with someone else. It was exactly what he wanted to hear from me. It excited him in ways that I thought was horrid and disgusting. It was a side of Jim that I had not ever seen. He wanted me to give him all the details of the sex act. Now what was I going to do. I was in this up to my neck and to tell him I made it up would have been deadly for me.

I did not have a fluent imagination so I began trying to share a story that had never happened. As I wove my way through the web I found myself trapped in, all I could think of was "what was next?" I had no idea how many times this lie was going to come back and haunt me and threaten my safety. I was giving Jim ammunition to use against me, as if he didn't already have enough. This lie was possibly one of the stupidest things I could have told Jim. As I finished my story, he physically and without a doubt, raped me right there. He was very aggressive and his excitement was frightening.

I know how loudly disputed me using the word rape would be in our society. Spouses don't rape their spouses. They are simply taking what is rightfully theirs to take. That is how the world thinks and that is sad. No still means no, even if it is saying it to your spouse. Jim did not ask nor did I invite it. He just attacked me and had his thrill while I laid back and cried. Damn him for taking from me the last element that was nearly sacred for me.

He seemed to take great pleasure and joy in his newly tried abusive behavior. He would say things like "there, show that to your doctor" or "let your doctor take some pictures of that." He was completely confident in the fact that I would *not* show anyone, including a doctor the physical sexual abuse that I had been dealt from Jim's fists and hands. There was pulling and stretching and twisting and even mutilation of my female genital area. Sometimes it caused not only unbearable soreness, redness and puffiness for days but also caused bleeding and scarring. The abdominal pain that came with his abuse was unbelievably increased every time he touched me that way.

I was sodomized with coke bottles or whatever he could get his hands on. He used more foreign objects on my vaginal and rectal area than I care to mention here. Suffice to say that many were objects not meant for any type of sexual games. Always, they caused me bleeding and excruciating pain all through my lower body. To me, by sodomizing me and doing the things that he now was doing, he was taking me as far away from humanity as he could. He was now taking the very last shred of my dignity away. By doing so, he could break me down to feeling as if I would be good for no one except for Jim. That is exactly what he wanted me to think.

My abuser was not finished with me after the violation of my body. He had to be sure that he had destroyed as much of me inside as he could. He would taunt me, as if I would ever do the things he accused me of. It was almost as if he were proud of what he had just done to me. He stood tall, boasting of what he had done to me. Jim had found the ultimate way to abuse me and to get away with it. It was "consensual" because I had not fought him or screamed out. What a husband and wife do behind closed doors is their own business and not against any law. He was well aware of this and enjoyed the knowing. He had, without any doubt, finally achieved his goal in humiliating me and he was very correct in what he had said. I would *not* be sharing this abuse, in spite of the horrifying pain that he had inflicted on me.

He was very interested in the "swingers" lifestyle and on more than one occasion, he attempted to make it happen for us. Sadly, he succeeded on several of those attempts. This may be an interesting lifestyle for many but it was not something I had any interest in. Everyone being alright with it was one thing but Jim knew that I was not compliant. That very fact made it even more appealing for Jim. After a couple of times of expressing my lack of desire to continue having sex with other men, I once again found it to be extremely "unhealthy" for me to tell him so.

He wanted me to have sex with other men so that he could watch us and then he could relieve himself at the same time. I am not really sure what brought that on. Maybe it had always been in his mind. The longer we were together, the more confident he got in the way that he abused me. The people he chose were men that I thought were my friends. They were people I thought of as only friends and had no sexual attraction to them and no desire to bed them. The thought of Jim watching wasn't a good thought in my mind nor was it really something I wanted to happen either. He pushed it all of the time and wanted to watch as he relieved himself. I became "compliant" for the sake of safety and peace for everyone.

I am not totally sure of what his actual expectations were of me at that time. I did find it interesting that his expectations were that I would always be a willing participant and that he would be the watcher or the director. As I found this to be a whole new type of abuse for me, I wasn't sure if it was sexual abuse or a couple experimenting. I know without a doubt today, that it was absolutely sexual abuse but the emotional degradation is so much deeper than that.

His confidence and knowledge that I would not ever share what was happening with anyone allowed him the free reign to do whatever he thought up in that warped mind of his. Until now, as you read this, 30+ years after it all happened…I have never shared this sexual abuse with anyone. It was sufficient for me to simply say that I had been sexually abused.

Working now with battered women, I can assure you that sexual abuse is a prominent piece of most victims' stories. The sexual abuse was extremely destructive for me. For me, like most battered women, the abuse was a very private event that a woman struggles with internally, privately and tearfully. We can't share with anyone how we feel inside and certainly not with our partner because they are the source of the pain. We don't share it with others because we are ashamed that we let ourselves endure it. It isn't even felt as "safe" to share it with the world because who is going to believe us? Who will believe that someone, to the outside world, acts as if they love you and says that they love you could possibly be capable of doing such things to you?

I guess I am still deeply ashamed, even knowing it was not my fault, for allowing this to happen to me. I also was a little taken back by the fact that I was somewhat relieved that the abuse had turned sexual. I knew why the sex had become his focal point for abuse and it was the same thought in my own mind. No longer would I have to lie about bruises and scrapes or broken bones. The scars that he would leave on me now were invisible to people outside of our home. They were marks and scars that would only be seen by Jim and me.

No-one would ever know of this abuse because I was too embarrassed and humiliated by his actions. The only time I ever reported anything was when medical attention was needed. Only when I was told that had I not sought medical attention I would have been dead in a few hours did the severity of it all become real. This, my private parts, had been the one un-abused part of our relationship and he abused every single part of my body. There truly was nothing left of the Connie that had married Jim Sarff. I was changed and would be changed for the rest of my life. I knew this without even having to think about it. The saddest thing is that the very last time an incident happened it was reported by someone else. I was too busy fighting for my life and being kicked and beaten to even think about telling anyone.

Chapter 8

Life and abuse goes on and on

In the later '80's and early '90's my world continued to change. At one point, and I can't tell you why, I tried to keep track of how often I was abused by Jim. I was not really surprised to find that it happened several times a week. Sometimes, months would go by without an incident and like a fool, the farther apart the abuse was, the more I allowed myself to relax. I even found myself beginning to believe that maybe our relationship had taken a positive turn. What a stupid thing for me to even allow myself to imagine. It wasn't long before the reality of the abuse that had always been would return in full force. Once again, the verbal abuse would start and then the physical abuse was never very far behind it. It truly never let up or changed; it just went dormant, like a cancer in remission for a while. It was there waiting to spring up and begin to terrorize my body and my soul.

At that time, we had six kids and we had pigs and cows running around to be taken care of. We had seven hundred acres of land that needed to be taken care of. Even if I had thought of having an affair, between Jim and our nonstop life at the farm, when would I have ever fit an affair in to my life? I surely did not have time for an affair and I didn't have the desire to have one. I already had one man that had transformed my life in to a living Hell; why would I want another man in my life. That one may have just been another Jim and done the same thing to me. One violently physical abuser was more than enough for this mother of six. At that time of my life, I had very little good things to say about men and I figured that they were all a pile of shit.

In the '80's I also found out that he had been having an affair. His disappearing from where ever we went was now making total sense to me. I am not sure how involved it was but he was seen sneaking out with this woman around town. If our life had been different, that knowledge might have bothered me or hurt me. The fact that he was with someone else was actually a relief for me. As long as he was out with her, he wasn't home sexually or physically abusing me. That all by itself was a blessing for me. As long as it wasn't me being hurt, I was good with it. That is how far I had fallen in my life. I should have been upset. I should have wondered if he was abusing her the same way he was doing to me. I also thought that maybe, I should have reached out to her and warned her about Jim. I did not do anything.

By this time in our lives, I had tossed away any thoughts that my life was going to change. I knew the abuse and the horrors I was living through were going to be my life. A sister in law of mine stopped by for a visit. It was so nice for me when someone would actually come to the farm. We were talking about my life and all that was happening to me. I told her that it was a terrible thing and that I was wishing my life away. I told her that when our youngest child turns eighteen that I was going to leave Jim. I told her I could not leave until then because Jim would take the kids away from me. He had threatened to take the kids from me before. His promise was that I would never see my kids again if I left him. He said he would go to the Social Services and deem me a bad mom and tell them I was sleeping around. The kids were the only reason I stayed. They were really the only reason I wanted to live. That was my life; they were my life and I would sacrifice and endure anything for them.

During the seventies and early eighties, things were very different from today. Couples didn't get divorced and just move on. The community saw everything and divorce was considered something ugly and unacceptable to many. You stayed married and accepted whatever came your way in the marriage. I was pregnant when I got married and that was bad enough and to entertain the idea of getting divorced was nearly unheard of. It was a social stigma and I couldn't destroy his name by divorcing him. There were not very many if any places for a woman to go if she were in an abusive relationship. For a woman to accuse and filed domestic abuse charges against her spouse was a no-no. I believe that Jim was the first man in our area to be charged with aggravated assault with a dangerous weapon used against his spouse. We lived in a time that was so totally removed from today's world. Even through the years leading all the way to 1998, things were hushed or swept under the rug. It was simply the way that things were then.

The mindset of women during the times I was being abused sexually and physically was taught us by our mothers. We stood by our man and protected him and he in return would do the same. Forcibly being made to have sex or having your spouse do things that you didn't want or enjoy was never considered "rape." I was Jim's wife and he was my husband, therefore whatever he wanted to do was considered alright. As my husband, he had the right to do as he pleased. Women didn't accuse their husbands of sexual assault and the courts would rarely, if ever, uphold a rape charge brought against one spouse by another. Even today, it is something that is very hard to prove unless the abuse has been violent.

Telling your "date" no and having them still take from you what you did not give freely is called rape. Your spouse doing the exact same thing; taking what you did not give freely is called "his right." It appears that the word "no" must only mean "no" if it isn't your spouse.

One of the problems I was facing was the changing of my stories. I had lied so long about where the marks or black eyes had come from. My stories were told and retold and never was there a mention of Jim abusing me in any way. Suddenly, I was supposed to change everything I had said and admit to lying about the injuries. My creditability was going to disappear and I might be viewed as a liar. These things often would cross my mind and scare me. I didn't want people to doubt my words and to cry wolf was certainly not a good thing.

I did now and then have thoughts about the lying. Was it truly possible that people believed the lies I told them? Couldn't someone tell the difference between a "fall from a tractor" and a severe beating? Could they look at me and believe me when I said an animal kicked me or the rake handle caught me? Were my words so believable that no one questioned them? I think I have said before that I prefer to think that way. It takes my mind down a bad road if I think any other way. For them to have not really believed me and still do nothing to help me seems too sad to want to believe. I know that people feared Jim, and I, more than anyone else in this world understands why. It doesn't take away the pain that my heart would feel if I knew that they all knew and said nothing.

If my words did not always ring true then it is a catch 22. I am left between knowing that when the truth came out, I would have to explain the lies and conveying to those that loved me why I could not speak the truth. If they were not totally believable then I am left wondering why more people did not come forward. I did ask myself sometimes where everyone was. I know that Jim had pretty much closed off any way for family to get to me. He caused such a "black hole" between me and those I loved. I lied to protect my children and myself from Jim's wrath. The truth was bound to come out sooner or later but still…

I did later hear that there were people very aware of what was happening at the farm. There were things seen by people that had to come to the farm for different reasons. Some people told their own family's to stay clear of Jim. They knew he was dangerous and that there were incidents happening that were not good. I guess it goes back to people not getting involved. They were doing exactly what I was doing. Staying out of harm's way by avoiding encounters with Jim. They were only doing just as I was striving to do for 30 years and it probably was the smartest thing they could do.

Life was moving forward no matter how badly I wanted it not to. I was over thirty now and had six children to love, protect and tend to. I was wondering if my life was ever going to change. Would the abuse one day just suddenly stop or was it to be a part of my life forever? Was Jim going to find new ways to abuse me physically and mentally? I really felt as if I had aged way beyond my years. Thankfully, I had my children to focus on and keep me interested in life and living. I wish that they could understand they were my life.

His threats were at times, frightening enough that I would be afraid to even sleep. He threatened to kill me and then chop me up into pieces so that he could bury me around the farm. There was always some kind of horrific threat that made me too afraid to go anywhere. He told me this would happen if I ever tried to make him accountable for his actions. That statement made me realize that his not wanting to be accountable meant he knew, without a doubt, that what he was doing to me was wrong. Not just wrong morally but also wrong legally. I knew then that he was very well aware exactly what he was doing to me.

Jim became very intently involved in the farm originations again. He was certain that he could organize and collectively bargain as a large entity, for a better price for farms and produce. The local offices he held, he worked vigorously to help their cause move forward. This of course left more work for me on the farm and off of the farm. It not only affected me but the children as well. Though the work was more again, it once again went easier when Jim was not there. We didn't have to deal with his yelling or criticizing everything that we did. There was always something changing in our lives and the children and I just seemed to go with the flow. Whatever the farm became, we adjusted and carried on as if it had always been that way.

In the '70's we stopped milking the cows and went to selling alfalfa and cutting firewood for income. In the '80's, we were very busy with a hog operation as our source of money. As the 80's rolled out and the '90's came in, we began to raise beef and farm the land. None of the children had ever worked away from the farm until after they graduated from high school. They were kept busy with the cattle and with the farming of the 700 acres of land we now worked.

Jim continued his work with the organization and was eventually elected to the National Board of Directors. Sometimes, I think that people have the mindset that abusers are under-educated, poor, lazy individuals that sit around and holler for a beer. They think of them as a low life that serves no purpose other than to be cruel and to scream. That is so very far from the truth, although the "low life" part certainly applies.

Jim was a very intelligent man with a plate full of passion for helping other farmers in any way that he could. He was extremely persuasive and convincing and a great public speaker. He always felt that he was looking out for the other guy. He had channeled all of his energy and his persuasiveness to the positive side of his life. I do still today; believe that he could have done so many good things for people. He was not afraid to "take people on" or confront issues he felt needed his input.

Jim had a powerful need for power and control. It affected every part of his life. I do know now, working in the domestic violence field, abuses can be from anyone including doctors and lawyers or the CEO of a huge company. Mechanics and pilots and the smartest, riches people in the world can all be abusers. There are no exceptions and no one is immune to domestic violence.

In the late 80's, our children started to graduate from High school. Some of them went off to college and some of them simply moved away. As each one left the "nest", it felt as if Jim had the need to divert his power and his control to those that were left to the remaining part of the family. I believe he was beginning to feel that his "Kingdom" was starting to change and perhaps... even maybe it was on the verge of crumbling away completely. His workforce definitely was changing. The only thing about Jim and our life together that was not changing was the abuse. It was ever present no matter what we were doing or where we were going to in life. The abuse of the one he called wife and swore his un-ending love to continued on and on.

Jim would occasionally take me along with him to his board meetings. I was more of a secretary than a wife on those trips. I took dictations and kept his paperwork organized for him. He went to Township meetings and county board meetings and anywhere else he could assert himself. He seemed to have a never ending list of causes or a reason that he had to be at the meetings. He wanted me to believe that his agenda was important to the survival of the farmers.

I watched and listened and soon found that many times, he had other reasons for attending a certain meeting. He would go just to intimidate someone that he felt had wronged him. He didn't care who it was or what position they might hold. He caused staff members and leaders to feel extremely uneasy just by sitting for hours and staring them down.

Fighting for a cause can be a great thing but raising Hell with people that were simply doing their jobs was not something good. There were times that he became so agitated and nasty that Deputies had to be called in to ensure safety. Jim was not bothered in any way by the presence of authorities. He carried on as if they had never arrived.

He was always finding a reason to turn things on me and become aggressively angry. He wanted me to speak up at his meeting so I did, once. It pissed him off and he told me to shut my mouth. I was damned if I did and damned if I didn't speak. I would pay for it no matter what I did.

One day, on the drive home from a meeting that had left Jim livid and ranting, he decided to drive very fast. He knew that it scared the Hell out of me when he drove that way. As we were approaching a bridge, he turned the wheel and aimed the car directly at the side of the bridge on my side. He looked at me and said "I could kill you so easily and make it look like an accident." His eyes told me that he meant it and I fully believe he was capable of doing just that.

On another trip home, he became angry with me for God only knows what reason. He suddenly kicked my door open on the truck and pushed me out onto a gravel road. We were traveling at thirty miles an hour and somehow, I survived with just some scrapes. I thought I was going to die that time. I couldn't help thinking back to the time I thought about tossing myself out of the car while it moved. Now, I knew exactly what that felt like.

I think that at times, he truly wanted me dead. I would think to myself "Why don't you just kill me and get it over with? Just kill me and this life of fear and horrible pain and the ugly varieties of abuse would be over for me." But as quickly as I thought those things I would tell myself "No." I wanted to live and raise our children. I wanted to have a family that lived a normal life in a house that was filled with love. I really didn't want to die at all; I just wanted the abuse to stop! These incidents, like so many others, always happened when we were alone. No witnesses and no body to tell about what Jim had done to me. It was a win, win situation for him.

~~~~~~~~~~~

In 1986, our eldest son graduated from high school. I had mixed emotions about being proud of him but at the same time, I would miss him when he went off to college. He came home most weekends and helped on the farm. One particular weekend, after he had spent time with some friends, he hugged me. He said to me "you know Mom, not everybody lives like we do." My response to him was "I know Son, and that is one of the most important lessons that you will learn out there."

We did have some good days and sometimes; even good weeks but the fear never left me. I was always on my guard, waiting for the next boot to drop. I tried so hard to think ahead and anticipate what he was thinking or wanting. With a mind like Jim's, it was a nearly impossible thing to do. I was always in "survival" mode.

I will be the first to admit that I am not perfect. I know that there were times that I was angry at what Jim was doing to me and I took that anger out on my children. There were also times that I confided some of what was happening to me to some of them. For doing that, I am still sad and will carry with me the guilt for having done so, to my grave. I had no one else to vent to or to share my pain with. There was no one that I could cry to because he had taken from me my family and my friends. The only people I associated with were Jim's friends and they were very seldom around.

The saying that "blood is thicker than water" made it impossible for me to talk with the people he allowed in to our home. Even if I had spoken to them, I was sure they wouldn't believe me. If they did, they were not going to cross Jim to help me. That had already been proven to me. I feared that they might even take back to Jim what I had told them and then, there would be Hell to pay for me. What happened at the farm was to always stay at the farm. Speaking to the wrong person would have been the same as chopping off my own head.

~~~~~~~~~~~~

In 1988, our first daughter graduated from high school. It was once again a time for celebration but also, it was a time of sadness for me. Each time one of my children left home, it was a time of reflection for me. I wondered if I had done the best for our children. I always felt as if I had short changed our children because the number one person that I needed to keep satisfied was Jim. To keep the peace in the house, the others, my children... had to take what was left after Jim took the life and love from me. I missed out on being the mom that I had always pictured myself as being. It doesn't get any sadder than that for me.

As we moved into the '90's, there were more graduations. Our second daughter graduated and she left the nest. Another empty bedroom always meant more sadness for me. I really missed my kids being home with me and it broke my heart every time one of my kids moved out. They were the very reason that I kept going and did not just say "To Hell with it all" and go away forever. They gave to me cause and reasons to go on living. By this point in my life, our oldest son was dating a wonderful young lady that he would later ask to marry him. Our family was excited and welcomed her in to the flock with love. Within months they became engaged and plans for a wedding were now in progress. My daughter and I planned a wedding shower for her that was to be held at the farm. What fun it was to plan and prepare food and decorate.

The day of the shower arrived and all was lovely and it was a special event for all of us. Then, the day was over and the night was there. The guests had all gone home; the adult children said their goodbyes and the three still left at home had gone to bed. The end to a perfect day... at least it should have been.

Jim and I went to our room that night and we talked about the day and the bridal shower. I was so happy for its success and I was pretty tired from the day's events. Not long into the talking, the conversation became extremely serious. There had apparently been some sort of interaction between Jim and his father earlier in the day. The more that he talked about it, the angrier he got. Somewhere in the midst of his being pissed at his father, I got drug into the mix and now, he was angry with me.

When Jim became angry this way, there was no slow brewing or body language that told me to be ready. It was sudden and instant and normally fiercer than had he taken time to think about it. He hit me so fast that I didn't even see it coming. He then pulled me by my hair and tossed me all over the room. He was leaving bruises all over me and intense pain. I found that neither the bruises nor the physical pain were any longer the worst he could do to me. My heart was filled with a sadness that was far worse than the bruises. My emotions and my soul were raw and the joy that had been our day was now gone in an instant. Though the next morning I was very physically sore, it was my heart that hurt the worst. Now, I went back to walking on eggshells again.

~~~~~~~~~~~~

In 1993, child number four was graduating. By the fourth graduation, it had finally started to get a little less emotional for me. That was not to say that I loved them any less at all. In part, it may have been that he did not leave home. He found work nearby and that allowed him to spend more time with us. I enjoyed the kids close to home and hated when I didn't see them for a while.

My kids helped me in so many ways. They made me feel safe because Jim was careful not to become too physical or to cause me any harm in front of them. When I have heard or read that they didn't see or hear a lot of the things that Jim did to me, I realize that it was by purpose. Jim, even in his angry moments, was much more aggressive and cruel when the kids were not around to experience it. To say that they never heard it would be stretching it but it was as seldom as possible and for that, I am grateful.

~~~~~~~~~~

1994 was a busy year for us. We had a daughter that was getting married in January. Anyone that has ever lived or visited Minnesota in the wintertime knows that it can be severely cold and terribly windy. The day of her wedding was no exception to that rule. Still, we enjoyed a lovely wedding and dance reception, despite the nasty weather. There were no problems and I even managed to finish out the day without being hit or kicked.

That same year, Jim and I were blessed with our first grandson and granddaughter. This was a totally new and exciting adventure for all of us. We were the typically excited and very proud grandparents and loved the babies very much. We doted on them as all grandparents do and welcomed them into our lives with open arms. The fact that the children were now the parents and that the house would one day soon be empty of them was bitter/sweet for me. I wanted only for my children to be happy in their lives.

I wanted them to know the love and marriage that I thought I was going to live, so very long ago.

By this time in my life, other thoughts had begun to manifest themselves inside of me. Thoughts about leaving Jim were becoming stronger and stronger. The idea of leaving my marriage and living peacefully was etching its way into my every alone moment. The fact that the kids would all be out of school and starting their own lives only added to my desire to go away from Jim. I had made the promise to myself that I would stay and endure so that our kids could have a two parent household until they all graduated. Those times were now coming full circle. These thoughts, though they gave to me a new hope of living without fearing for my life, always faded when reality took over.

I remember asking myself how I could even imagine doing such a thing. After-all, I was stupid, incompetent, and I could not do a single thing but "pitch shit and pick up rocks." Jim had reminded me of that for all of our life. I had no money, no vehicle, no job and not enough intelligence to get any of that. How could I exist, even if it were to just be myself I was taking care of? Jim had chiseled; more correctly would be to say he beat that into my brain so much, I believed it.

~~~~~~~~~

In 1995 and '96, two more grandchildren were added to our family. 1996 saw our youngest daughter graduate from high school. We celebrated that event as we had all of them. The preparing for the graduations was always a good time, no matter how many times we had done it. I made home-made cream mints in pretty shades and shapes. It had by now become a tradition for me to make mints in the desired colors for the occasion.

Our adult children and grandchildren always came to celebrate the occasions as a family. Some of them brought friends as well, some of which called our home their second home and I was "mom" to them. I loved every minute of those moments in our life. But unfortunately, something inevitably happened that left things unsettled. A couple of hours before the graduation ceremony, our granddaughter fell off of a bench in the kitchen. Sadly, our eldest daughter spent the evening in the E.R. with her baby girl. Fingers were pointed and somebody had to be at fault for the accident. In our house, the word accident did not ever apply or even exist. Someone was always going to be to blame. This unfortunate accident put a damper on the joys of the day.

Our youngest daughter also found work within driving distance of home. She stayed with us for a period of time before venturing out on her own. By this time, our work force had dwindled down and that meant more work for the rest of us. My daughter was expected to come home, after working all night, change her clothes and go to work on the farm. The same was expected of our son that was working outside of the home. I understand that we did not charge them for rent or food and therefore some help was a reasonable expectation. There was simply no thought given to the fact that they needed rest after working their away from the farm jobs. It was not a thought that would have entered Jim's mind. If it did, he didn't bother to mention it.

~~~~~~~~~~~

Our next wedding took place in 1997 and once again, the festivities were a huge family event. The wedding was held in our little country church that was just two miles from the farm. This was the same church that the kids and I had been attending since the early 1980's and we dearly loved the minister and his wife. The minister had tended to weddings and baby dedications for our family and had become a dear friend and special part of our lives.

During this time of our life, the verbal and emotional abuse was still very active. Jim had perfected his mode of emotional abuse and knew exactly what to say to cause the deepest hurt that pierced my soul. It seemed that the physical abuse was a bit lessened, although still present. When I think back now, I remember still being hit or punched but much of the physical abuse was now mostly over-looked by me. It was less severe and therefore, in my mind, it wasn't very serious according to my survival mindset. I had learned by then what was worthy of my concern and what was simply routine abuse. I hadn't yet figured out that it was all serious and all worth my concern.

There was always such a sense of relief when Jim would go away to his meetings in Iowa. Sometimes he would be gone for two or three days and it was heaven on earth for me. Even if it meant more work for us, the work was pleasurable when he was away. It certainly beat the hell out of being screamed at or cursed at for being "stupid."

Our youngest daughter moved out on her own so it left me and the two youngest sons to care for the farm. Jim was there from time to time to help. Our responsibilities peaked out during this part of life and we worked very hard to complete the tasks set before us by Jim. Working the fields, getting the crops in and tending to the beef cattle took care of most of our time. There was little time left to do much of anything; not that it really mattered. I never left the farm without Jim and he kept a close watch on me, no matter where we were.

The abuse that I had endured and considered just a way of life had come increasingly or perhaps a better word to use by this time was "annoying." It is sad to think that I had reached a point that his abuse had become a simple "inconvenience" for me. That is a place that I know now, no woman should ever be at in her life. It is terrible that it took me 30+ years to figure that one out.

With our last son in his junior year, life was as it was always going to be for me. I wanted for him to finish his schooling so that he had a chance to live. I watched as each child slipped away from home and found their own place in the world. I cherished the grandchildren and looked forward to each visit. I prayed with all of my heart that none of my children would follow in the violent, abusive ways of their father. Peace and happiness was all I wanted for them.

The knowledge inside of me that I took everything that Jim could toss at me, {and that can be taken in both the literal and the "pun" mode}, so that my children could grow up as near normal as possible, was enough to bring me a little smile. I gave to them every chance to live like any other kid they knew and hid the scars from them while I did it. If I did in fact make mistakes along the way and I am certain that I did, the knowing that everyone of my children escaped Jim's truly most violent wrath, sustains me. The cost was only some blood and tears and the payment was my children's love and the grandchildren.

~~~~~~~~~~

When 1998 rolled around, I was still thinking daily about getting away from Jim. With or without children at home, his abuse was not ever going to stop. I was his punching bag; his squeeze ball that you see people carrying with them to relieve their stress. I was the place he came to whenever life overwhelmed him and he needed to "relieve" some of the stress. My purpose had been shown to me and it was only to serve him, raise the children, to give him sex in whatever manner he saw fit and to roll with the punches. I was not a wife to him but a person to keep nearby in case he needed a "violent abuse" fix.

One particularly nice beautifully warm and sunny July afternoon, still in 1998, Jim became angry once again. He didn't reach his really iconic pissed until he discovered that there was no fuel in the vehicle. He didn't even have enough to get him from the farm to the nearest gas station. His rage turned into a tantrum and he went off about finances and how the gas tank should be full all the time. He told me that there should be a reserve tank on the farm. His pleasant departure and the nice sunny day in July quickly became a thing of the past.

Jim began his normal screaming and cussing at me. He shouted orders about the work that he wanted done while he was away. He warned me that I had better not screw anything up or break anything. If I did, he said there would be Hell for me to pay when he got back. Those words were nothing new to me and I was use to hearing the same speech every time he left. I listened attentively, like a "good" wife should do, mostly out of fear that this was going to change to physical. He shouted at me to go get him some 5 gallon gas jugs from the barn as he was walking towards the combine. He began to siphon gas to get him to the station to fill the vehicle.

The next thing I knew, Jim was ordering me to get under the combine and watch the jugs fill. I was to let one fill and then replace it with the next jug. I was told not to spill a single drop of gas while transferring the jugs. As he walked off to pour the gas in to the car, there I was, sitting under a combine, watching gas jugs fill. Something suddenly happened as my mind began sending me a thought. What was I doing sitting under this combine? At that very moment in my life, under that damned combine waiting for another jug to fill, I made the decision that I was done with this relationship. I was going to be gone by the time that Jim returned from his trip. I took the final jug of gas to him, watched him pour it into the car and then go into the house. He showered and he got into the car. I stood outside, watching the car head down the road. This was to be the last time that I would ever see that site again.

That very night I began to put my things together. A family meeting was called and the children that were able to come were told of my decision. I told them that I was done and that I could not and would not live like I was anymore. I was leaving their dad for good and would not be returning to the farm. There were of course mixed feelings and tears and a lot of fears for both me and Jim. All the tears and words in the world were not going to make me change my mind. I had to do this for my own good.

I told them that I had to go because 30+ years of being beat and verbally abused needed to come to an end. The moment had finally happened for me and I was not going to pass it up. The offer from a friend of our daughters for a place to stay was taken. I had no money, no car and no plan except to leave for good.

In the next two days, I did all of the jobs that Jim had left for me to do. I was still in that "please and appease" him mode. I didn't really know anything else. I packed and I sorted and I cried while questioning my courage to go through with leaving. My children and their spouses brought trucks and trailers and I loaded up my life onto the trailers and away to storage it all went. I was finished and I was finally breaking away from a 30+ year abusive relationship.

I and a couple of bags left my home of 24 years that day. I left a home that I had loved for all of those twenty-four years. It was the place filled with memories of graduations and bridal showers and that two of my babies had been born in. I was also leaving a house where I had been beaten and assaulted physically as well as mentally and sexually violated in the most disgusting and horrid ways. It was a home where I was raped by my own husband, time and time again. This place I called "home" also had left me wondering if I would live through the next beating or wake to see my children's faces again.

My middle son and my youngest son moved out of the house on the same day that I did. I felt shame inside of me for breaking my own promise. I had not made it to see my entire family graduate before I left. I would have to carry that shame with me for the rest of my life. Leaving was something that I had to do and I felt that it needed to happen right now. There was not going to be another chance like this one.

I left Jim a note, and with a final glance back at my home, I left. It was the end of a lifetime of pain and sorrow and I was praying that my new life would be different. I wanted a life of love and warmth and safety from anymore abuse. I could not have ever imagined that there was more to come. What happened at my apartment never crossed my mind. I truly felt that I was free for the rest of my life. My Lord, how terribly wrong I was.

Chapter 9

Knowing the man

I think that to understand some of Jim's issues, you need to know the man behind the charming smile. He had a way of manipulating and intimidating that was scary. Born on St. Patrick's Day, 1949, in Long Prairie, Minnesota, he was one of six children born to the Sarff family. He was born a descendant of a founding family of Eagle Bend. He had a competitive spirit inside of him, almost from the day he was born. He was a member of the FFA {Future Farmers of America} and spent the better part of his childhood working the family farm with his siblings.

His father and mother owned and maintained a large dairy and crop farming operation. In 1982 they divorced and went their separate ways. Jim's mother never remarried before she passed away. His father remarried three times before his death in August of 2000. His childhood was wracked with the very same abuse that was so prominent in our lives. Jim once described his mother as a liar that was abusive to everyone. She frequently told the children just what a bad person their father was. This took its toll on Jim.

Jim loved his father and for the most part, Jim did have a respect for his father. He learned from him the trade of a farmer and took that knowledge and made a life for himself in the trade. Because of his father's recent death, Jim did not want to discuss his father when asked for more details. There were questions asked during the trial and he spoke of his father's death and the timing. His father passed away right in the middle of the abduction. Jim kept his thoughts to himself concerning this until he was giving his last statement at his sentencing. As for life, the life that he lived was just that... life.

Although Jim himself talked very little about the life he lived at home, his siblings were more open about their lives. Through their words, one could see how Jim came to be the abuser that he was. Because a person experiences abuse as they grow up doesn't mean they will be the same. To the best of my knowledge, none of his siblings were abusive to their wives or children. Jim happened to be the one that followed in the same path as his father.

His brothers spoke of abuse they witnessed from their father. It was abuse that was felt by their mother as well as themselves. They knew of Jim's volatile temper and of the abuse that he rained down on me. The family had concerns about my safety and well being but that was as far as it went for them. The biggest thing that stood between them and helping me was the same as most that knew Jim. Put simply...they were afraid of their brother and did not want a confrontation with him. That left me pretty much alone as far as help from Jim's side.

Another of Jim's siblings told of the abuse that went on in their home as children. Strange that she stated that their father came from a moral, upstanding and idealistic family. She was certain that it was the terrible abuse that their mother lived with daily that brought an end to their marriage. More of Jim's "learned" ways were seen in the statement from the sibling.

She remembered spending many nights hiding from her father and stated that she still has problems sleeping at night. Her father blamed her for some issues that he had and made things her fault. She had the responsibility of taking care of Jim and remembered that he was a difficult child. He was and still is extremely strong willed and went after whatever he saw that he wanted. There was little bonding between their father and themselves but Jim was strong inside and he moved past that. The blaming that was so deeply a part of the verbal and physical abuse from Jim, once again, can be seen in his forming years.

Even when we started getting serious, Jim said very little about his family or his home life. It was pretty much a known fact in the town that his father was not a nice man. He abused his wife and at least one of the kids and did not stop at simply mentally abusing them. He was prone to violence and beat his wife. There was a restraining order that kept his father away from his mother. His continued harassment and physical abuse was part of Jim's life. He had the broken leg, well; he was on crutches for some time at school. I saw him with a black eye but like me, he always had a reason for it happening. His reasons were of course lies to hide the truth. He never told me but he did tell a friend that that leg and eye came from his father beating him.

I am not blind to the fact that what Jim did to me was a learned action. He was following in his father's footsteps and didn't know or at the very least, he did not care that he was. The things that he would do to me were things I am sure he watched his father do to his mother. It does not make it alright nor does it condone his actions in any way. It is simply a stated fact. Jim spoke with his father when and only when he deemed it needed. He would ask advice concerning he and I but as far as I know, that was as much as he did.

Never were his siblings unkind to me in any way. They tried very hard to keep social avenues open for me. They visited seldom but were unhappy with what Jim had done to our lives. One of his brothers kept in contact with my parents as much as he could. He tried to relay life happenings to my mom and dad when-ever the opportunity arose. This of course pissed Jim off fiercely but I don't think they cared. Sadly, in their efforts to keep my family informed concerning what I was doing and all of the things they were no longer privy too, it came back to haunt me. "The road to Hell is paved with good intentions," I am told. This perhaps personifies those that had reached out to help me in any way during those years of torture. Their good intentions and their desire to try and help me... sent me straight to the Hell that was Jim's anger and fury.

Whatever was done to try and stay in contact with my parents was seen as a direct slap in the face to Jim. Disrespectful, arrogant, uncaring were the only things that Jim could see through his fogged over glasses. He cared nothing for anything except himself. That was all that mattered to him and he made that clear both verbally and physically time after time.

Whenever money got tight or the farm work was hectic, I was right there in front of him to feed his need to hurt. He started his anger issues long before me and they continued straight into our life together. In looking at Jim and reading all of the things he did to me, I can only say that his life and our life together were just a reflection. We lived the mirror image of the life he grew up to think was "normal." I don't think that he saw things any other way.

There were things that happened in our lives that I was not even aware of sometimes until I saw it in the newspaper. He would go to town board meetings and county board meetings. He would just sit in the room and glare at people. He would verbally threaten members but kept it just on the side of legal. His threats were not held in any specific place and he threatened everyone from the county assessor to the county attorney. He was like a big bully on a play ground. He took what he wanted, when he wanted it and no-body would stand against him.

Even when he was being tested by the state, he had a way to make himself look as if he were perfectly normal. In their evaluation of Jim, they felt that Jim was very rigid and uncompromising. He was a highly ambitious individual who displayed a low tolerance to frustration. They felt he had a very suspicious nature and trusted no one but himself. This was a man that was evasive and defensive and could disassociate himself from anyone, in an instant. He told them that I was an incompetent dependant that could not think for myself. Jim talked down to people that he felt might appear better than him. This was simply Jim's way and he learned from the very best.

The evaluation went on to say that although he expressed a love for me and the children, he lacked the empathy or understanding of the emotional consequences that his assaultive behavior had on his wife or his children. He displays a deep seated, unrecognized hostility and rage that he is unable to come to grips with.

During a recitation in 1977, Jim displayed little to no emotional effects concerning his admitting to beating me. He felt I was to blame for any difficulties he had and that I had caused my own beatings. He left the impression with the evaluators that his abusive behavior was justified and that he was fundamentally, guilt-free regarding his own behavior. The study found Jim to be an "explosive and angry individual who was very capable of doing great bodily harm.

"Mr. Sarff does not respond well to therapy and seems to be quite angry and hostile and on numerous occasions has shown anger in my office. He has admitted to killing some of his cattle in a fit of rage by running them over with his truck. He also admitted that he threatened to kill his wife and her attorney." These were not issues that had suddenly manifested themselves after Jim and I had become a couple. They were deeply rooted and had been inside of him for a very long time.

Jim was thought of by the people of our town as almost two different people. Each was equally intimidating and both sides held a dark side that kept most people at bay. His moods changed as quickly as the weather and had the potential for the most menacing actions. Like huge clouds that darkened slowly, the storms that hid inside of him could burst open and flood you with inconceivable acts. He hid his spiteful side deep inside, at times, so deep that he appeared to be nothing but kind and helpful. He was the charming gentleman that had a quick, witty response that caused people to like him. He helped farmers that were facing farm foreclosures while he was head of the Todd county NFO. He was known to love and adore his grandchildren and even collected coins for them. He was part of the local tractor pulls and involved in a little bit of everything.

The Todd County Attorney said that Jim was known in the community as an opinionated, headstrong person that was a bit of a loner. The township knew him well as he showed up at so many of the meetings. Jim nearly always had something to say and rarely was it positive. The attorney also said that he was an "idea guy" and energetic as well as a great fund raiser. They knew him as a man that was always good at working with the young people.

Funny how differently this man I was married to looked from outside of my world. People either didn't see the monster that he could be or they simply chose to look past that side of Jim. The NFO's state president at that time thought Jim was a "great guy." He told the papers that he had always gotten along well with Jim and that he thought everyone else had too. "A leader among men" the president called Jim. I look at the description and cannot help but wonder how they could not see the Jim that I saw. They saw only what they wanted to see and the rest of Jim was simply pushed aside. The views and thoughts of the town were just whispers amongst one another. It seems that they were never spoken loud enough for anyone to help me.

That same man was also the one that most avoided as much as possible. He had made a habit out of threatening people and intimidating them any way that he could. He had a camera that went everywhere with him. If he had an argument with someone or they simply pissed him off, he would take their picture. He made certain that the person knew he had taken the picture of them. It was Jim's way of saying "hey buddy, I have proof so don't mess with me.

There were incidences that were logged in the police records and Jim didn't seem to care. He used the police to his advantage and would not hesitate to press charges against anyone that crossed him. Although the authorities wanted to lock Jim up, they were bound by the law to follow through on charges he had filed against people that dared to touch him. As the devil knows the bible, word for word, so did Jim know the laws and what he could get away with.

He got into an argument with a man we will call "Fred." {I do not use actual names as I do not want to hurt anyone while telling my story.} Fred was angry because Jim had arrived uninvited to a party and began harassing the guests. Jim told Fred that if he ever caught him with his back turned, he would certainly kill him. Jim went and got his camera but Fred met him at the door. He kicked Jim in the head. Jim, of course, called the police and filed assault charges against Fred. The authorities had no choice but to fill out the paperwork. Fred was cleared of all charges except for the kick in the head.

Jim never forgot anyone that had given him problems, no matter how long ago the issue was. He kept it all in his head and used it whenever it suited him. Many years later, in court on unrelated charges, Fred encountered the darker side of Jim. Jim sat in the court room and glared at Fred. Fred was later quoted as saying "He came looking for me. He just sat there in the courtroom and stared at me. He was harassing me and getting away with it. That man was always plotting something."

A reporter that worked for one of the newspapers in our area also came up against Jim's dark ways. No one was excluded from his list of people that he would vex. "Fran" told people that he would threaten her concerning some of the things she would write. He would remind her that she drove home alone, a lot. He would tell her that he would not want his wife driving alone that way. "Something bad could happen" he would tell her.

When the Todd County attorneys were asked why Jim was never charged with these threats, their answer was simple. "He never threatens when there is someone else nearby enough to hear him. He makes certain that he is alone with whom-ever it is he is threatening. "Jim Sarff is an extremely clever man and he is smart. He knows exactly how to do things without worry of legal issues He cloaks some of his threats so that they are sitting on the edge of legal or illegal."

There was story after story about Jim's reputation in the town. People that owned businesses said that he was smart about how he dealt with matters. He never had a checking account, or any other type of banking account.

He held no credit cards and always paid cash for whatever it was that he purchased. He knew how to dicker and rarely backed down if there was something he wanted. He would sometimes intimidate the owners until they gave in to his demands. He had no issues with standing in front of someone, finding a way to make them feel about half scared and waiting them out.

As for having the cash, though often times I have no idea where it all came from, he carried large sums of money with him at times. To take out several thousands of dollars at a time, serialized one hundred dollar bills and pay for an item, was not unheard of. Merchants had talked about it and some had seen it themselves.

He was a hard man and he could shut someone out of his life in the blink of an eye. He had no issues with being estranged from his family or an entire town. He could survive on his wits and make things happen by his "gift" of manipulation. I was not that way. I needed people and yearned for family and friends. I begged to be part of something outside of the farm. None of that matter to Jim. He did not care about anyone else's needs or wants. They meant absolutely nothing to him. If it wasn't going to help Jim in some way, it wasn't important to him.

His own blood meant little to him. He could and did close the door to them for many years. I have spoken of his distancing himself and me from family members. He did it so easily and so callously at times. Once he wrote you off, you did not exist in his world and he was perfectly content with that. It was not something he ever gave a second thought to. His siblings truly meant very little to him. It was not a happy home that Jim left and there was no real closeness between him and his family.

Jim was sued by his brother for monies not paid back. It was a very strange relationship that Jim had with his family. They communicated through letters and even the mail told of uncertainties and confusion. Kind words that were mixed with accusations showed there was something deeply disturbing in the way Jim faced his family. I believe that if Jim had allowed the doorways to their family relations to remain open, the others would have visited more often.

His brother, knowing of the strained relationship with Jim and my family, once showed my mother a picture. He had seen her at a meeting in town and showed her a picture of a great-grandson that she had never seen. She looked at the picture and cried. The brother was later heard saying that he knew he had stepped over a line. It was a line that Jim had drawn and the brother felt strongly about the way that my parents had been treated by Jim. The fact that he had cut off all ties to my family angered many of my family and Jim's family, as well.

"I do know that there will be families that are unhappy with me for what I did and what I am saying now. I feel that no one should be treated like Connie's parents have been treated by Jim. It just isn't right at all." The brother stepped away from Jim in his life. Some of it was the lawsuit but a lot of it was Jim himself. His brother had seen enough of Jim's madness, as he referred to Jim's ways. He said that family members had tried for a very long time to get Jim to seek counseling. Everyone was aware that Jim had some very serious and dangerous issues. Well, everyone, apparently, except for the State, who found nothing wrong with him nor did they find him menacing. Sadly, his brother wanted to reunite with Jim. There was no way that Jim was going to allow that until he himself made that decision. "I feel very, very angry at Jim and I have plenty of good reason to feel that way. I just wish he could find help. It doesn't feel right to me not being in communication with one another" the brother had said.

Jim trusted no one and he went out of his way to let people know. Most of his distrust was with the people that he was closest too. Places and times that I would have preferred to be alone, Jim would make sure he was with me. The few times that I did go to a doctor for a simple check up or because of one of Jim's fits, he always came in the examining room with me. I am sure there are husbands and wives that just naturally do that. I was very aware of why Jim did not let me go in alone. He wanted to be nearby when I spoke to the doctor. That was the best way for him to be sure I didn't say anything about the beatings.

It seems strange to me now that after so many years of beating, Jim still didn't fully understand. Following me around like a hound dog; going in with me at the doctors, were things he did not ever need to do. While he was being sure I didn't tell anyone what was happening at home, he totally failed to see the truth in that matter. I was never going to tell anyone what he was doing to me at home. I was far too frightened of him to say anything to anyone. So scared was I to "rock the boat" or give him reason to hit me that I made certain myself that I did not say anything. He was one hundred percent safe and he didn't even know it.

Jim's reputation was finally getting noticed aloud. People saw and they knew what was happening to me and yet they did nothing. It was like something whispered about in their homes or the privacy of an office. Never was it spoken about loudly but it was on everyone's lips and in everyone's home. None of the town was going to step up and say a word to him or upset him. He had once again accomplished exactly what he had set out to do. Now, he controlled my life and the people around me and their lives. He was gaining in strength throughout the community and that was not always a good thing for me. How could I not be aware of his intentions or the reason he did things a certain way? He had me so brainwashed that I didn't see the bad things he was doing or maybe, I didn't want to see it.

Chapter 10

{Enough is finally enough!}

There is nothing more frustrating to me than to have a woman finally step forward just to have a county attorney say that she doesn't have a lot of credibility. That statement alone is one of the reasons that more women do not seek help from the public or the state. The battering and accusations that she may have to endure by coming forward are at times, more frightening than the domestic abuse it's self. The life I lived and the abuse I experienced were too harsh and too real not to tell my story. The sadness, the turmoil, the unimaginable fear; the incredible blind eyes and negative response to a battered woman like me has got to find a way to make something good happen. I hope and pray and I want this story to open the eyes and the doors for the millions out there that do not know where to go or where to turn.

The number of calls to a crisis call center is bigger than one might imagine. They are staggering and maybe half of those callers seek actual help for what has happened to them. One other thing that I might mention is the fact once you have been through something so tragic, it lives with you for the rest of your life. The violence and the shredding of your dignity and self worth is life changing. You live with fear and sounds that are just that, sounds, and those sounds cause you to jump or look behind you. You are a different individual, whether it is good or bad, because of the things you endured. A great deal of where you end up is how you follow through with life. Changing all that you have known as a way of life and your home structure, determines whether you are a winner or if you got beat. Who supports you, if there is any support, is very important to your survival.

Seeing returning abused partners is something not uncommon in my line of work. Many times, the return is because either the victim went back to the abusive relationship or walked out of one abusive home and right back in to another one. They have not figured out that they do not deserve to be treated abusively and that they did not do anything to cause the behavior of their partner. There have been women that have come to me and have been in six or seven abusive relationships. One after another, back to back, they have walked into the fires of abusiveness. They tell me "But, I do love him and I need a man in my life." I can't help but think "Really?" This woman is suffering from brain damage because she has been hit so many times and yet here she is.

I do understand them, even if it does astound me. I don't know what happened that day; the day I just decided I was done. I had decided that I was not going to live with the abuse anymore. My life, my family, everything that was dear to my heart except my kids had been taken from me. The self-esteem and dignity that was once mine, no matter how little, was stolen from me. These were stolen years that I can never get back. What Jim took from me over the 30+ years we co-inhabited was forever lost to me.

It was on my daughter's birthday in 1998 that I made that decision. I remember saying to myself that enough was finally enough for me. As I mentioned a few chapters ago, I called the kids and told them I wanted a meeting. I know I spoke of this before but my thoughts expanded on this important turning point of my life. I feel that it warrants more explanation. I hope that you will bear with me as I remember the details. Jim had left for the day and I told the kids I had something I needed to talk to them about.

Strange how your mind works when you have been controlled for so very long. You forget your identity and you focus on trying to make the abuser happy. Jim had programmed me to be the way he wanted me to be. I was in that "robot" mode that caused me to do things without even thinking. I didn't need to think for the past thirty years. Jim had done that for me.

I knew what he wanted done and how he wanted it done. I was on auto-pilot and went about my day the same way every time the sun rose. The only deviance from the automatic mode I lived in was when he beat me. Even that wasn't out of the ordinary by this time but it was not a part that I ever simply shrugged off. It was just something I had come to expect though.

Because of those very same thoughts, I went out and did Jim's "to do" list that he had left for me. I made sure it was all finished and chores were taken care of before I had the kids out. I had already started the process in my head. I would work during the day and then at night, I would go through my things. I would pick out the clothing and other needed items that I was going to take with me. I was very aware that once I left, I wasn't going back. I also knew that after I left, Jim would not have allowed me to come back in to the house to get anything. I knew the most likely thing that would happen to the things of mine that had been left behind was that Jim would destroy them. He would ruin the things that were precious to me just like he did to my mother's wooden chest.

Jim was going to be gone for three days. It was a very rare window of opportunity for me and I was going to use it to my advantage. All of the kids came to the farm except one. She lived a far distance from the farm and I didn't call her as I knew she wouldn't come. I told them that I was finished and that I was going to leave. One son was still living at the farm at that time. We met at my son's and I told them I could not handle their father anymore. One daughter had called a friend of hers and told her I was leaving. She asked the friends advice as to what we should do. The friend offered me a place to stay for a few days. Jim was going to be home later that same day. I needed to get my stuff out of there before he got home. I prayed that he would not come home early. That would have changed everything and the repercussions of him finding me packing would probably cost me my life.

We began loading things and took a load to the storage unit. I packed up a few personal things to take along. After gathering all that I thought I would need to get by for a while, we left. My daughter took me to a cabin in Douglas County, where I was going to stay. They dropped me off and I went into the cabin and began pulling all of the shades closed. I was "locking down the hatches" so to speak. I knew that Jim was going to be furious when he got home. I left him a note telling him that I could no longer live the way he wanted me to live.

He got home somewhere around 7:30 I suspect and the first thing he did was read the note. He immediately went over to my son's house and wanted to know where the Hell I was at. My son told Jim that he did not know where I was and that was a true statement. My son had made it clear that he did not want to know where I was going. He knew that he would be the first stop for Jim when he got home. "I do not have the ability to lie to my father and so it is better that I not know anything about your where-abouts." I told him not to worry about it and that he would not know where I was going.

Not getting the answer that he wanted from our son, he made a call to one of our daughters. He didn't get down to Burtrum, where my daughter lived until very early the next morning. He knocked on her door and again wanted to know where I was. She told him the same thing as our son had. She swore she did not know where I was. Jim told her that I had left him and that he was going back to the farm. He told her he was going to burn every building and then that he was going to kill himself. He was furious and very angry that none of the kids would tell him where I was. He did not believe that they were telling him the truth.

I got a call that night from one of my daughters telling me that her father was back. That was very late night and they told me to be very careful. I went through the house and locked all of the doors and the windows. I went to the bathroom and then back downstairs. One by one, I turned all of the lights off in the house. I lit a candle in the cabin so

I had enough light to see. I went back upstairs to the bathroom and sat down on the floor. I spent the night in the bathroom, sleeping on the floor next to the bathtub. I lay there all night, barely sleeping and when I did sleep, I would suddenly wake and sit straight up.

The fear that engulfed me that night was unbelievable. My entire body could feel the effects of the horror that was now mine. I try once again to find a way to help you understand what the feelings; the emotions were that had totally consumed me. Try as I may, words will not convey to you this feeling, that even now as I tell you about it, causes my whole body to shake.

Try to imagine the darkest place on earth. Liken it to a cave that has no exit, buried deep inside of a mountainside. It is cold and wet and there is little sound except for the beating of your own heart. From somewhere in that silence, you can hear movement coming from the darkness. It sounds like someone or something moving across the floor. Footsteps, coming closer and getting louder with each moment, echo in your ears. You know that something is waiting for you in the darkness. Its breathing is shallow and you can hear a low growl coming from the abyss. You are too terrified to leave the cave but at the same time, petrified to stay where you are. All the while you try to sleep, the sounds and the feelings that someone is nearby, standing next to you in the darkness. You jump because you could swear someone or something has just touched you. You wait, your mind racing and your heart following suit, for whatever is hidden in the night to jump out of the dark and devour you. There is no peace and there is no security. That is perhaps as close to the way I felt that first night alone as I can convey to you. The night seemed to go on forever for me as I waited for the sound of a door opening and seeing Jim walk in.

The following morning, my daughters called me to tell me that Jim was back at the farm. They said he was beginning to burn down the old buildings and threatening again to kill himself. I told them that there was no way that Jim was going to kill himself. I told them that the farm was his whole life and that he was simply trying to guilt someone into telling him where I was. I stayed at that cabin for two nights until another cabin came open for me. The owner and his son came over and asked me what I wanted to do. They told me that if I wanted to stay, I was welcome. They offered to get me some food to eat. I told them that I was not sure if I should stay in one place very long as I figured that Jim was going to find where I was staying. I felt like a wanted criminal, hiding from the authorities. Something was very backwards about the way I was thinking and how sad it was that I had to feel that way. The owner offered to take me to Saint Paul with him and his son and I said yes. That seemed like the smartest and safest move I could make at the time. I thought I might look for someplace to work down there.

Not ever being a big town or city girl, the city was very scary for me. I came from "small-town, U.S.A." and was not accustomed to the big city. I wasn't afraid to go outside for walks or anything like that. My fear was because of the huge, tall buildings and the hurry and rush of the busy city. I stayed there for several months until one of my grandchildren was going to be baptized. I wanted to go to the baptism and I borrowed a car from the man that owned the place I was staying at. We had the baptism at the church Jim and I were married in.

Jim came into the church and sat down beside me. He began to start crying and the effect on me was only anger. I had reached a place in my life that his tears did not break me down. There was a time before all that I had endured, that his tears would have reduced me to mush. I would have done anything he asked of me back when we were young and in love. Now, they only made me angry because I knew the evil that was behind those tears.

After the church service, we went to my son's house for a family gathering. Jim spent most of his time outside in the yard. He was trying very hard to talk me into returning to the farm with him. I continuously told him that I was not coming home. My son left the same time I had left the farm. Jim had called him and promised him the moon, pretty much. My son fell for Jim's lies as I had for 30 years. He only stayed with him for about a month and then he left. He realized that everything that Jim had promised him was not going to ever happen.

I stayed with my daughter for a month or so where I got a job at Wal-Mart. This was the first job that I had since 1978. It felt good to be working again and I felt a sense of freedom. I was extremely nervous about starting the job. I had convinced myself that I would not be able to do the work. There was something inside of me that challenged my abilities to do anything outside of the farm work that I knew. Of course, I also knew that the truth was that I had been knocked down and broken so much over the years. There was no self-esteem left in me. I felt the stupid and incompetent and the worthless that Jim had pounded, or more accurately, beat into my brain. There was no belief that I could actually do something without Jim telling me how to do it and when to do it. Once you reach that place in your mind, it is very difficult to stand back up and to be your own person again. There is such a fear inside that it almost causes you to not take that baby step. The fear of failure or of having something terrible go wrong is strong. I found myself battling the demons of my past just to make myself go to this new job.

Walking into the store for the first time was an indescribable feeling. I wanted to just stand at the door and yell "Freedom" at the top of my lungs. I suddenly believed that I *could* do this work and that I *could* survive without Jim telling me what to do. We had two vehicles from the farm and Jim had given me one of them. I used it to go back and forth to work. Of course, as life would have it, shortly after starting work, the transmission went out on the car. I needed the car and so had no choice but to replace it. I worked at Wal-mart for about six weeks but it was autumn and I knew that winter would be there soon. I knew I needed to find a job closer to where my daughter lived.

I started searching the classifieds for anything that might work for me. There was an ad in the paper for a housekeeper. That was something I really felt I could do as I had done it since I was fifteen. I got dressed and headed in to town. When I got to where the ad was for, I walked in and told them what I was there for. The gentleman was very kind but told me that he had just given the last position to the woman who had passed me on my way in. My heart just sunk and I could feel the sadness and loss taking me over. I thanked him for his time and turned to walk out the door. He asked me to wait for a moment and I asked him why. He informed me that he wintered in Florida and that he left Minnesota in mid-September. He told me he needed someone to be a night manager while he was in Florida.

The fear of trying something new always seemed to be just below the surface of my thoughts. I knew I had to shake the destructive mindset that Jim had pressed in to me. It was the one thing that could and would ruin me if I allowed it to keep controlling me. It was scary to think that even when he was not near me, his control over me was still very evident. I needed to work and I needed to shake those fears and feelings of being nothing good to anyone.

I told the gentleman that I could not do the work he was offering me. He questioned me as to why and I told him I had never done anything like what he was looking for. I had no idea at all how I would do the work. I was unfamiliar with the computer and the phone or any of the other equipment that he had. How sad that I was unknowledgeable about such things as a phone. It was one of the "luxuries" that Jim removed to further his control over my life. Those things should have just been second nature to me, but they were not. I thanked him and prepared to leave once again. He told me not to short-sell myself and wondered why I did not want to even try.

"You need a job, right?" he asked me. Of course I needed a job and I told him so. He asked me to come in the following day and told me he would train me personally. He was going to be there until the beginning of October that year and so he had plenty of time to get me trained before he had to leave. He worked and lived in the motel and would be there to help me if I had any troubles. He lived in one of the rooms in the motel. I finally agreed to take the job and walked out. I felt as if I was on cloud nine. Here was a man that did not even know me that trusted me enough to give me a job. That was huge in my world and it felt so good inside. He showed faith in me that I myself did not possess. It was the most amazing feeling that I had felt in twenty years and I loved it.

I returned home that day and told my daughter the great news. I was excited to be working at the Super 8 and was on my own the end of October when he left for Florida. I was able to live in the apartment in the building. Once I was trained, I loved every minute of the job. I enjoyed working with people and the public. In the winter, if the housekeepers could not get in to work because of weather, the housekeeping was up to the manager and that was me at that time. The pay was low but I loved the work and that helped. My friend was also hired and so I had someone that I knew to talk with and that took away some of my anxieties.

I bought a car with the money I was making and had given Jim back the Jeep. After I had fixed the transmission on the Jeep, Jim had decided that he wanted it back and I didn't argue with him. I tried to buy insurance for my car and ran into a problem. They told me that they would not insure the car unless I put Jim's name on the vehicle papers also. I told them there was no way I was going to put his name on my car. It was after-all, my car. After fighting with them over and over, I was told that they were not going to change their mind. I ended up putting him on my insurances, even though he was never going to drive the car. I realized, about that same time, that I was not gaining with finances. I had paid the car off but that was all I really had to show for the hours I was putting in at the motel. I was back to that feeling of "can't survive on my own" and that scared me.

A friend asked me one day why I had not applied at a print shop nearby. I wasn't aware that they were hiring and I told the friend that I couldn't have a job like that anyways. In response to their questioning why, I told them because you have to be able to do certain things and I didn't have the skills. Again, I was selling myself short and feeling exactly as Jim had "trained" me to feel.

I think that people have the mindset that once you are away from the controller that everything inside of you just reverts back to before the abuse. That thought is an absolute false impression that people not educated in domestic violence or that have never experienced true control have in their minds. The fact is that after twenty plus years of being controlled, not only mentally but physically and sexually, it does *not just go away.* The actions of a controller are not unlike the methods used to brainwash a person. Repetitive reminding that you are ignorant or useless, after many years will cause you to believe those words. Jim being gone or at least out of my life at that time, was not enough to wash the feelings away.

I don't even know that 30+ years has erased it all. It has lessened and I have found a belief in myself but gone or erased from my thoughts... never, I am sure.

My cousin was working at the same place at the time. I decided that I was going to give the job a try. I took a written test that they required and waited to see if I would hear from them. A few days later I received a call from the company asking me do come in and take a drug test for them. They had decided to hire me but the test was needed before I could begin work there. I was overwhelmed and a bit awed at the wage difference they were offering me. I was going to go from $5.00 an hour to close to $9.00 dollars an hour. That was huge for me as it would be for anyone but for me, it was another freedom call.

Life was changing for me and I was excited about it. I worked at the print shop full time and still worked for the motel part-time. Something more was going to change in my life and I had no idea of the road this job was going to take me down. I met knew people and during my training, a man that was going to be huge in my life was my trainer. He taught me what I was going to need to know to run the machines that put books together. This man would one day come face to face with the reality of Jim Sarff.

David John, the man that called in the abduction of me from my apartment on February 19th, 2000, would work with me, train me and become my lover. There was no possible way that neither he nor I could have imagined the terror and the horror that was waiting for us in the not so far away future. David was in the National Guard and had been married once. Something seemed to "click" between us and we got along wonderfully. He was a good man and I found myself very interested in him. We worked rotating shifts then so I didn't see him a lot at work, once I had been trained.

Often times after work, people would get together and go out for social drinking. I am not much of a drinker now and I was not a drinker in the past. I wasn't sure if I would really fit in with the crowd, so to speak. When I was asked to join the group for drinks, I wasn't sure if that was something I really wanted to do. At the same time, I wanted to be accepted and liked David very much. I decided that it might be nice to mingle a bit with people and get to know them. It was also a reason for me to get outside of my apartment and live a little.

The socializing was something that Jim had stripped me of and it left me uncertain how to really mix with other people. I put some of my fears aside and accepted the invitation. I found that I truly enjoyed going out with these people. We would drink a little… some of them a lot, and then I would go home for the night. Never once did I ever think that knowing David would end the way it did. I could not have even fathomed that Jim's actions, on that horrible night in February, would impact so many lives.

The after-math of what Jim did would be felt by everyone I ever loved. It would change lives forever and bring with it fear and distrust, drawing an invisible line between families. Like our own personal civil war, brother would disagree with brother, sister with sister and mothers and fathers would be separated from their children, forever. A distance would slowly fester and some of those children that I took beating after beating for, just so I didn't lose them; would turn away from me and wash their hands of everything.

I do not believe that you can live in a home, filled with abusive and violent actions and not know it was there or say that you didn't see any of it. Some may try and block it from their memory and others may call what transpired just lies or just a story. I know that what happened to me and my family is real. The events that led up to me finally finding freedom, I endured and lived because my children were more important to me than anything. I wanted them safe and wanted for them to grow up in a nice normal family. Taking the cruel punishments from a man that swore he loved me was worth it, as long as I had my children. A person does have a breaking point and when enough was enough… I left. I wish it had been "enough" just to leave. I so very much wish that David John had not been a victim of Jim's actions. I just wanted to live a normal life for once. Jim was determined to make sure he still had me and made it very clear that he was never, ever going to let me go.

~~~~~~~~~~

Time passes quickly when you finally find a place to call home. I was comfortable and feeling as if I belonged somewhere now. My life was different without Jim telling me how to or when to do things. I had found a confidence within myself that I don't know I ever had. It was new and exciting and I wanted to be just normal. The abuse was still in my mind but I could go out and share my time with others and enjoy.

   After getting together with co-workers for several months, all the while drawing closer to David, he finally asked me if I would like to go to a movie with him. It was mid-December by now and I said yes. I was extremely anxious to see what the world had to offer. I had not been out to a movie or anything even close to a date in thirty years. I was very nervous about our first few dates but enjoyed the time with David very much. He and I became very close and found that we shared many of the same interests. He was a Beatles fan as I was and the "oldies but goodies" were a connection for us also. He would come to my house and we would share our music and talk.

  Sitting with a man and being able to interact with the conversation felt nice. My past experiences as far as talking wasn't like what David and I were doing. I could freely voice my thoughts and give my own opinions. I didn't need to flinch or sit waiting for the fist or weapon to knock me out. There was no yelling or degrading… no beatings or reminding me of how stupid I was. This was plain and simply talking and I loved it.

  In January, our relationship grew much more serious. It had turned intimate for us and I was again happy. I enjoyed feeling emotions from a partner that didn't come with pain or violence. A few weeks into January, David stopped by to tell me we would have to back off of the relationship. I could think of nothing to say back except to say alright. Inside of me, I was hurting. I realized that we weren't a "couple" but I felt amazingly close to him. He had made me feel like I had not felt in what seemed like a millennium. David was kind and he was gentle and he was everything that I imagined a lover would be. He would compliment me on how I looked or things that I did. That was something that even when we were dating, Jim never gave to me. The very fact that David made me feel as if I mattered was enough to hold me forever.

I finally found the strength and courage to ask him why we needed to break up. David said that Jim had come to visit him. He felt that Jim had been watching us because he knew when we went to each other's homes. To know what he knew, he had to have been watching us closely. David told me that we could still talk at work and go out for drinks with the co-workers. As far as our seeing each other intimately, we would need to let that go. What I had found and wanted so very much, Jim had found a way to rip it right out of my reach. Even after all of this time, he still was controlling my life. I thought I had been given the chance to move on and was doing exactly that. Now, out of no-where, Jim was back to destroy the serenity that I had found in David. I felt now as if Jim was going to continue to dominate my life and that there was little to nothing I could do to stop him. He was determined that if he could not have me, nobody else was going to have me either. I didn't blame David for backing off nor did I doubt that Jim had the ability to intimidate someone to the point of fear. I had lived with that side of him for far too long to not know and understand.

David and I did not see each other outside of work for several weeks. I found myself missing our relationship and the intimacy we had shared. We talked one day about our relationship and decided that we would be alright. We resumed our relationship and heard nothing more from Jim. Life seemed to be settling and I was moving forward. How long it would last I didn't know. One thing I was certain of was that somewhere in the shadows, Jim was still watching us. Whether we saw him or he made contact with us, he was there, like a stalker of the worst imagination. I could not have known that in a very short time, Jim was going to make him-self very visible to me.

On February 18th, 2000, a family member got married. I had not been back in the family very long and I was looking forward to the wedding. For me, it was a chance to get back with my family and spend time with them. I thought it was an awesome thing to be able to see my family whenever I wanted to. That was something Jim could not take from me ever again. Those were my thoughts at that moment. I had no idea where Jim was or what he was thinking. I only knew that he was not anywhere near me and that was good enough.

I borrowed a dress from a friend of mine that I worked with. I went over to my daughter's house and she fixed my hair up nicely. My daughter came to my house and picked me up to take me to the wedding and the wedding reception. I had a few drinks at the reception and stayed there until midnight. I was having such a wonderful time with my family. My sister told me that she had to work the next morning and would need to get going. She offered me a ride to my house and I accepted. She asked me if I would like to come home with her but I declined. I was planning on taking the grandkids to the movies the following day. She dropped me off and went home. I had no idea that the next time I would see her was after an ordeal that would be with me forever.

I found that I was not really ready to end the night and decided that I would go back to the reception. They weren't ending the gathering until one o'clock and I wanted to visit for a while longer. I got into my own car and drove back to Pier 71, which was the local dinner club and where the reception was. I remained there, visiting and having a great time until they were closing the bar at 1:00 a.m. I drove home and got ready for bed. I was sitting in the living room listening to some music. David was on his way home from spending time with some of his buddies from the National Guard. When he passed by my home, David noticed that the lights were still on. He decided to stop in and visit. We sat for a while, talking and laughing and then things began to get more serious. We went into my bedroom and made love before falling asleep. It was after 2:00 a.m. when we fell asleep.

Chapter 11

{The Abduction}

Author's words: Life is often a mix of excitement and joy and expectations and surprises. Not every surprise becomes a welcome, nor is it always a beautifully fond memory to go back to from time to time. Sometimes, life is filled with one bad thing followed by something worse. To escape terror, for even a fleeting moment, seems like an impossible quest. The past may seem behind us but "behind" is also not always a good thing. In the darkest of night, when the rest of the world is sleeping, our past can come slithering back without us seeing it coming.

Connie Sarff {Nelson} lived a life that was filled with the worst kind of fears. She was not afraid of strangers because she was never allowed to associate with them. She didn't fear her family or friends because the man that she called husband had closed her off from having contact with them. Simple things like talking or walking in a field had become scenarios that our nightmares are made of. She endured a lifetime of beatings and cursing and hospital stays, her face and body scarred from the atrocities that were inflicted on her. Inward injuries to her body and to her mind had become just a part of life for her. She had come to believe that nothing would ever change and that her nemesis would follow her to her grave.

Connie took everything that her husband could throw at her, literally, and still, she stayed. Her love for her children and the desire to be a family was stronger than her husband's punches. She is a survivor and hopes that her story will show others that they are not alone and that there can be a light at the end of the tunnel. Please read on and follow her through the life changing ordeal that put her on the nation's news and in newspapers across the United States. This is the story of her abduction and kidnapping at the hands of her estranged husband. The fears that were her constant companion and her means to stay alive are documented in police and FBI files.

This is a story, that had the proper actions been taken years before the abduction, Connie might never have been taken from her home. Too many times, vicious, domestic violence goes un-responded to and the perpetrator is left un-punished. They are free to do over and over again what Jim Sarff did to Connie. She is but one of thousands that are caught in an abusive home. She speaks out here for the victim and reaches out to help others in abusive relationships. This is her tale of abduction, told by her-self, local authorities and the FBI agents that brought her back home.

February 19th, 2000 at 3:30 a.m.

Approximately 3:30 a.m., on the morning of February 19th, 2000, I woke from a deep sleep. I cannot even tell you what it is that woke me. I thought that I had seen a light coming from outside of the bedroom. David was asleep and I didn't want to wake him. The light flashed in front of the bedroom door again. My apartment was situated so that you came up the stairs; it was a second floor apartment and had a landing at the top. Taking a left at the landing, my door was directly ahead. When you walked in to my apartment, you walked right into the kitchen. Off from the kitchen was my bedroom so I could see if there was light in the kitchen. It had been dark when I fell asleep and now, I could see clearly that there was a light of some sort in the kitchen.

I remember being terribly tired and I didn't want to get out of bed. I tried to forget about the light and go back to sleep. The light flashed in my eyes again and at that point, I knew something was not right. I got out of bed and walked to the door of the kitchen. As I entered the kitchen, I walked right into Jim. I stared at him, trying to grasp what he was doing standing inside my apartment. He asked me why I was there and I told him that I lived there. I asked him what he was doing, standing in my kitchen. I don't recall what his answer was but he then asked me who was in the bedroom. He wanted to know why I was standing in front of him naked. I gave him some answer and then told him to get out of my apartment. I told him that he needed to leave and that he had no right to be here.

Jim looked as if he were a million miles away. He stared at me and then shook his head. He told me that he was not going anywhere. I shoved against him, trying to move him backwards towards the door. I informed him that I was going to dial 911. He shook his head and told me I was not going to call anyone. At that time, he reached out and grabbed my arm. Dragging me outside of the apartment, Jim shoved me down to the floor. His anger flared and my mind reeled. Everything he had ever done to me, all that I had moved forward from as best as I could, was all flooding back in to my mind. I was so scared and still trying to comprehend what was happening. It was so overwhelming and I didn't really know what to think.

Jim began his assault on my body right on the landing. He didn't seem to care who heard my cries or who saw him beating me. I remember struggling to get free of his grasp and then heard Jim hit the neighbor's door with his hand. Then as he kneeled above me, I hit the same door with my hand three times and I remember I was hitting it hard. I wanted someone to come out and help me. I needed help to escape Jim and I didn't care who it was that helped me. I called out for help and waited for what seemed like an eternity and no one was answering my calls. I was near hysterical by now as Jim continued his assault on my body. Finally, the man in the apartment of the door I was pounding on opened it. I asked him to help me and Jim told him to get back inside and to mind his own business.

The heinous crime that was unfolding right outside my own door was something I had never imagined. I thought my apartment was a safe place for me. Behind that door was where I locked out all of the dreadful things that Jim had done to me. I had told people time and time again that I did not feel I had anything to fear from Jim any longer. Although I knew without doubt that he was always watching me from somewhere, I felt that was as far as it would go. The papers had been filed for the divorce and I was simply playing the waiting game. That is what I really believed and I had no reason to think otherwise.

Now, within inches of what had once been a place of refuge, I found myself being ravaged viciously by my estranged husband. Eighteen months of life without being kicked or smacked or struck by whatever object Jim could find had ended. The life was being crushed out of me and there was no one to help me. I cannot convey to you the fear or the horrible sense of being violated that filled my soul. I can only tell you that it left me completely lost and confused. I didn't know how he got inside my apartment or how long he had been inside.

The man at the door that could have helped me did exactly what he was told. When Jim saw him open his door, he barked at the man and told him to shut the door. Jim also told the man to mind his own business. The man closed the door and made what was happening outside his door... just go away. I did find out later that the man had suffered from mental health issues due to time in Viet Nam. I also discovered later that the man had been in trouble for being an abuser himself. A worse person could not have opened the door than this man. I heard the door close and then my world began to fade. I felt as if my life had just ended for me. I remember nothing that happened from the landing to the outdoors.

The next time I was awake, I found myself in Jim's Jeep. I was lying on the floor of the Jeep, still totally naked and cold. I remember hearing the rattles from the body of the Jeep. I remember thinking that he was going to take me out to the lake and dump my dead body there. The lake was at the edge of our property and I was certain that was where he was taking me. I don't know that I was fully conscious while I was lying on the floor. Some of my thoughts I am sure were more unconscious thoughts.

My memory then goes to feeling the vehicle moving and asking Jim for a drink. I was so very thirsty and needed something. I was freezing on the floor and my neck and throat hurt very badly. Jim tossed a Viking team blanket over me but it was short and left my feet sticking out the end. They were absolutely frozen and hurting. Jim handed me a bottle that I thought was a two liter bottle of Mountain Dew. It was not the Mountain Dew I was hoping for. The bottled had some fiercely nasty tasting liquid in it that tasted old and stale. I almost gave him the bottle back but I was so thirsty that I drank it. I have no idea what it was and probably never will know. I blacked out immediately after drinking from the bottle. I have often wondered if there was something in the bottle that knocked me unconscious again because I slept for a very long time.

When I woke after hours of sleep, we were nearing Albuquerque, New Mexico. For some reason I thought we were in South Dakota. I don't know why that state came into my mind. I realized suddenly that I was fully clothed and I don't know when or where we stopped. He had to have dressed me while I was asleep and then placed me in the front seat. I looked outside the window and saw the sign that said we were in Albuquerque, New Mexico. I remember asking him what we were doing in New Mexico. He told me that we were never going back to Minnesota. That was the only thing he said to me. He would not talk to me after that time. He drove on in silence until we got to the border of Mexico. We stopped for a short while and then crossed over the border into Mexico. I was fully conscious by that time and knew my surroundings, though the landscape was completely unfamiliar to me.

Before I tell you about Mexico and what happened to me there, I would like to go back and tell you of the actual abduction. The words that you read now will be from other sources as I was knocked unconscious before being taken from the landing to the Jeep. There are many versions that may be worded differently but the story and what happened after I was taken remain truthful and accurate. There is sadness within me as I look back on that night. Lives were again changed forever and one that was extremely important and precious to me… took his own life. This is the events from the moment I lost consciousness and into the search for Jim and me.

~~~~~~~~~~~

Fifteen minutes after Connie's abduction from her apartment, co-worker and boyfriend, David John would dial 911. This was to be the start of a man hunt that would go on for two weeks. Police and FBI agents, along with family and friends would embark on a search for Connie and Jim Sarff. Calls would be made and reports of seeing Jim's vehicle reported, but no solid evidence as to their whereabouts would surface. Authorities told reporters that of the 100+ calls received by the department, only one was ever considered solid and worthy of investigating. There was some confusion as to the license plate number but investigators got things straightened out. A copy of the 911 call, made by David John is presented here also.

911 Call received from David John 02-19-2000

{Phone ringing} Q; E 911 operator

QQ: Long Prairie Police

A: David John

A: Hi, yea, I think I would like to report a kidnapping or something

Q: O.K. and who is calling?

A: My name is David John

Q: David John?

A: Right

Q: O.K. and who has been kidnapped?

A: Um, my girlfriend. It is the weirdest thing I...

Q: How old is she?

A: Um, 47

Q: O.k. where do you live, David?

A: I live on 6th street but I am not at my place.

Q: 6th street in Long Prairie?

A: Right

Q: O.k., where are you at so an officer can...

A: {inaudible} Long Prairie

Q: pardon me?

A: 6th St. NE in Long Prairie

Q: What is the house number?

A: Um, I don't know. You know the big apartment a block off of 27, just a block north.

Q: O.k. the apartment just off of 27?

A: Right on 6th street. It is a big brick building.

Q: O.k., I am still thinking of it but I can't...you are not on, are you Todd 27?

A: No, no, no, no, I am on 6th street

Q: You are on 6th street and I am trying to think of a brick...

A: A block north of...

Q: Hwy. 27

A: Right

Q: And it's, does ************ own that yet?

A: Geez, I don't even know who owns it

Q: Are you upstairs or downstairs?

A: Upstairs

Q: And that would be 6th avenue, NE. I don't know which house you are at right now but I am trying, O.k. and who is your girlfriend?

A: Her name is Connie Sarff.

Q: Oh, oh, so you think he came and got her or what?

A: Boy, I don't know. I was asleep...

Q: Was she with you last night and stuff?

A: Yea and I heard a rumbling, just now, about fifteen minutes ago, ten minutes ago.

Q: And she is gone?

A: Yes, she is not in her apartment anymore.

Q: So you are upstairs. 700 or 726

QQ: 26

Q: Could you please go to 6th NE, it is a block north of 27; it's a duplex house, older brick home, upstairs apartment. He doesn't know the address. Reference to a missing female. O.k. David, what is your middle name?

A: Barrett

Q: Barrack?

A: David John

QQ: 10-4

Q: How do you spell your middle name?

A: B-A-R-R-E-T-T

Q: o.k., what is your middle name?

A: That's it, Barrett

Q: I mean, what is your date of birth?

A: January 15th, 1959.

Q: O.k., do you live with her?

A: No

Q: What is your address?

A: ********************************

Q: 6th street north?

A: Right

Q: O.k., and what is your phone number?

A: ****

Q: An officer should be there shortly and you can just explain to him. This just happened ten, fifteen minutes ago?

A: Yea

Q: Has Jim been giving her problems?

A: I don't know

Q: Oh, she don't say anything, huh?

A: No

Q: O.k., an officer is on his way over there, o.k. David?

A: All right

Q: O.k., bye

As stated in a report filed by the police officer sent to investigate the incident, he spoke with David John. He arrived at approximately 4:04 a.m. on 2-19-2000. David John had told the dispatcher that he had heard a disturbance outside the apartment of Connie Sarff. David thought that Connie had merely tripped or bumped into something on her way to the bathroom. He laid his head back on the pillow and began to fall back to sleep. He heard a man's voice call out "No, you don't" and decided to get out of bed. Searching the apartment and not finding Connie inside, he then made the decision to call the police. In less than ten minutes, an officer arrived at Connie's apartment. He went upstairs where he was met by David John. He saw human feces on the floor, just outside of Connie's apartment.

David John began to speak with the officer concerning the incident. He told the officer that though he did not live there, he had been spending the night with Connie. He spoke of the sounds he had heard outside the apartment and said that he knew it was Jim Sarff outside. He also noted that Connie must have been taken while wearing no clothes as she was naked in bed. He had called as soon as he realized that she was missing and knew she had been taken because her vehicle was still parked outside. David John was extremely fearful of the fact that Jim may have abducted Connie. He was known to be violent with Connie, David told the police.

After the officer told David to secure Connie's apartment, he told him to go home in case he was needed for questioning. The officer went back upstairs and spoke with the man that had opened his door during the scuffle. The man said that he heard the knocking on his door and went to see who it was. When he opened his door, he saw a man lying on the floor of the hallway. It appeared that he was struggling with another person. When he was told by the man on the floor to shut his door and mind his own business that is exactly what the man said he did. He claimed that he did not open the door again and the sounds in the hall had quieted. He told the officer that he did not see the other person that Jim was holding down. He did believe that that if the man were to appear before him again, he would know the man's face.

The officer was informed by dispatch that they were familiar with Sarff and that he had a long history of abusing his wife. The dispatcher added that the abuse was extremely violent and that Jim should be approached as such. Because of the prior arrests and the knowledge of Jim's violence, the police chief and the Sherriff were both contacted. They met at the police station and spoke of what the officer had observed. The officer was instructed to video tape interviews with both David John and the man from the apartment next to Connie's. He returned to the crime scene to look more closely at the apartment and stairwell.

The first thing he noticed was that the feces was no longer in the hallway. The man from the apartment told him that he had flushed it in his toilet. Going back to the outside of the building, the officer noticed what appeared to be two drag-marks in the snow. The drag-marks led from the outside door to across the parking lot. They suddenly ended at the garage near the apartment. He called in for assistance and then photographed the drag-marks. He also found shoe prints that were believed to belong to the suspect. Those too were photographed. None of the prints were clear and there were no prints from a second person. Connie had been dragged the entire way to where ever she was taken. He did a complete search of the area, hoping to find some clues as to what had actually happened. There was what appeared to be blood in the snow where Connie had been dragged. This added to the concern that her life was in danger.

The front door of Connie's apartment was removed by pulling the pins in the door. Having no key to access the apartment, the police were left with no other choice. After examining and photographing the interior of her home, the door was replaced to keep the crime scene secure. David John and the man from the apartment were both taken to the police department and videotaped interviews were taken from both men. The Bureau of Criminal

Apprehension {BCA} had been notified so that they could process the scene. An all points alert of an "attempt to locate" was sent out and the search for Connie and Jim was to begin immediately. Gathering more evidence and speaking with people in the area was also part of the procedure.

There were many people that had observations into the investigation. A woman that lived across the street from Connie's apartment told officers that she had seen an older pick-up truck around 11:00 PM. The driver was a male and she recalled that the truck was loud, as if it had no muffler. She had seen Connie's car being driven away at around midnight. She did recall that three weeks prior to the abduction, she observed a man, tall and thin, looking in the windows of the apartment building. He had walked around the building, stopping to look in each window before finally leaving the area. She said other than what she told the officers, she had seen nor heard anything unusual the night of the abduction.

Photos were shown to the man from the apartment but he could not make a definite identification as he had thought he could. He thought that two of the photos may have been the person in the hallway. He stated that the difference was that the man in the hallway was clean shaven and had no mustache. Because of his uncertainties, his thoughts on which photo the man might be were dismissed. As a side note, one of the two he had chosen was Jim's photo.

Reports had come in that Jim had called his sister only a few hours after the apparent kidnapping. He informed her that he had killed Connie and was going to kill himself.

Somewhere around that same time, he called one of his daughters to tell her that he and Connie were fine. The confusion at trying to sort all of the facts left officials struggling to get searches for the couple under way. Witnesses reported seeing the Sarff vehicle on Interstate 35, near the Twin Cities later the same day. By that time, Jim had been officially charged with kidnapping Connie.

The search for Connie began with some locals looking for her. The law enforcement said later that they were not looking for Connie to be alive. They believed they would find Connie's body somewhere close to her home. The Long Prairie Police Department, the Todd County Sherriff's Department, the BCA {Bureau of Criminal Apprehension}, and the State Patrol were all called in on the investigation. The search was conducted both on the ground and in the air. Private Citizens flew over as much area as they could while trying to find Connie.

With all search warrants in their possession, the Deputy Sherriff was able to get on with the search of the outside area. A search plane was sent up to look at the area that surrounded Connie's apartment complex. The DNR also took part in the search, sending out snowmobiles to conduct a ground search of the area. Efforts were being made to find Connie, though no evidence as to where Jim had taken Connie was being found.

A deputy, along with one of Connie and Jim's sons, searched the family farm a bit deeper. A gravel pit that was at the end of the property was searched. There were fresh footprints that showed someone had entered and exited the gravel pit very recently. There was some concern that perhaps Jim had taken Connie to the pit and disposed of her body. There was no evidence other than the footprints to indicate anything other than someone walking around there. There were no drag marks, like those that had been found outside the apartment complex. The airplane and the snowmobile that the conservation officer was using also turned up nothing on the farm.

Their son's farm was only a mile and a half from Jim's. The police decided to have a look there also. The son had no issues with them searching his property as well. There were no fresh tracks of any kind found and his farm was cleared just as Jim's was.

The search was actually initiated when the police realized that Jim was for certain missing also. When the Law Officials spoke of Jim's past, they realized he might be dangerous and people were informed not to approach him if he was seen. They were to notify the police as soon as anyone saw him. Over one hundred calls came in to the department in the next few days. Only one or two were considered to be of any use. Officials at that time still believed that Jim was somewhere in the area. There was little reason for anyone to think otherwise. His jeep had been seen in the Lakeville area and then again in Owatonna. This gave way to the police believing that Jim had not left the area or Minnesota.

A warrant was issued to search the Sarff property in an effort to learn more about the suspect and look for evidence concerning the abduction. Authorities were hoping to find something that might tell them where Jim may have taken Connie. Three photographs were removed from the residence along with a notebook that had been lying on a table top. When the search was finished, family members stayed at the residence to wait and see if Jim would return. The warrant covered an extensive area of the farm which was searched by several different Law Enforcement Agencies. A search plane was flown over a large portion of the area near Jim's farm by the Sherriff's Department. The DNR continued to assist in the search still using snowmobiles and looking for Connie on foot. No evidence to further aid in the investigation was found by either.

Later in the day, a search warrant was obtained for Connie's apartment again. Minnesota Crime Alerts and teletypes were also sent out in an effort to find Connie and Jim. The Jeep was posted everywhere and police still channeled calls reporting that the 1993 Jeep Cherokee had been seen. After the apprehension of Jim, it would be realized that most of the calls would have lead to dead ends. It was also learned that one of Jim's daughter had informed him that the phone at the house was tapped. The authorities were waiting to tape record any messages that might have come in.

At 11:30a.m., the officer spoke with the Pastor of the Assembly of God church Connie worshipped at. The Pastor told the officer that Connie had been coming there since around Christmas of 1999. She had made acquaintances with several of the people there and was especially fond of one of the ladies there. Connie had met her through the ladies stay at the Super 8 Motel that Connie was managing at the time. The two had talked for a few nights while she was staying there and the woman had invited Connie to her church. Connie was a regular there and only missed service if she had to work that day. He said that he and his wife had visited Connie's apartment shortly after she became a member. They spoke mostly in general and though Connie did mention the abusive relationship, she did not stay on that subject very long. The pastor felt as if it were an embarrassment for Connie to speak of her past. She made no indications at all about being afraid or about herself being stalked. He never once, during their conversation, felt as if Connie felt she were in any kind danger. She did not mention her relationship with David John. She spoke highly of her children and told him they had been very supportive of her decision to separate from Jim. She appeared to be very happy to be working and was excited about starting her new job at the print shop. It was going to mean more money for her and that would make life easier.

The officer did return to the apartment of the man that had opened and closed his door to Connie. He showed him more pictures of six different people and asked if any of them resembled the man he had seen outside of his door. He picked a man out of the photos but commented that the man did not have a mustache. He looked at the pictures again and chose another person. He thought that might be the man he saw earlier. He then told the officer there was just no way to be positive. He had chosen Jim first but by choosing the second man, his choosing could still not be used.

A woman came into the police department the day of the abduction. She mentioned that she was concerned for the safety of her friend, Connie Sarff. She had heard some talk on her scanner and decided to come and talk with authorities. The woman said she knew that Connie was attending a wedding for a niece and that she had received a call from Connie. Connie had asked her to come to Pier 71, where the reception was being held. The woman was unable to attend but that it sounded as if Connie was having a good time.

This woman was aware that Connie had served Divorce Papers to Jim about two weeks prior. Within the past month, she said she had seen Jim driving by the motel where Connie was working. She watched him drive around the building several times before finally leaving. She did give the officers one of Connie's daughters names and then she left.

It seemed as if people were hearing about the abduction through their scanners even before family had been notified. The abduction was not something that Long Prairie had ever experienced and exactly what procedures needed to be put forth was new to the Todd County Sherriff's Department. The early time that the abduction had occurred also caused actions to be slowed.

Connie's family was not informed of the abduction officially until later in the morning. People of the town knew before her own family had knowledge of the abduction. Her parents were visited by an officer at their home. They were told of Connie's disappearance and that everything possible was being done to locate her. Her parents called

Connie's sister, Bev and told her of the happenings. At the time, Bev was working a security job she had. The family got together to discuss what could be done to help. It did not take long before the house was filled with well wishers and people asking how they too could help. There were family members from both sides of the family, Jim's and Connie's side, that were asking what they could to aide in finding where the two were.

Authorities seemed less than anxious to have family members helping with the investigation at the time. They were busy interviewing people that may have had knowledge of where the two might have gone. The family, estranged as they were, seemed the least likely to have information that the police or Sherriff's Department might have deemed useful. They did talk with family daily, according to the Todd County Sherriff, in hopes that one of the six kids might remember something that would give the authorities a direction in which to pursue the missing couple. They also had hopes that perhaps Jim would contact someone in his family.

The Sherriff's Department was quoted as saying that the investigation was frustrating. They really had no idea where to even start looking for Connie and Jim. "It is frustrating for the department. It drives us crazy. This is a mystery and we have to solve it as quickly as we can. It is like a jigsaw puzzle and we only have a few pieces right now."

There had been two calls from Jim to his family shortly after the abduction. He told the family member that he had killed Connie and that he was going to kill himself. There was no indication as to where he was or where he planned on ending his life. The following day he called another family member stating that he and Connie were both alive and well. He told the family that he would be contacting them again soon. No word was heard from him after that call.

Facts that were known on that first day of the abduction were fairly limited. Jim Sarff had for certain taken his soon to be ex-wife from her apartment. Connie Sarff was for certain taken from her apartment, naked and against her will. Evidence left behind at the scene told authorities there had been a struggle and that Connie was dragged from the apartment complex to a vehicle. Witnesses saw her being beaten and held down on the landing outside of her door. From the end of the drag marks, the facts ended.

The first day was going to come to an end soon. There had been no sign of Jim or Connie other than the sighting of the vehicle. The plate was only a partial but it did match Jim's vehicle. Where Jim had taken Connie was unknown. Whether or not she was alive or dead when he took her was not known. If alive, the extent of her injuries was left unknown. What Jim's reason for choosing that night to take her from her home was a question that nobody was certain how to answer. The unknown left many fearful for Connie's well-being based on the couples violent past. Jim had shown far too many times that he could and would hurt Connie in the most horrific ways. So many questions were still left to be answered and no-one had the answers.

The only one that knew where Jim and Connie were was Jim himself. Connie herself didn't know until they arrived in

Albuquerque. Were his intentions to go to where he ended up from the beginning or did he end up in Mexico just because? He was going to make sure that Connie did not leave him and that she had no way back to Minnesota. The days would turn into weeks before she would know the taste of freedom again. Her ordeal in Mexico was finished but the tale of her weeks in Mexico was only just beginning. Connie's life would remain changed forever. She had questions and statements and video-taped interviews to deal with. She had to find a way to return to her life while she awaited the trial that would explode across Minnesota and make Connie Sarff a household name for a time.

Chapter 12

Mexico and beyond

I remember the disorientation that my entire being was feeling; confused and extremely tired. My body hurt in every place you could imagine. When trying to recall some of the events, it is difficult at times. My mind absorbs the feelings and fears and they have remained with me through the years. Though many things are unclear about the abduction and all it entailed, what Jim was capable of was certain for me. I knew that wherever we were, I had to play by Jim's rules if I was going to live long enough to be rescued. I wanted to live and to see my children and parents again. I wanted to be safe in my own home once more. Knowing Jim the way that I did, I had no doubts that I was to do exactly what he told me to do or suffer the consequences.

I was unsure what day it was when I woke. I knew now that we were in Albuquerque but I still had it in my mind that it was the nineteenth of February. Truthfully, it had to have been the following day because the miles from Eagle Bend to Albuquerque would take no less than twenty-two or twenty-three hours to cover. I believe now that Saturday had come and gone and that it was Sunday, the twentieth. I was dressed by this point and still, as I stated before, have no idea where we stopped to get me clothes. Other than the socks that were Jim's and his jacket, I had never seen any of these clothes before. I remembered that I was naked when he attacked me in the hall. Obviously I was not given the option to gather any personals. My eye glasses, bifocals that I used for reading were also not with me.

Some of what I write here is from knowledge learned after I was found. I do recall the drive across the border. Faint memories come back of him smashing my head against the truck window. At no time was there a safe time for me. By that I simply mean that at any given time, without reason, Jim could start kicking or hitting me again. There really was no rhyme or reasoning to his violent outburst. After 30+ years, I had still not fully learned what triggered his ferocious behavior. The very air that you and I breathe was sometimes all it took for him to start his assaults again.

We stopped at a gas station so we could get something to drink. I began to look my own body over. Jim was still refusing to say anything except that we could not go back. He told me that Minnesota was gone and that there was no way to go back there for us. I wondered what he had done that was so horrible that we had to hide out in Mexico. I knew he was totally capable of killing someone and that thought crossed my mind. Had he killed someone before coming to take me away? Who had angered him so badly that he took their life? I tried to refocus my thoughts. I wanted to ask him how I had gotten to where I was but I was too afraid of him. I think maybe I was afraid not to know but at the same time, I was scared to death to hear the truth. I let it go when he would tell me not to worry about it. I could not help but think that I might never see my family again. I wondered silently when he was going to pull in somewhere and just kill me. I was certain that was what he had planned to do in the first place.

There was a terrible pain in my neck and my shoulder. I could feel scratches on my throat and what felt like scabs all over me. I could not remember the events that had led up to my sitting in a truck with my very soon to be ex-husband, going over the border in to Mexico. I had no idea where the redness and the marks on my body had come from. I assumed something had happened between Jim and me; something violent from the way that my body felt.

I tried to move my arm and I found that it would not move without help. I had to lift it with my other arm to get it to move at all. There was no feeling in my arm or my hand. I looked at Jim and asked him what had happened to my arm. I explained to him that I could not move it. He stared at me for a minute and then offered to rub my hand for me. He never gave me a reason why it was that way. He passed it off as he had done every time he had hurt me. I think I knew in my mind, just from his reaction, that Jim had violently abused me once again.

My feet were very sore and swollen and they hurt very badly. My feet were cold and swollen and the shoes he had bought for me were new and so they were tight anyways. I tried to take them off so that they didn't hurt so badly but they would not come off. I had so many questions to ask of him but the fear inside of me simply would not allow me too. He seemed hell bent on something and I didn't want to do anything to set him off again. The last place I wanted to find myself was stuck in a truck, a millions miles from who knows where, with a pissed off Jim. Jim suddenly started the truck and we drove away from the gas station.

We drove until we had reached the ten mile boundary that would require us to have passports. It was supposedly the only way to get deeper in to Mexico. I had no idea how we were supposed to do that since I didn't even have identification on me. I had nothing on my person to say who I was or where I came from. That is a scary place to be and it leaves you with emptiness inside your body. I don't think that my being without any identification was any part of a "master plan" of Jim's. He was just making decisions as things happened. Suddenly, I was absolutely a no one and if Jim decided to do anything to me, dental records were going to be the only way to identify me. We drove down a road that was littered with Hispanics trying to dig their way through tunnels and climb over huge boulders to get in to the United States. It is one of those things you read about and hear about but unless you have seen it, it is hard to imagine.

So many things crossed my mind during those first few days we were in Mexico. I really had no way of knowing what day it was or how long we had been gone from Minnesota. Because of the amount of time that I had been sleeping…unconscious would be a better word for it, I had lost all track of time. A new day or another dark, cold night was the only measure of time that I had to go by. We slept in the Jeep most of the time and during the day, we would just walk. I couldn't even try to tell you where we were walking. I think I was still too scared to care about what place we were at.

My only real two thoughts were getting back home to my family and surviving long enough to do that. I had doubts that either of those things was going to happen for me. Those first few days were filled with anxiety and fear of the unknown. My body was still so sore and tired and my arm was not going to work no matter how hard I tried or I wanted it too. I had no clue as to how I injured it or how long it would be before it was useable again. I say "no clue" but in truth, I had a pretty good idea of where the injury came from.

I tried to talk with Jim in as calming of a voice as I could. I didn't want to shake the hornets' nest that I knew laid just below the surface. I had so many questions I wanted to ask him but they were questions that could wait for the right time to be asked. I don't know, to this day, if a "right time" existed inside of Jim. When I would ask him if we could just go back home, his answer was always the same. He would look at me, staring sometimes for a while before he answered me. "There is absolutely nothing to go back home too. That is a place we will never see again." Those words frightened me more than I will ever convey to you in words.

Your home is that safe place you go to lock out the world. As I sat with Jim, waiting to see what his plans would be for us, I thought about my children and my parents. I wondered if they knew I was gone. Had my sister been notified and were they looking for me? They had no idea where we were and I was certain that Mexico was not going to be a place they would look. I worried about the kids and if they were out searching for me. My sister would be support for my mom and dad but I still worried about her and them. I thought again about that safe place I called home. No longer would it be that for me. Jim had found a way to come in and completely erase all securities for me. What should have been a place for me to relax in would now be a memory of bad things. I wondered if I would ever find a place to call home again.

People asked me so many questions after I was taken away from Jim. There was concern but there was also wonderment as to why I had not tried to escape from Jim. Were there moments that I was left alone that I could have used to get away? Did I try to call anyone or notify authorities of the abduction? All very fair questions and thoughts that I may have had myself if I was outside, looking in. It is always easiest to toss doubts and questions out when it is not you that is in the situation.

I guess it might be a little bit like the game shows you see on television. You sit in your easy chair, watching the contestants trying to guess a word or answer some question. The answers all seem so easy from where you sit. You shout out the answer long before the contestant gets it. You are amazed that they didn't see the answer sooner. You shake your head and say to someone "I need to go on that show. I could win some big money." If you find yourself on that show, suddenly, you are the one that someone is yelling out the answer to from their recliner. Being put on the spot or having questions thrown your way from people that did not just experience what you have endured leaves you wishing there were simple answers to their questions.

No, I did not try to get away. I could give you a million reasons why I did not make an attempt to get away. They all make as much sense as the questions do. I can also answer the question with a question for those that asked me why. Where exactly was I supposed to go? How was I going to explain to whoever I might bump into that I was being held against my will? Fear was still my constant companion. The fact that I was in a country that I did not speak their language was for me a huge barrier. Trying to explain to someone what was happening that might not understand my words made little sense to me.

As I said before, I did anything to not provoke Jim. I imagined suddenly bursting out with "I am being held captive by this man beside me. Please help me." I also immediately thought about the possibility that the person would have no clue as to what I was saying. What I would have been left with was a very pissed off Jim and the damage that would certainly come with my doing that. I was going to have to pay for such an action and I wanted to live. Being in a foreign country left me extremely vulnerable and open to anything Jim chose to do to me. Jim could easily kill me and leave my body hidden somewhere. It could take a long time to be found and then what? Would they pursue anything in Mexico or would I just become another statistic? These are just a few of the thoughts that went through my mind each day.

I won't say that it wasn't Hell for me. It was that and more while I was being held against my will. I dealt with the abduction in the very best way I thought I needed to. I kept to my faith and hopes that perhaps we might achieve the goal we did in fact achieve in the end. I guess that one of the things that stayed with me was my thoughts of God. I knew there was a higher being than me and that eventually, he would help me out of this bad situation. The end may have been reached only by grace and God's helpful hand, but I stayed alive until it did happen. That was my number one priority the entire time we were in Mexico. It was a learned action for me after the 30+ years of Jim's cruel treatment.

I later heard that the Sheriff of Todd County had backed my words and given me hope that the rest of the people asking, would understand. His words were "battered women will do what they have to do in order to survive. In this case, Connie was taken against her will and obviously had fear inside of her. I believe she did what she had to do in order to live long enough to be rescued from her captor."

His words meant then and still mean so much to me. I had no idea what Jim had in his mind when he took me. I wonder today if Jim even really knew. I don't think he really had a plan when it all started. I can't tell you why he chose to go to Mexico. I think it was more of an afterthought for him. Once he had taken me from my apartment, I think that every movement was ad-libbed.

I share my story with you because I believe that it is important to convey to you the multitude of fear and pain suffered by battered people. I say people because whether it is women or children or men, they are not as alone as they may feel. I know the feelings they live with each and every single day. I feel their fear and I hope that something in my words will give them strength to endure. I hope someone finds the courage to seek help and free themselves of the terrible life that is domestic violence. My wish would be that not another person ever had to experience the life that I lived with Jim.

During our drive through the back roads of Mexico, Jim continued to inform me that this was where we were going to be staying. He told me that we were never going to go back to the family. He said I was not going to be working anymore and that my job was now finished. He told me that the life we had known was now over. We were never going to see our grandkids or our kids again. As he spoke, my mind kept searching for answers. I wanted to know what he had done so terrible that we had to be on the run for the rest of our lives. Why did he feel that we had to hide out forever? He never, ever once offered up an answer to any of my questions.

Jim offered no words as to what he was thinking about. I would have little bits and pieces flash back at me. I wasn't getting a full picture yet as too how exactly I got to the vehicle. Those memories were lost to me, it seemed. I could remember parts of the day before he had taken me from my home. I did have a brief thought about being taken outside of the apartment complex. Other than that, it was all a blur to me. I wanted to push more but something inside of me told me not too.

After 30 some years, you know how the person with you might react to feeling badgered or cornered. You know exactly what makes them happy and learn that the "trigger" is life itself. Here I was a passenger in his vehicle, with nowhere to run and no one to call for help. Jim got pissed at me over nothing several times while we were in Mexico. He would blame me for something that had happened or scream at me for doing something he didn't like. It was actions and words that I thought I was free of. I was sadly wrong, just as I was wrong to believe that I could let my guard down in Minnesota.

When he got angry with me in the vehicle, he would grab my hair in his fist. My hair, for some reason was wet. He would bury his fingers in my hair and then shake my head violently. He would shake it so hard that I would become dizzy and disorientated. He would smash my head against the window, over and over again. When he was finished with the torture, I would look and see his hand filled with my hair. He would literally pull handfuls of my hair right out of my head. The pain was excruciating and he knew it... and he did not care. Any one that has ever had their hair pulled, even if in playing, knows how tender and sensitive the scalp is. It hurts like Hell! My pain meant nothing to him. Why would it? After all, wasn't I the one that did something to make him angry? That was precisely what he was thinking the entire time he was hurting me.

The time spent there was strange and unpredictable. We would go from him beating me half to death to him taking me to a circus. Yes, we actually went to see a circus while we were in Mexico. Does it get stranger than that? He would use this "nice to me" time to try and sweet talk to me. He would tell me how much he loved me and hug me to him. He would tell me how we needed to make it work and that a little effort on my part wouldn't hurt. It was truly just a freaking nightmare. I could hardly believe the words he was saying to me. I thought he was as finished with our relationship as I was. I figured he knew that I was done for good. The papers had been filed for the divorce and I was ready to finalize things between him and I. I thought that by my being with David, that Jim would understand where I was concerning our life together.

David John... I didn't know what had happened to him that night. I don't know if I had even thought about him at the time. There was so much going on and trying to please Jim all the while was exhausting. Time was going by for us in Mexico but very little had been accomplished. Days turned into weeks, though I really didn't know how many had passed. It seemed like an eternity to me. I only know one thing for certain about the entire ordeal. I was ready and waiting for all of this to end with me going back to my life before Jim showed up at my apartment.

Thoughts do run through your mind and you wonder if anyone is looking for you or are you just assumed dead. I knew my family would be frantic and I worried about my parent's health. My life with Jim and all that he had put me through had been extremely hard on my mom and dad. My mother worried constantly about me and my father wanted to make Jim pay for every time he had struck me. For far too many years I fought to keep our family in one place. I gave up my life and my dignity, along with my family and friends so that the kids would have a home with both parents loving them and watching over them. I am not sure if I accomplished that for them. I don't know if they truly knew where their father and I had been in our life together.

Would the way that I was taken from my home in such an aggressive way open their eyes to the reality of it all? Was seeing my face, along with their fathers face, plastered all over the news and the news papers enough for them to understand? I prayed for their safety and I prayed for my mom and dad and my sister. I also prayed that God would send somebody to rescue me. I felt that I might actually not see the U.S. again and that my children would not hear me tell them how much I loved them ever again. What a terrible, worthless waste of pain and sorrow that would be if this was where it was all going to end for me. I wanted the pain to stop and I wanted desperately to live.

I think that one of the things that passed through my head was that after this, there would be no more secrets. Everyone in our town was going to know what had been going on for all of the years that Jim and I were together. What they might have suspected or known was no longer going to be a whisper. I thought that maybe that was not such a bad thing. Perhaps with the world knowing, I would be safe. I also thought it might be a good place to start with a clean slate. Everybody in the world would already know our darkest secrets.

I will stop here for now because I don't want to get too far ahead of what was happening back in Minnesota. There were plans being put in to play to try and locate Jim and me. These things, I was not aware of and came to know what had transpired only through friends and family and of course through the articles that were being written about the abduction. I was happy to learn that so many people had come together when they learned of my abduction.

Chapter   13

More… From Minnesota

Day one had passed by and there was little more known about the abduction than was known the day Connie went missing. Warrants were out and interviews were being done in hopes of finding her and Jim. During a search of Connie's apartment, three photos had been taken by the investigating officer and the Sherriff. A hand written letter from Jim was also taken into evidence. Jim's residence had already been gone through the day before. Two photographs of Jim and a notebook that was sitting on his table was taken.

The day of the abduction, the phone call was received from Jim stating that he had killed Connie and was going to kill himself. Police were unsure of the validity of his words and continued their search. The day after the abduction brought in new words from Jim who had called his daughter on the 20th. Their daughter called the Todd County Sherriff's Department to tell them she had heard from her father. The call had a strange tone to it and a question that left them all bewildered.

"I am fine and your mother is o.k. Did they catch the other guy, yet? I will be calling back at a later time." There was more to the conversation than she told them at that time. Why he had asked if they had caught "the other guy" was uncertain. Police did not suspect anyone else in the abduction of Connie. No second person was ever seen at the crime scene and the authorities were not looking for anyone other than Jim and Connie.

At 3:45 p.m., the daughter gave the Sherriff's department a voluntary statement regarding the phone call she had received. She was staying at her father's farm when the call came in. She stated that she answered the phone and a voice asked her what was going on. She recognized the voice as that of her father, Jim Sarff. He then told her, "This is your dad." She asked him where he was but he didn't answer the question. Instead, this was the time that he asked her if they had got the other guy. She asked him again where he was and he still did not give her an answer. Jim asked her what was going on and she told him that the police were looking for him. She told him that his face was all over the T.V.

It was quiet for a moment and she thought he hung up. Jim then told her that her mother and he were doing fine. After he told her that, he said that he would be calling later. As he was getting ready to hang up, she told him that there was a phone tap. She thought he had hung up before she finished the sentence. The police then informed the daughter that they would be setting up a tape recorder to record any other calls that came in from Jim or Connie.

Authorities were struggling to piece the events of Connie's abduction together. They contacted anyone that might have had contact with her or Jim the night prior to the incident. One of their sons was very present during the investigation and seemed to be willing to offer up as much information as he could. He spoke of the close relationship that he and his father shared. He told authorities that he and his father had spoken the night before his mother was taken. He said he and Jim had spent the better part of the day before the abduction talking about events that were approaching.

"We talked about birthdays that were about to happen. He was excited about the family getting together for my children's birthdays in the next few days. There were two birthdays and my sister is due to have a baby. We spoke of attending an NFO meeting later this week in Ames, Iowa. Dad spoke of a partnership with my brothers and me and was enthusiastic about that issue."

The son held back tears as he spoke to authorities concerning his father's mind-set that night. He saw no indication in his father's actions or his words that would have led him to think his father was planning to do anything concerning his mother. He was still intending on going to a meeting in Sauk County and a speaking engagement in Iowa. Cheery and in a very good disposition was what the son considered Jim's attitude the night before he took Connie. The son was sure that Connie had filed for divorce but that no papers had arrived yet.

"I am telling you, this was not a man that was planning any kind of abduction. He talked about the divorce and said that he wasn't going to do anything about it until he got the papers. I do not believe that my father is in any way harmful to my mother."

Court records for 30+ years indicated and actually proved that the statement made by Connie and Jim's son was most probably, untrue. The abuse that had led up to the abduction was evident throughout the six children of Connie and Jim's life. Although some of the abuse may have been hidden from the children, there had to be abuse that was seen and heard by them. Stating that his mother was not in any danger with Jim was questionable and authorities did not slow the investigation based on the son's words.

Family and friends met to discuss what they could do to aid in the search for Connie. Her immediate family did not share in Jim's sons feelings about Connie's welfare. They had seen too much abuse from Jim to believe for even a moment that Connie was safe with him. A cousin to the family had been ever present and active in the search. He checked in daily with the authorities to see where they were at. He would then relay the messages back to Connie's parents and sister. Her parents were distraught over her being taken and kept to themselves and her sister.

Many of the town's people had tied yellow ribbons throughout the town, showing their own support and concerns for Connie. They, at times, feared the worst and hoped for the best. Outside of her apartment there were yellow ribbons tied to trees and to her mailbox. Friends of Connie were coming forth to tell of the abuse that knew of. One person that knew Connie, though he did not live in Long Prairie, spoke with the investigators. Employed by a food service company, he stayed at the motel that Connie was employed by. Over a period of eighteen months, he had built up a casual acquaintance with Connie.

"I felt that I had gotten to know Connie very well. She spoke of her family more often than anything. She told me how much she loved her children and her grandchildren. I was aware of the conflict between Connie and Jim and she told me that she was afraid of him. I met him on two or three occasions when he would come by the motel. She told me that she had been abused by Jim for many years and that he was extremely possessive of her. She did not tell me of any recent abuse and Jim always seemed very appropriate when he was visiting the motel. Connie said that Jim had told her that he was in therapy for his anger issues but that she did not believe him. She spoke of distrust and told me that on more than one occasion, she was certain that Jim had been in her apartment while she was working.

Connie was a good person and she liked her job at the print shop. She very much valued her friendships. She did tell me that at Thanksgiving, she was with David. Jim found out and became very angry. He apparently called David John and had gone to see him also. She did not give me the details of that particular meeting. Connie was very much afraid for her safety and friends had encouraged her to get a restraining order. She made the statement that she had just found friends and now, Jim was chasing them all away from her.

Another witness stated that she had been sleeping in her apartment when a loud noise woke her. She said it sounded as if someone were falling down stairs. "It was not the falling as if you were bouncing off the walls. It was more like something thumping down the steps, one at a time." When the sound reached the bottom of the steps, whoever it was would have been directly outside of her door. She said that she did not hear anyone coming down the stairs after that. About five minutes went by without any sound; no noise and no talking. She then heard a tapping sound that happened four or five times. She did not know what the sound actually was. "It sounded like a hand hitting the side of a pant leg."

She spoke of hearing someone speak outside the door. She thought that the voice said "sick 'em, Dog." It was for certain a male voice which was followed by a dragging sound. About two minutes went by when she heard someone come back inside and go up the stairs. The person then came back downstairs and left the building. She tried to wake the person in the apartment with her but got no response. When asked if she ever went outside or called 911, she said she did neither. She also stated that she heard no car doors slamming or car engines starting.

She was asked if she knew Connie and she wanted to know if she drove a green car. When told that Connie did drive a green car, the woman said that she had seen Connie coming and going on the day before she was taken. The woman indentified Connie from photographs shown to her by the investigator. She could not say that she had seen Jim, after being shown some photos of Jim. She said that she didn't think she had ever seen him before.

The town, devastated by what had happened, had no idea that another tragedy had occurred. This was a sad incident that would leave the town even deeper in sorrow and devastation. While the searches continued and people fought to process and understand what had happened, in the quietness of an apartment... a life was lost. Though at first, passed off as totally unrelated to Connie's disappearance, this death was no doubt partly brought on by Jim's decision to take Connie away.

~~~~~~~~~~~

In the wee hours of the morning, on February 19th, 2000, a man lay sleeping in Connie Sarff's bed. Connie's friend and lover, David John had spent the night with Connie on the night of her disappearance. Hearing the voice of Jim shouting out, he listened to Jim say "oh no you don't!" Minutes later, too late to do anything for Connie, he dialed the 911 call that would set off a search for Connie and her estranged husband, Jim. He told the operator everything he knew and explained the he believed that Connie had been taken from her apartment against her will.

On the morning of February 21st, David John apparently took a gun and killed himself. When investigators arrived, they were met by two individuals. One of them explained that they had gone to David's residence because he had failed to show up to work. Unusual for David not to show up, they became concerned. When they enter the residence, they found David dead. There was a rifle near his body.

Being aware of the association between David and Connie, the authorities quickly secured the scene and notified the crime lab from the BCA. Security was set up and the crime lab was allowed in to do their job. At the scene, a letter was found on the floor explaining his suicide and the special conditions he wanted for his final arrangements. A .250 caliber rifle was located by his side and a box of shells was also found. Several other documents were taken from his residence and the items as well as the residence were dusted for prints. David's body was removed from the residence and the home was secured. As is per normal, an autopsy was performed and it was decided that the gunshot wound was self-inflicted.

David John had taken his own life and the reasons were written in his letter. Prior to his death, David had been given a physical and blood had been discovered in his stool. Further tests revealed that David had bladder cancer. Surgery was scheduled for the 22nd of February. Co-workers said that David seemed comfortable with the news and said little about it, but a close friend of his said that she knew better. She was going to go with David to the hospital on the day of his surgery. She told investigators that David was very worried about the procedure. He didn't know how aggressive the cancer was and it scared him.

David had been plagued by tragedy before and after the cancer had been found. His uncle had died a week before the surgery. David and the uncle were very close, sharing a love for guns and railroads. A younger brother's death in '94 and a broken relationship with a girlfriend were part of his sadness. He was also not going to be able to join his National Guard colleagues on an assignment overseas because of a back ailment. He feared that the ailment might cost him his future in the Guards.

"It wasn't like the guy didn't have anything on his shoulders" a friend was quoted as saying. "There were many things that weighed on his mind."

"He would never ask for help so you just had to do it for him" said his best friend. "There was a lot of good packed in to that six foot five inch frame of his. If you met him and were privileged to be his friend, you had a friend for life."

The friend that was going to the hospital with David described him as a soft, shy person; with puppy-dog eyes that made women just love him. "He did not have a single mean bone in his body. You could not excite the guy, no matter what the circumstances were. He was always under control."

David had been married for four years and then divorced. He served in the National Guard for fourteen years, where he was well liked by all. He was the calming force behind his team in the Guards. When he was not working at his job, he was fixing up old cars or collecting music or volunteering for Honor Guard for the burial of local veterans.

David spent the night of February 18th, drinking some beers and shooting pool with friends. It was the final night out before he would have surgery. One mile down the road, Connie was attending a wedding. Sometime after 1:30 a.m., David left the VFW and headed presumably home. Along the way, he stopped at Connie's apartment, just two blocks away from his home. It was only a mere two hours later that he was making the 911 call to inform them that Connie had been abducted.

David was only one hour late to work. One hour was enough to send the two co-workers to his home. The door was unlocked and the men let themselves inside. Thinking David was just sleeping on the couch, one of the men moved closer. He grew afraid when he touched David's shoulder. He saw the blood and the rifle. At that point, "All of the life fell out of me" the friend was quoted as saying.

In the three page suicide note, David didn't mention Connie or Jim by name. He did apologize to his friends and family because he felt responsible for the deaths of two people. David believed that Connie and Jim were both dead and he took that responsibility onto himself. Friends that knew him well had no doubt that he took the entire blame for Jim taking Connie that night.

"I should have been there for her. I should have done something about it." Those were the words that he spoke to his friends following Connie's disappearance. He felt he had allowed it to happen or at least caused it to happen for being with Connie. He had no way of knowing that more than a week after he was buried next to his brother that Connie and Jim would both be found alive.

"This was a senseless thing for David to do," his ex wife told friends. "His family and friends are numb and crying for this loss."

Although the authorities had said there was no connection at all to David's death and Connie, they later recanted the statement. "Obviously, there is a possible connection or relationship to the suicide and the Sarff's but we will make no comments concerning the matter at this time."

~~~~~~~~~

Investigators were still trying to work through two separate and yet seemingly connected incidents. They were no closer to finding Connie or Jim and information concerning their where-abouts was non-existent. They had interviewed a dozen people and found very little that was worthy of being called a lead. Sheriff's department people as well as the local police department were still searching for live bodies. They had no reason to believe that Connie or Jim were dead.

Charges were filed on the 22nd of February and a warrant for Jim's arrest was issued. He was being charged with kidnapping. The complaint filed for the warrant stated that Jim had taken Connie against her will for the purpose to commit great bodily harm and/or to terrorize her. The state penalty for kidnapping is 40 years imprisonment and/or a fifty-thousand dollar fine.

Two sightings of the vehicle that Jim was driving led the authorities to believe that Jim had not left the immediate area. His vehicle had been seen in separate areas with the most recent location being Owatonna. This call in was considered to be a true sighting and authorities had dropped the notion that Jim had switched plates on the vehicle. The area was searched but no further calls were received from anyone seeing Jim or the vehicle. The search area was increased to include Iowa and Wisconsin, on the chance that Jim had in fact left the state.

The son that had been the most accommodating to the search had told the authorities that some tools were missing from the farm. A spare tire had been removed and left at the farm. He wanted to find a way to contact his father and ask him to return home with his mother. He used the media to try and appeal to his father, in some way hoping that Jim would hear his words and come home. He still believed that his mother was in no real danger from Jim. He was certain that if his father would just return that life could go back to normal for them all.

He spoke before going to the media about his father's frame of mind prior to the abduction. His father knew of the impending divorce and told his son that he would deal with it when it happened. He said that the worst part of it all was that he still loved Connie. He said that he loves her and yet she just left.

The son went on to say that it was not a clean break for his mother and father. They had gone to Alexandria, Minnesota in the days before the abduction took place. They had run some errands and stopped to have a sandwich at a fast food restaurant. From what the son could tell, everything was fine. The day before his father took his mother out of her apartment, Jim had spent an exhausting day baling hay. He then spent the evening finishing up farm chores and doing some paperwork. The son said good night to his father at about 8:30 the evening before everything happened.

Their son said that he did not know how or why the abduction took place. His father seemed very excited about everything that was coming up in the very near future. He had travel coming soon as Jim was preparing to speak with the NFO in Ames, Iowa. There were family gatherings planned in celebration of family events such as birthdays for Jim's grandchildren. It made absolutely no sense to the son why his father would ever do such a thing. He felt that after all that had happened; he needed to speak publically, asking his father to come back.

A news conference was organized for the son to speak to his father. Authorities were in total agreement, based on the knowledge that the trail was cold, in looking for Jim and Connie. Nothing had been heard from Jim since his call to his daughter. The son, teary eyed and looking worn down, spoke to the cameras. It was 3 p.m. and the Todd County Courthouse was filled with TV cameras. His message was seen by most television stations, radio stations and the newspapers in Minnesota.

"Dad or Mom, if you can hear this, and I hope that you can, after three and a half days of thoughts and prayers, we the Sarff family have decided that we would go public and ask and beg our Dad to turn himself in to whomever he feels safe so that we can, as a family, have our mother and father safe once again. We know that as a family there have been many mistakes but it is time that we put an end to this ordeal. And we again beg you to turn yourself in, please."

Jim and Connie's son made a very heart-wrenching plea to his father to turn himself in. "Dad, if you are out there driving around somewhere, please do turn yourself in. Contact us so that we can help you through this. I pray and beg for you to please come home. Let us hear from you so we know that you are ok. Or you can just come and turn yourself in and end this once and for good."

Their son's voice cracked when he began to speak of the many family things that were so close. He reiterated that he could in no way believe that this was happening. There simply was no sign and no one was looking for this to happen. With tears again running down his face he said "I have to believe that neither of them has been harmed. I've got to believe that, I really have to."

After the son spoke to the public, the Todd County Sheriff's office announced that the search had in fact been expanded. The search area would include Wisconsin and Iowa where Jim had friends and family. Unsure of his whereabouts, the search continued to be done both in the air and on the ground. The Sheriff told the public that they were continuing endlessly to try and find any leads to follow. He described the search and trying to trace Jim's calls as a "nightmare."

The days continued to pass and no further information was found. On the twenty-fourth, Jim's brother came into the police department to give a voluntary statement concerning his brother, Jim. He spoke of his family and of growing up in a very verbal and physically abusive family. He told the police that he was ten years younger than Jim and that he remembered the abuse in his home. He said that Jim and their father had an extremely verbal and physical relationship as was the violence that their mother endured throughout their growing years.

The brother stated that Jim and his father argued constantly and that the fights would more often than not, become violently physical. That same physical and mental abuse was carried over into Jim and Connie's marriage.

The brother stated that Jim was a very possessive man where Connie was concerned and that he knew of the violence that went on in Jim and Connie's home. He also said that leaving was the very best thing that Connie could have done. The brother stated that he was afraid of Jim doing something to him or his family. He was certain that Jim was capable of hurting someone badly and that he was afraid for his safety and the safety of his family and his brother. When asked if he believed that his brother was capable of actually killing Connie, he answered quickly. "Absolutely, yes!" was his answer to the question. The brother had no idea, not even a guess as to where Jim had taken Connie. He feared for her life; and his own.

A daughter was called to see if she had heard from her father again. She said that she had received no more calls from her dad or mom. She also stated that she felt that her father might show up at her residence. When asked why she felt this way she responded that it was a gut feeling and nothing more than that. The investigator took no further actions after talking with her.

Trying to cover all possible scenarios, the investigators talked to family members. There was not as much involvement as Connie's parents and sister would have like to have seen. The communications were kept to a minimum and family wasn't always sure what was happening with the investigation. Much of searches were unknown to the family at the time and none recall a walk through as a large group. They had expected to see more interactions between themselves and the authorities. Some felt as if they were being pushed back away from the investigation.

DNA was needed to confirm Connie's indemnity in the case that she was not found alive. Cotton swab samples of DNA were taken from Connie's parent's mouths. They would be used only if needed. The family was all questioned and most was recorded either on video or tape recording.

~~~~~~~~~

On February 25th, the FBI was finally called in on the investigation. The county decided they needed to outreach much further and that the FBI would be able to give them a longer "arm". The Long Prairie Police Chief said that the FBI would be working the case at the request of the Todd County authorities. The county had spent six days working through the investigation and leads were not even trickling in.

"When you add minds, it brings in additional perspectives as well as perhaps new ideas. We have asked the FBI to look at what we have done and give us their thoughts. We still speak daily with the family and are hoping that just one single memory will turn us in the right direction."

With nearly a week of time already passing, authorities said they were no closer to finding Jim and Connie than the day they began searching. Many issues complicate the investigation, leaving the police, the Sheriff's department and the FBI with zero leads. The phone calls were untraceable so no one knows where Jim might have been when he phoned his sister or his daughter. The fact that Jim hated banks and did not trust his money to them also made it hard to trace his whereabouts. With no spending trail to follow, Jim and Connie could be states away or they could be sitting somewhere, right under the authority's noses.

"We quite often use credit card or ATM uses by a person to follow their movements. With Jim not using anything electronic to pay for food or gas, it simply isn't working. There is still so much about this case that we do not know," was the Todd County Sheriff's response to questions concerning the couple.

"It has been terribly frustrating for all of us. We are aware that with each passing day, it becomes harder to locate the two of them. Our inability to find Connie or Jim is beginning to drive us a little crazy. This is a total mystery and we have to solve it very soon. The only things we know are this. Jim Sarff absolutely abducted Connie Sarff. Connie was without a doubt taken against her own will. Jim is very capable of inflicting terrible harm on Connie. The longer we search, the harder it will become to find them, alive or dead."

Chapter 14

Found In Mexico

Mexico was supposed to be a place that you went to for vacation. It was the quaint little towns and romantic music and all about a get-away place for couples in love. That is what Mexico was *supposed* to be all about. For me, it was a nightmare… it was a freaking nightmare. Everything about the drive to Mexico and crossing the border was like a horror picture. There were no romantic little café's with men in sombreros, singing to you while you dined. There was no Cantina, where the floors were dirt and the walls were made out of clay. This was a place of hell for me. I was not a visitor or tourist there; I was a prisoner.

Jim never answered me half the time when I asked him a question. He would grunt now and then as if that were all the answer I was going to receive. I was certain of only one thing as we drove around. I did not want to set the beast inside of him on fire. As long as he drove, he was relatively calm. Calm for me meant no hitting or bruising. It meant not having my head smashed into the window or the dashboard just because he decided to do so. Quiet was sanctuary to me and I knew that all too well.

We were approaching what I believe to have been the second week in Mexico. Jim drove out into the desert. This was pure desert with no ditches or ravines. It was simply desert to road as far as I could see. He suddenly stopped the vehicle and got out. I knew he was angry but for the life of me, I could not tell you why. This was nothing really new for me by this time in my life. It was just a look or a feeling that I got when Jim was in a mood. I hated those times because it was never going to be good for me.

Jim started walking away from me, out further in to the desert. I was sitting in the vehicle, watching him walk away. This was another time that I truly dreaded because I wasn't ever sure what it was that I was expected to do. Was I supposed to just stay in the car or did he expect me to get out and follow him. If I chose the wrong answer, it was going to mean a beating or worse for me. I was scared to death to ask him and he wasn't telling me anything. I decided to stay right where I was.

Strange things go through your mind after so many years of violence. There is no longer a love that wants to protect. I had no feeling of loyalty towards Jim any more. In fact, my thoughts at that very moment were anything but loyal. I sat in the vehicle, scared and cold, wishing that he would simply keep walking. I wanted Jim to walk out into the desert and never come back. I even had thoughts that maybe by luck; some wild animal would find him and eat him. I didn't care what got him or how badly it hurt. I just wanted Jim to walk until I could not see him anymore.

The words I am saying here may seem harsh and cruel to some. They may not sound like the kind of words that a wife should ever have for her husband. After all of the years I sat in pain or worked when I should not have even been out of bed; the things I thought about happening to Jim were nothing. Whatever he would have felt while being attacked by some desert creature, would have been far less than the pain he had inflicted on my body throughout our years together. Truthfully, they would have been more merciful for him. At least if the creature killed him and ate him, his pain would be over forever. I never got to realize that peace. I so wanted Jim to not ever return to the vehicle again.

   Jim walked for a while longer and then he did return to the vehicle. He kept asking what he should do or where we were to go. I still had not put things together in my head yet. I still didn't even know why we were even in Mexico. I didn't plan the trip to Mexico and I certainly did not drag myself out of my apartment at 4 a.m. I was just an unwilling passenger and I didn't know how to answer him or what he wanted me to say. I told him I didn't know if he had money. I didn't have a clue what his plan was. He never answered me but instead, he just got back into the vehicle and drove back to where we had been. There was no violence and no yelling at me this time. All I could do was silently thank God for that.

   About three or four days before we were found, we drove into a little town. We had slept in the vehicle some nights and a few nights in motels. Jim paid cash for everything while we were there. I was never totally sure where we were at in Mexico except that I know we stayed in Naco at least a couple of nights. I am fairly certain that we were in Cananea at least once. We shopped at some garage sales for clothing in Naco. Jim wanted to go further in to Mexico but there was a checkpoint in between where we were and further into Mexico. It was just a shack by the side of the road but it was manned by Mexican authorities. Jim didn't want to have any confrontations with anyone that might be looking for us.

We came to the town of Agua Prieta, Mexico from Naco. There was very little there to see. Mostly we saw little shanties with dirt floors and it appeared to be a very, very poor town. We pulled in and stopped at a park that had a school on one side of it. We got out and walked around the park before sitting for a time. Again, Jim asked me what we were going to do as if I had an answer for him now.

My mind was some place other than what we were going to do. I was looking around, trying to decide if I could escape somehow. I didn't speak the language where we were and that was a huge disadvantage for me and my getting away from Jim. I was afraid that I might approach the wrong person or that they would not understand that I was there under duress. What if they didn't have a clue as to what I was saying? Then what was I going to do because all that would be left would be Jim and I. I didn't even want to imagine Jim's rage if I said something and then was left to only him. Those fears absolutely stopped me from stepping up and saying anything to anyone.

I didn't want things worse than they already were for me. At least I knew somewhat what I could expect from Jim. I could handle him a little bit and at least knew things to offer him that would relax him for a while. I had experience with Jim where as I had no idea what the reaction from one of the locals would be. The wrong reaction could have been devastating for me.

One night we went in to a pool hall and sat and watched the night life going on there. At that time, we were sleeping in the Jeep. It mattered very little to me where I slept, as long as Jim left me alone to sleep. I was so very tired all the time and wanted to go home. The next morning, Jim attempted to start the vehicle but it would not start for us. Knowing it would take very little for Jim to get upset, I worried when the car did not start for him. The longer he messed with it, the more frustrated he became. I felt myself getting nervous because I knew what normally followed his anger or frustration.

There were honestly very few times that I was surprised by what Jim's reaction to a situation was going to be. This time, I was shocked to not feel his wrath across my face or his fingers wrapping themselves around my hair. He just looked at me and told me that we would try and cross the border into the U.S. in the morning. He said he could get some parts that he needed to fix the vehicle. The night finished without any pain and for that I was grateful.

The following morning we got up and walked to the swing gates that go from Mexico to the U.S. The border patrol was standing there when we arrived at the gate. He stopped us and asked Jim what he was doing. Jim told him that we were staying in Mexico and that our car had broke down. He told the man that he was sure he knew what he needed to fix the car. We were allowed through and went to an auto store to get the part.

I think now about the terrain that we walked across day after day. This wasn't like walking around Eagle Bend or Long Prairie. This was desert and there was little more than brush and sand or rocks to walk on. You see garbage and bones of dead animals along the sides of the roads. I later learned that the Customs people try to discourage people from visiting the area we were in because of the high drug-trafficking that goes on there. We were actually lucky that we were not approached by bad people or wild animals as we slept in the desert at night. I really do not think that Jim had made a plan to head to Mexico to hide. If he did, surely this was not the place that he had in mind. I think it was something that just came to him. None of this really matters, I suppose. We did survive for several weeks and that to me was all that was important.

Getting back to the auto store, when we arrived at the store Jim talked with a clerk inside. It was in the afternoon on Friday and Jim seemed comfortable inside this store. He was joking with the clerk and asking him if he knew any cheap mechanics around town. The clerk informed Jim that there were a lot of good, reasonable mechanics in Mexico but that didn't interest Jim in any way. I watched as Jim became a little more aggressive as was his way once he was relaxed. He insisted that the parts he bought were to be made only in the U.S. I don't think the clerk was impressed.

Jim asked the clerk right to his face if he were an American Citizen. The clerk sort of chuckled and then smiled. He told Jim that he was not a citizen and whether that was true or not, I do not know. What I do know is that I watched Jim yank his money back, smile at the man and say "then I won't be buying anything from you." We did need the part or at least thought it was the part we needed and so Jim bought it. That was the end of that visit for us. I never spoke a single word the entire time we were inside the store. We returned to the car and Jim put the part on. Of course, that wasn't the problem at all. Now he was even more upset. We had no choice but to go back across the border.

We had been seen and definitely noticed by more people that we thought at the time. As investigators began questioning the people of Agua Prieta and the surrounding area, it became clear that we stood out. We were seen eating at the Centro Café and were seen sitting in the Jeep near a park. We sat on a bench that was beside a shoe shine stand at one time or another. The man that ran the stand told authorities that we seemed very normal.

A small grocery store owner had a different view of us; or at least of me. She said that we had walked past her store several times. She didn't think much of her recollection of Jim but she did remember me. She was quoted as saying "We get a lot of tourists here but this woman was not one of those. She did not look like a tourist for sure. She was like she was looking for something. All the time I saw her, she was like she was looking around for something."

Each time that we crossed into the United States, I wanted so badly to run. I wanted to just start running as fast as I could and never look back. I didn't care what happened to Jim. I wanted my freedom and I wanted my family. Over and over, for years and years I was without my mom and dad. Years went by with barely a word spoken to my family because Jim made it a taboo. And now; now he had even separated me from the only reasons I had endure his punishments. He stripped me of the one thing that was good in my life. I wanted to talk with my children and to hear their voices again.

As you read this tale of disastrous events, take a moment and look at your children. Where-ever they are, imagine for just one moment that they have been suddenly taken from you. Now feel your heart as you hear someone tell you that they are gone forever. Listen to the words that say there is nothing to go back too. Add to that image that your parents and your siblings are also gone forever. You are being told that everything you ever loved or lived for is now only a part of your past. They are lost to you and you to them. Think about that and the emotions that well up inside of you. Your children are gone forever. It is the saddest, loneliest feeling you will ever know.

I had asked Jim every time we crossed the border if I could call my daughter. He of course absolutely would not allow it and each time it tore me apart. If you have seen your children grow into adults; seen them marry and give you grandchildren, imagine that you will never see those babies grow in to adults. You are not going to watch them play or hear them call you grandma ever again. That is exactly what Jim told me was to happen. He made it clear that my life back in Minnesota was erased and that I would not live that life ever again.

Did I want to run away from him? Did I pray each and every day that somehow I would be free of Jim? I cried for my children and grandchildren. I longed to hear my mother's voice and to see my sister smile at me. Hell yes I wanted to run but where was I supposed to run to? Was I supposed to run out in to the desert or try to tell someone that would have no clue as to what I was saying that I had been kidnapped? Where was I going to go and who was I going to tell?

The question "why didn't you try to escape" at times just makes me angry. How easy it is to sit on the side-line and toss questions out at someone. To simply assume that to escape was something that was simple is to prove that you were not the one in the situation that I was in. "Walk in my shoes?" If those people that were so flippantly tossing the questions out there had done that... they would not have even bothered to ask.

People asked me time and time again why I didn't make an effort to get away from Jim. I didn't because I didn't know how. I did not run because there was no-where to run to. I did not leave Jim's side because, though he may have been my abductor, he was also the only protection I had out in the middle of no-where. I was afraid for my life and I was tired and cold. I had been physically, violently hurt too many times and was a bit shell-shocked. How badly I want you to know how much I wanted to be free. It wasn't that simple to get away. It had never, in 30+ years, been simple to run. When I finally did run, I was left questioning if I would ever see my home again.

Where we were and the element of being alone with someone you love in a place like Mexico should have been something so special. Romance and the night life and seclusion from the world around you sound intoxicating. It should have been a place that left good memories to look back on for a lifetime. Memories were certainly embedded into my brain for a life time; not the memories of romance and fun though. Jim managed to not only make my life a living hell but to also make certain that I would remember that hell for the rest of my life.

Something else that was taken from me throughout the years of abuse was my trust in anyone. I certainly did not trust the judicial system or the authorities. Too many times I had tried to reach out for help only to watch Jim walk away nearly conviction free. When he was given time or any type of punishment, it was either "stayed" or "revoked" or he only spent a short period serving a sentence. Crossing the border as often as we did, I had no faith that the men we passed each time were going to doing anything to help me. Another reason that I did not try to get away from Jim was exactly that. After all that had transpired, why would I have any reason to trust these men? I never said a word to anyone. We walked around on the U.S. side again and came back to the vehicle. The gas did not fix the issue either and his frustration levels were peeking. My level of anxiety climbed as his frustrations got worse.

He told me that we were going to go back once more and get what would fix it. It was very cool that morning. The temperature was now in the forties because it was early morning. Jim had on a long sleeve shirt and I had on a sweatshirt we had picked up somewhere. Jim had a leather coat with him and threw it over my shoulders. My hand was hanging at my side still. I could not do anything with it and so I tucked it under the leather coat. That is how it was when we were crossing in to the U.S. that morning.

When we reached the border, the border patrol asked us where we were going. Jim told him we had bought parts for the car the previous day and that they did not work. He told him we needed to get another part to get the car running. The man looked at me and asked me if I had a weapon under my coat. The way that I had to carry myself and cover my arm drew attention to me. It was totally unintentional and not something Jim or I even thought about. He asked me to take my arm out from under the coat and I couldn't. Whatever Jim had done to my arm and neck had left me with a useless arm and hand.

After staring at me, the man stepped forward a little. He asked me for my identification, which I did not have, obviously. I told him I had no I.D. with me so he asked me my name. I told him who I was and then he asked Jim for his I.D. Jim had no choice but to give it to the man. The guy ran it through his computer and it came up that there was a warrant out for his arrest. The warrant said he was wanted for kidnapping.

Two border guards suddenly showed up and the female grabbed me. She pulled my hands behind my back and the man put Jim's hands behind his back and led us into a holding cell. I felt like some hardened criminal that had just been apprehended. Each of us was put in to our own cell. I will tell you that holding cells are not very comfortable places at all. There is a bench and a toilet in the corner. It is strictly for keeping someone until arrangements can be made to move the person. There are no pillows or blankets or any of the comforts of home. I was tired and worn down and we had been sleeping in the car and I was sore. With everything that had gone on and not knowing what was wrong with me physically, I was physically and emotionally empty.

On March 4th, 2000, just outside the little town of Agua Prieta, Mexico, we were found. Strangely and perhaps a bit poetic, the town's name means Plaza Luck. It was across that border, in Douglas, Arizona that my freedom arrived. Maybe I should call it rescued but at the time, with handcuffs on, it didn't feel much like I was free. After being placed in the holding cell, I felt more like the criminal than the victim. I just wanted to know what was happening and still worried about retribution from Jim if they released us.

I wasn't sure exactly how to feel and was scared as much as I was relieved. A room or a cell or a box; it would have mattered very little to me at that time where they put me. All I knew at that time was that I was not going back to Mexico with Jim. That was at least my hope. For a moment, I really was free from Jim and his clutches.

After I was placed in my cell, I heard a knocking on the wall beside me. I looked at the wall and said out loud, "what the heck?" I heard Jim's voice coming through the wall. He said to me "Connie, what are we going to do now?" My only response to him was "I don't know." That was the last that I spoke to him. At that point, the events of the trip and all that had happened hit me hard. I laid down on the stainless steel slab and fell asleep after talking to Jim.

After spending two fear filled weeks in Mexico, wondering what each minute would bring my way, I thought about home. I thought about whether I would ever go back to my family, my friends, my kids or my grandkids. I wondered what had really happened because I could only remember bits and pieces since that early Saturday morning on February 19th. I was so terribly confused, as if I was in someone else's nightmare. How could all that they were telling me really have happened?

Back in the cell, we had been held there for what seemed like forever. After a time, {I don't know how long as time had stopped meaning anything to me} they took Jim out of the holding cell and placed him in the county jail. By this time, Jim had already asked for a lawyer and was not open to be interviewed. The next thing I knew, the FBI was there and wanted to interview me. I remember being so very tired and wanting just to leave. They were as kind as they could be but my emotions were running high.

I listened as they informed me that I had been "allegedly" abducted and that I had been missing for two weeks. I began to cry and was trying to take all that they were saying into my brain. It wasn't going so well. They asked me if I thought Jim had any medication with him. I told them that he had a bottle of an over the counter sleep-aide with him. Jim had mentioned the pills to me earlier in the week. I am certain that he had put some of them in the drink that he gave me and that is what knocked me back out again the night of the abduction. He gave that to me two times and the second time left me without any memory of what happened after I drank it. The interview was almost un-ending for me.

Authorities took me out and asked that I verify for them that the vehicle they were holding was the one we were in. They must have towed it from Mexico because I know it was not running when we left it. I told them it was Jim's vehicle and that we had slept in it many nights.

After the FBI and the police had finished with their interviews, I had a feeling that I still didn't have the whole story. People were being evasive and telling me they couldn't share with me until I had given my entire account of what happened. They didn't want to influence my recollection of what had transpired. They didn't seem to understand that my recollection was not good and they had little o worry about concerning my memory.

I was transferred to a woman's shelter in Sierra Vista, Arizona. I stopped at a hospital first because of the numbness in my arm and hand. A Special Agent spoke with me just before I went into the hospital. He asked me if I had been sexually assaulted by Jim at anytime during the two weeks I was gone. I wasn't sure how I was supposed to answer that question. Jim did not so much force himself on me but I was nervous; and actually, I was scared to death. I told the man that I had consented to having sex with Jim out of fear. I did not want to face any consequences that might have followed me saying no to Jim.

I also had red scaling skin on my feet and I was hyperventilating and weak from all that had happened to me. I remember thinking that I was having a heart attack. It was now believed to be an anxiety attack. The doctors looked at my hand and were at a loss as to what was causing me to not be able to use it. My fingers were purple and red and it hurt very badly. They pretty much just told me I would live and then, without knowing the issue, they were releasing me. The officials also were afraid that I had been having a heart attack. It was for certain just anxiety. An hour later I left the hospital with my arm in a sling and no diagnosis on my feet. It turned out to be frostbite but I guess a doctor in Arizona wasn't familiar with the signs.

At the shelter, I wanted to just collapse. I was exhausted but still needed to fill out a little paperwork. I did the minimum and then showered. I found some night wear and went to bed. I thought I would sleep like a baby but I was still very anxious. Sleep was very intermittent at best and Sunday morning couldn't come soon enough for me.

On that Sunday morning, about 11 a.m., a deputy from my home county in Minnesota and a man from the Minnesota BCA came back to talk to me. I was glad to see them because I knew that they were my ride back to my home. That was really all I wanted to do, was to go home. I did not realize what I had ahead of me that Sunday before I could go home. I didn't know that it would be another day before I could really leave this nightmare behind me.

The officers began the interview by telling me I would be audio and video taped. They wanted me to tell my story exactly as I remembered it all from the day I was kidnapped to present time. I shook my head and cried. Two weeks of my life was gone, to never be reclaimed. I remembered only about a third of what had actually happened to me. The facts that I would learn upon my return home would be more over whelming than I could have ever imagined.

It was not until later that evening, when the interview was nearly over that the officers informed me that David had died. The circumstances that surrounded his death took the breath out of me. I was already drained from the two week ordeal, the capture/rescue, the hospital, a restless night and the grueling interview. I was reliving and trying to remember the events of the past two weeks and missing my family. That seemed like enough already to me but it wasn't finished yet.

Suddenly I am being told that someone I looked forward to seeing again; a man that had befriended me and taken me with all of my baggage, was gone forever. I was over-run by the guilt and sadness for his family and friends. I felt sad for myself and the loss of a man that listened to me and never once judged me. He was my dear friend and I grieved deeply for that loss.

The next news shared with me that night was that I would not be going home yet. The officers needed to interview Jim first. My heart sunk and it was once again because of the man that had started all of this. It was just one more reason to want to be as far away from him as I could be and to be home again.

Although many people were brought in to continue the investigation, there were never any true leads to where Jim and I had gone too. Family had continued to gather in different houses and when my family drove down highways, they now searched the fields they passed. I had tried so many times to contact my kids or my sister but Jim was not going to allow that to happen. Without contact, the family had no way of knowing whether we were dead or alive. Jim always appeared worried that someone might be looking for us. Of course someone was looking for us! He had taken me from my home and dragged me across the United States. Did he think when he took me that people were not going to look for me?

Our being found was the biggest news to hit Douglas, Arizona since a gang of Satan worshippers had been caught there a few years back. Although at the time of our apprehension the man that found out who we were never showed it, he was ecstatic. He stayed very professional and said that he was happy we had been found alive. A colleague of his later told the press that he had been very excited about the event. A female guard told him "Way to go, my friend. You may have just saved that lady's life." The truth is… he truly might have done just that.

Chapter 15

The return home

A concerned people's thoughts

After our return, people talked of how they worried and searched for us. Some thought we were dead and others refused to believe anything except that we were alive somewhere. No one ever thought of Mexico and the investigation never reached out that far. If not for the warrants and my bum arm, I don't honestly know what would have actually happened to me. I do think about it from time to time. I wonder if he would have tired of the run and simply ended it for both of us. Would we have kept moving further in to Mexico until we had nowhere else to go?

I received a letter from a woman that had been involved in the call concerning the abduction. She remembered thinking about how very cold it had been the morning Jim took me. She thought about how scared I must have been and how the cold must have felt to me. Truthfully, I don't really recall a lot of that morning. Most of what I "remember" comes from words I have heard from others. It is a good feeling knowing that people's thoughts were with me the entire time that I was missing.

The woman that wrote me said she had been in training at the time the call came in. The woman training her was a very patient, well seasoned dispatcher. The trainee had told her trainer of the call that she had just received. She said the caller had gotten disconnected the first time. She began a search of the number that had called. During that time, the caller had redialed and explained who was missing. The caller was of course David John. She remembered how terribly helpless she felt and that she could sense panic taking her over. The trainer remained totally calm and gathered the needed information from David.

Here, in her own words she said "So many feelings came over me. I wondered who could do such a thing to anyone. What could I do to help this woman? And then the address hit me hard. Oh my God, this was directly across from my house. I panicked and called my roommate and told her to look outside the window. I asked her to monitor any activities she might see. She also worked for the Sheriff's Department so it was all very legal. I could let her know what was happening. As the details of the crime scene came in, I was engulfed in sorrow and worry. I wondered where she could be and who took her and why? I wondered if she were dead or alive. I said a prayer to assist me in helping this woman who so desperately needed help. We were briefed by the Sheriff and told that it could go either way. The woman could be dead already or was alive and needed to be found. Weeks went by and neither the department nor the FBI had any leads. I prayed every night for this woman who had been taken against her will. I prayed that she would be given the strength to endure whatever was happening.

I do recall when the message came in that she had been found alive and was now safe. What a feeling of relief washed over me at the news. I was thankful that prayers had been answered and could not help but think what an amazing woman she must be. Her family filled the lobby, waiting for any word concerning her being found. I know her personally now and I was very right in saying that she was an amazing person. She had so much strength and that strength brought her home. Connie Sarff is an example to all that have endured life's extremely hard and cruel times."

It is letters just like this one that allow me to know that people were out there, praying and searching and doing all that they could to find me. My family and friends listened every day to hear if I had been found. Never did they believe that I was dead. Jim had left no trail and had taken me to a place that no one would think of. I think back now and am amazed at how easily Jim and I crossed in between the United States and Mexico. We were free to come and go as we pleased. If not for the arm, who knows what would have happened in the end.

I know that as the details of our life became public, my children learned things that I had tried to shield them from throughout their lives. I didn't want them to grow up thinking of their father as a monster. I wanted them to have the life that all the other kids they knew and grew up with had. It was terribly hard on the entire family and I know this to be true. Our "dirty little secrets" hitting the front page of every newspaper they picked up left them bewildered and uncertain what to say or do. The entire world knowing wasn't the issue. It was the fact that the people that knew myself and Jim and our children, knew. It was the up close and personal that was going to affect our daily lives. Hard as it was, I hoped with all of my heart that it might help them understand in some way why I left Jim.

I read the words of my children and it leaves me extremely bewildered and at times, saddened. I don't know who believes and who doesn't although some have not been shy in letting me know that answer. I struggle to process the fact that my children grew up in the same house that Jim and I lived in and yet... some still look away from me. The denial that I lived for the length of our marriage is the same that some of my children bear. To be able to "pretend" that none of the abuse happened is beyond my own comprehension. A kidney no longer in my body and scars that will never completely fade, are the reality of what was endured for my children's sake. What I did, I had to do if I was to give them a life as close to normal as normal could be applied to concerning Jim and my relationship.

When we were found, there was a great relief for my family and all those that were following our saga. People were elated and sighs of thankfulness were breathed, I am certain. But some of my children only wanted life to "get back to normal." I feel some days that they would have liked to have swept it all under a rug and to just move on. I understand, I do truly understand their want and desire to have this all go away. It is not going to go away, ever. The events that landed me in the hospital so many times are real and they will be real for a life time. To imagine them away or believe that they did not happen is something I find impossible for me or my children to do. They are grown and have minds of their own. I cannot force them to believe nor would I ever do that.

I was quoted as saying "Everybody knows all of our dark secrets now. Maybe we can start over with a clean slate." I wonder today if the slate can be cleaned and as for the start over; I am unsure where my children were then or are today concerning that statement. I guess I will leave that decision up to them.

The time spent in Mexico was at times frightening. I didn't know most of the time what Jim was thinking. I was unsure what it is he wanted of me. I did what I was told and that seemed to keep him at bay for the most part. It was a matter of survival for me and the actions were all focused on exactly that; surviving the ride. Sometimes, what we love and cherish out-weighs the pain we suffer to keep them. I felt my family was the most important part of my life. I still believe that but it in no way condones what Jim did to me.

From this point, the story will be told by me and the author. The newspapers kept a close vigil on what was happening to Jim and me. People talked a lot about my return but there was very little talk about Jim. There was great relief at us being found and especially the fact that I was still alive. The authorities tried to treat me as well as they could. They needed to talk with the FBI to find exactly what the details of the warrant were.

Funny, I look back at where we had been and think how ironic. We had just spent two weeks surrounded by the very people that Jim so often criticized. He condemned people that were trying to get into the United States through illegal entrance. The truth is that the only difference between them and us was that we were going in the opposite direction. While they were risking everything they had to get in to the U.S., Jim was doing his damnedest to get in to Mexico. Our jeep was still sitting right where it had broken down, a few feet away from the border until authorities towed it to the U.S. side.

While we were in Mexico, I did little to try and blend in with the local people. I wore shorts and a tank top. I also sported a baseball cap which no woman wore in Mexico. It was also still winter so to see a woman wearing shorts when it was barely fifty degrees outside sort of made me stand out. Later I was to learn that when authorities spoke with some of the locals and showed them my picture, they would smile and nod. They called me the lady with the shorts and hat. They told authorities that they had seen me many times, always with a man beside me. The man was obviously Jim and they recognized Jim's photo as well as mine.

The reports had reached Minnesota and they now knew that we had been found and were alive and safe. My sister called right away and wanted to come to me but they told her no. They did not want to expose me to what had been going on there or to too much of the abduction yet. My daughter also called and though she was 9 months pregnant at that time, she wanted to come to Arizona also. She too was told that she could not come to me. I was told that the people from Todd County, meaning the authorities, were not coming down to me until Sunday. They actually took a flight out to where I was, almost immediately after they were notified I had been found.

I will follow with more of what happened to me in Arizona when the details of what was going on in Minnesota after we were captured are told by news reports and me.

~~~~~~~

{At approximately 10 a.m. on Saturday, March 4th of 2000, the authorities received a call from the Douglas, Arizona Police Department. They were told that Arizona had Jim and Connie Sarff in custody. They informed the Todd County Police Department that Connie was well and safe and that she would be moved to a shelter. Todd County confirmed the warrant for Jim and asked Arizona to hold him until they could get to them. They also confirmed that she was not a willing participant and that she should be treated as such. The Sheriff was told they were not sure how Jim had kept her against her will. She appeared to be in good shape except for a slight hand injury. It was not known yet, the extent of her total injuries.}

One hour later, a cousin that had been the speaking connection between Connie's family and the authorities, was notified that Connie and Jim had been found alive. He was told that she was in good health and was being held in Arizona until the right authorities could get to her. He immediately called Connie's parents, who were staying in St. Cloud with Connie's sister.

"This was exactly what we all were praying would happen. Sadly for others, they do not always have a happy ending. I just told the family that they found Connie and Jim and that they were both well and alive. I could hear Connie's mother screaming with excitement in the background. They were all very excited and very glad to have her back." The family all gathered at the cousins home to await further news about Connie.

There were many excited comments being made concerning Connie being safe. Jim's brother said aloud, "Praise God" when he heard the news. Cousins of Jim's actually drove to his brother's house in Eagle Bend to give him the news. "I just want to see Connie and Jim in the flesh, that's all I want right now. They are both alright; a little worse for wear perhaps but they are alive." The brother had tried to reconcile with Jim after not speaking to him for more than three years.

Connie's father spoke briefly about their feelings concerning Connie being found and possibly coming home soon. "We are relieved but apprehensive about the days that are to come. We are still very concerned for her safety. Jim is still not put away and that worries me. It has been a very rough two weeks and we know that many people, thousands of them, have been praying for her. I have not spoken to my daughter yet. I do know that she is worried about everyone except for herself. There are people that have a family member abducted and never seen again. We are very grateful and thankful for her return."

There were some people that still feared the wrath of James Sarff. He had left a lasting impression on those that had encountered him along the way. Although there were neighbors and acquaintances that viewed him as a youth leader and farmers friend, none called him pal or buddy. When asked what their thoughts were, a few agreed to speak only if their names were not mentioned. There was still then and at present time, fear of retaliation from Jim.

A co-worker of Connie's that spoke on the condition of anonymity said "She didn't want the farm; she didn't want any of it. All she wanted was a chance to make a clean break. I didn't know of the abuse until it was outlined in the news after the two had vanished. I had no idea what she had endured. She is the sweetest, kindest person you could know. She always put people before herself. When I see her again, I am going to squeeze her."

A battered woman's advocate also commented on the finding of Connie and Jim. "Regardless of what Connie Sarff wants to do, I do hope that prosecutors pursue all charges against Jim Sarff. I am certain that Connie did what she felt she had to do to survive long enough to be rescued during her 15 days in Mexico. When a woman is in danger, survival instincts kick in. She will find herself doing whatever she must to keep from being murdered. Connie Sarff is one of the very lucky ones to have survived."

Church services on Sunday, where Connie and Jim were members for many years, revolved mostly around Jim and Connie. The Parishioner spoke of the elated feelings that they had been found alive."Now, things will have to take their course. There are things to be righted. We will pray that they both will turn their lives over to the lord and let him take control."

Part of that day's service at the small country church was to include a baby dedication of one of Jim and Connie's grand children. The media didn't want to miss a single chance to write about what was the biggest news for miles around. The Parishioner asked reporters and photographers to leave before the services began. He told them that the Sarff children felt the dedication was something private and didn't feel it needed to be filmed.

Jim's brother said that he believed that the children were becoming overwhelmed by the media coverage that the case had drawn. He said that he and his wife had spent the better part of Sunday discussing the events of the past two weeks. He said they were still trying to absorb it all.

Both towns, Eagle Bend and Long Prairie, went out and placed yellow ribbons all over the towns once again. They wanted Connie to see how much they had missed her. Jim's brother went out and gathered all of the ribbons and placed them all around his house, just outside of Eagle Bend.

"Connie and Jim are going to see now how much we wanted to see them back and how much we love them," said one of Jim's brothers. He said that the outpouring of sympathy from friends and neighbors had been essential in helping the families of the missing couple get through the ordeal. "Words would never convey how thankful and blessed we are to be surrounded by the people in this country," the brother said. He had witnessed the effects of violence between Jim and Connie and acknowledged a wide range of emotions with them being found.

"It is impossible to deny what has happened. I assume that Jim will not be around for a while. As a family, we have to talk to each other, support each other and be strong for one another. Our entire family has an enormous amount of healing to get through. We are looking forward to seeing them both. I feel very sad for the children as they are the ones that are truly feeling the impact of all that has happened. It has been so rough on all of them. There are many elements and dynamics that have made this more difficult. I am just anticipating all of this can be worked out and that we can get back to at least some semblance of a normal life."

The brother, who had not spoken to Jim for nearly three years, said that he did try to reconcile with his brother recently. He wanted to be supportive of his brother and of the children.

"I have searched my heart and my soul to find the strength to support Jim in whatever way I can. I believe inside of me that I have found that strength. Every family has something they would just as soon not talk about and not dwell on. It just so happens that my family is in that very situation now. Our lives and family have been brought into the light so much more than we would have wanted it to be. We are a very proud and passionate family and sometimes that can work for you or against you. I can only hope that Jim gets the help that he needs."

He spoke openly from his heart concerning the issues surrounding domestic violence.

"My wife and I both hope that this case can be used to highlight the need for more attention to the existence and problems of domestic violence in rural Minnesota. Domestic violence is something that no one wants to talk about. It is something that everyone knows everything about and yet, they never say a word about it."

The brother continued to speak, his heart filled with every emotion imaginable. "I was raised in this community and have spent most of my life here. I always knew the community had good people in it. My family wouldn't have settled here if they had not liked it so much.

It took me a while to go downtown after Jim and Connie had disappeared. When I did, I was relieved at the outpouring of support and genuine caring. After living here for so many years and facing a crisis of this magnitude, it truly showed me what wonderful people we were surrounded by. It also showed me that the people understood that what one person does is not always a reflection of the entire family. Despite the ordeal and all of the things that have been brought to the public's awareness, I really can't imagine living anywhere else but here."

The brother wanted people to know how much their actions meant to him and his family. "A simple thank you will never feel like enough. The entire community has touched our hearts. We now really know what having a church family is really about. The past two weeks have been a stream of prayers for Connie and Jim's safe return. My wife says it shows what the power of prayer can do.

One thing is for certain about this ordeal; there has to be a constructive outcome to it all. Some kind of good has to be brought forth and right now, we are searching for a way to turn it into something positive. There is a real need to bring more attention to domestic violence in the rural areas."

The brother said that he and his wife planned to contact the legislators to ask for more money to be allocated for educating the public about domestic violence. He also wanted to see more funds that could be used towards creating more shelters and crisis centers in the farming community. He said the need for safe houses and better communications was a "must have."

"Out in the middle of no-man's land, things go on that go unseen or if they are seen, nobody says a word. Violence and horrible abuse goes on each and every day and yet we have turned a deaf ear to it all. If they are seen, they are looked on by eyes that pretend to be blind. That is why women feel they have nowhere to go and no place to hide from the abuse. They need to know there is a place that they can go to and find safety."

As news of our discovery circulated in Long Prairie, residents were expressing their surprise as well as their relief. They wanted answers to what had really happened to me. They were curious as to what the next steps were to be now that we had been found. One co-worker of mine said that she didn't want to think anything, one way or the other. "I just kept hoping that they were alright. I think that honestly, many people thought that she was gone forever.

What a wonderful surprise to find she is alive and unharmed."

~~~~~~~~~~

On March 5th, Jim asked to speak with the agents that had flown to Mexico. They met with Jim and read him his Miranda Warning. He said that he fully understood all of his rights and then agreed to give the agents a statement. Later, during the trial, it would be debated as to whether the statement was admissible. Jim did not have a lawyer present at the time of the statement but has asked to talk with authorities anyways. His answers to the questioning were extremely vague. He insisted that no wrong was done and that all that happened was consensual. He gave contradicting stories concerning the abduction itself.

"I thought that she was dead and so I took her to my car."

"Connie came with me voluntarily and without refusal."

The two statements absolutely contradict each other, leaving authorities to be wary of Jim's words. You can't have a "willing" person and think that they are dead at the same time. It doesn't work that way. Eye witnesses had already stated that Connie was definitely not a willing participant and that she was struggling to get away from Jim on the landing of her apartment hallway. Drag marks through the snow also said she had not gone willingly. Jim was already confusing his stories, making his statement questionable at best.

"After I placed her in the vehicle and began driving, I saw her move. That is when I realized that she was alive. At that point, I pulled off the road and held her."

In Jim's statement, without his attorney present, he began to tell the Todd County Investigators and the Bureau of Criminal Apprehension {BCA} a little more about the early morning events that led to the alleged abduction. His lawyer did try to get the statements tossed out but it was ruled that Jim had shown an open willingness and desire to discuss the investigation. That was before the main trial.

Jim told them that he had gone to Connie's apartment only after he had received a call from someone that he could not identify. Again, Jim told of events that there was no way to verify. He said that his wife, who was living in an apartment in Long Prairie, had gone to a wedding on the night in question. He drove to her apartment and then walked upstairs to her door. When nobody answered, he pushed the door open and stepped inside.

The fact that he knew where she had been and when she came home confirmed what Connie had told friends. She was being stalked, her every move monitored by her soon to be ex-husband. The divorce papers would arrive at his farm a day after he took Connie.

Jim said that he saw Connie standing in front of him and she was naked. He said that he asked her what she was doing and that she told him she was sleeping with some guy. {This was also later disputed by Connie who said no such words came from her mouth.} Jim said that he knew that the man was David John, the same man that would, two days later, take his own life. He knew him to be a co-worker of Connie's that she had gone out with several times.

Jim told authorities that Connie was very, very mad that he was standing in her apartment. He said that they began to struggle when he tried to get into her bedroom. He said he remembered Connie pushing on his chest and him telling her he would never lay a hand on her. {Connie also claimed that he was lying about that too.}

For reasons unknown, there were parts of Jim's answers that were deleted from the transcripts. He did say that he remembered getting up from the bottom of the steps, with Connie on top of him and trying to lift her back upstairs. He did not want to just leave her there that way.

Because his car was right outside, he said he and Connie went to the car where they then drove to the hospital. He turned away from the hospital because he saw police cars. He panicked and drove directly to the nearest highway and just kept driving. At some point, he phoned his sister to tell her what had happened. The two of them decided to drive south because it was warmer. In saying that neither of them had a real plan, he again mixed up his story. He had already said that he thought she was dead.

Jim said that he had spoken with David John once at David's house and then again at a local bar. Jim said he seemed to be a nice guy and a gentleman. He felt that they had come to an understanding that worked for both of them. He didn't feel the need to pursue the issue any further. In learning of David's death, Jim did comment about what happened.

"There was no reason at all for that to happen," referring to David's death. "I feel sorry for him and for his family. It is sad but I have lost everything... I have lost everything."

The charges that were filed against Jim were Federal interstate kidnapping. He would remain in the Cochise County jail in Bisbee, Arizona until he could be arraigned and transferred back to Minnesota. He was denied bail as the court felt he was a flight risk. If the convictions stood as kidnapping and crossing into another country, Jim could have received a sentence of Life in prison. The charge of interstate domestic violence carried a sentence of up to 20 years in prison.

Jim would waive the extradition rights and return to Minnesota. He made no formal statement during his 10-minute hearing at a District Court in Tucson, Arizona, other than to acknowledge a question from the U.S. Magistrate. He spoke very briefly with his attorney. U.S. Marshalls would be assigned to bring Jim back to Minnesota within a week. It was expected that he would be held in the Twin Cities, where he would be arraigned on Federal Kidnapping charges. The felony kidnapping normally carries a maximum penalty of 40 years in prison and/or a $50,000.00 fine.

When the Sherriff was asked his thoughts on the penalties, he did not hesitate to answer. "I hope that Jim gets the maximum allowable penalty. The evidence and Connie's testimony could result in even more charges being filed. With the FBI being involved in the case, they should file federal charges against Jim. Although I do hope to see him given the stiffest sentence, our first priority right now is to ensure the safety of Connie Sarff. We all had assumed the very worst but every day we continued the search for Connie. We looked for any shred of hope that she would be found and continued our search. Evidence was simply not coming to us. We were searching for two people that was not even in the Country anymore. Nothing we saw gave us any reason to believe that Jim Sarff had fled the Country."

The Sherriff went on to say that he wanted to get Connie and her family reunited as soon as it was possible. Paperwork was filled out and arrangements were made to fly back to Minnesota with Connie. She had been seen by the local hospital and was waiting at a women's shelter in Sierra Vista, Arizona.

One of Connie and Jim's sons had spoken with Jim and said that his father seemed… "o.k." He also made a comment concerning the media coverage and the stories that had been becoming much publicized. It was neither an admission nor a denial to the articles. It was however a statement that left one leaning towards the stories being more fact than fiction.

"What happened twenty years ago, happened twenty years ago and we can't change that. It will be nice when all of this is just old news." Many people were surprised by the words spoken by a son of Connie's. The lines were being drawn and the distance between siblings was taking shape amongst her family. No one would be more shocked or shattered than Connie herself to read those words.

Time would pass and years would go by for everyone involved. As for the "old news", the scars and the pain that Jim inflicted on Connie would never be "old news" to her. The fear that one day he would be free and may not have been finished was not ever going to be "old news." Connie endured a lifetime of domestic violence for the love and sake of her children. That also was never, ever going to be just "old news."

On March 6th of 2000, Connie Sarff, accompanied by Federal agents and the Sheriff's department, boarded a plane that would take her back to her home and back to Minnesota. She would leave behind the desert and the man that had, for 30+ years, made her life a living Hell. There would be trials to attend and people to see. She would relive her ordeal over and over again for family and the media. She would have pieces to pick up and a friend to silently say goodbye too. How she would return to life as it once had been was still unknown to her. She would cross that bridge when she reached it. There were more uncertainties than there were solid ideas. The only thing that everyone could count as a truth; Connie Sarff's life had been changed once again, forever.

Chapter 16

Back home

On Monday, March 6th, authorities picked me up and off to the airport we went. As I boarded the plane, all I could think of to do was to thank God because I was alive and I was going home. Though in some ways the flight felt like forever, the flight actually went fast for me and we landed at the airport in Minneapolis. I wanted to do so many things, like see the kids and family but I was still very drawn down from everything. Time went by quickly and yesterday was gone; giving way for the tomorrow to finds its way to me.

Tuesday, March 7th, 2000 was probably just another day to a billion people. It was a day like any other day with people hustling off to work and then rushing back home to their families. The afternoon and evening, on that very day, was anything but "just another day" for me. It was a bit of a fourth of July as far as my life was concerned. That day, a long time ago and yet just yesterday at times, was the time that I stepped off of a plane in Minnesota. Scared and unsure, I was not certain how I would face the media and all of the questions that were sure to come. I only knew that for that moment, all I wanted was to disappear someplace quiet and away from the onslaught of cameras.

I was escorted through the airport with a deputy on one of my arms and a BCA agent on the other arm. They wisped me through the airport where the cameras were flashing in my eyes, making it that much harder to see where I was going. There were reporters shoving their microphones in my face, screaming questions that I was not going to answer. Every one of the reporters wanted the "Scoop" and wanted their paper to be the first to tell about my arrival.

Strange as it may seem, my mind wandered for a moment as I stared into the crowd. I knew for certain what I was seeing, and even more so, I knew what I was not seeing in the crowd of unfamiliar faces. I saw no faces of my family anywhere in the crowd of people. There was no family waving or screaming as I walked past the people gathering all around us. I knew that we were meeting at a private place to try and avoid the media frenzy and yet… When I look back now, I wonder what the media and the television audience thought when they saw no family there to meet me. I could almost see the headlines reading "No family at the airport for Connie Sarff."

I did learn later that the authorities had asked my family not to meet me at the airport. They wanted to get me through the airport as quickly as possible. They knew the media would be relentless in their quest for the scoop on the story of Jim and I.

I was taken by the BCA and the Todd County Sherriff to an undisclosed place where I could gather my thoughts. I asked that the place not even be revealed to my family right away. I wanted so badly to see them all. I wanted to hug my children and hold them close to me. I wanted to hear their voices and look into the faces I thought that I might never hear or see again. I had stayed alive because I loved them and I wanted to live to see them.

Freedom takes on an entirely new meaning when it has been taken from you. I look around the world today and I see people fighting for their freedom. Whether it is freedom from tyranny or bondage or just life itself, freedom is a word that becomes something cherished once you lose it for a time. I fully understand those that wish to have the right to make their own decisions. I can easily relate to people desiring to walk where they want and say what they want to say without fear of retribution.

For 30+ years, those things had been taken away from me. My choices to go where I wanted or see who I wished to see were not mine. All that I did had been dictated to me, and in a not so very nice way, by Jim. Stepping off of that plane, feeling the ground under my feet; not looking back and seeing Jim watching my every move, was freedom for me. I needed to rest and I needed some time to think but I also needed to be back with my family again.

Family was anxious to be reunited with me and there was much to be said by so many well-wishers. A lot of what was said I would read about or hear from the news and my family. My cousin, who had been instrumental in keeping the family informed of any news, told the media that I had been taken to a "protected site" until I was ready to meet with family and talk.

"She wants some space and that is very understandable. Connie has spoken to her sister and to one of Connie's daughters. She plans to contact the rest of the family when she is ready to talk. For now, she just needs time to rest and get her thoughts together."

I was driven to Monticello, which was the "secret meeting place" for me to meet with my family. Two of my daughters and a son in law picked me up and brought me back to Todd County. As the evening came, a couple of my other children came by to see me. It didn't take long to see that a division in the family had already been established. Some of the kids had already chosen to support their dad while others would support me. This was just the beginning of a new trauma that our family would now face. Even after all of these have gone by, we still live with that same separation.

For a few days after coming home, most of my time was spent going to doctor appointments and interviews with law enforcement. The doctors wanted to determine what had really resulted physically for me from this assault and abduction. What they found would play an important part in the trial.

The Long Prairie Police Chief had scheduled a time to talk with me and set up a question and answer type video. I was still not a fan of the authorities and any trust in them was at its lowest. For far too many years I had suffered and then watched Jim walk away unscarred by his actions. Telling me that he was "locked up" held very little value to me. I had been there and done that once before also.

I think back to that time and another thing both saddens me and confuses me at times. I think that I was still in the "protect and defend Jim" mode at that time. I was too uncertain and distrusting to believe that when the dust settled, I would not find myself staring into Jim's face. I believed that I would be left alone to deal with the anger that was certainly going to be his. Of all the things that I had done, or not done, as was often the case; this was one that would leave him brewing and scheming. In my mind, he was still sitting somewhere trying to think of ways to punish me for betraying him.

I still felt very alone and vulnerable, even being surrounded by FBI agents and sheriffs and BCA authorities. It wasn't the then and now that I was scared of. It was the time, after all of the authorities were not at my side that scared the Hell out of me. Every time that the door opened, I wondered if Jim were standing on the other side, waiting to pounce on me like an angry tiger.

There was still a lot of talking going on in the town. People were glad to know I was safe and that I had returned home. Our son had spoken to Jim on Sunday and told the media that Jim was concerned about some birthdays that he had missed. That thought pattern told me that he was already moving on. He was catching up on the family matters and the media coverage. I don't know now, nor did I back "then", understand how his mind worked. Jim simply dealt with whatever came his way. He took it as life and moved on and never looked back. Well, he never looked back unless it was to use the past against someone.

The verbal abuse that I was given by him and the violent rages that ripped my body inside and out were to Jim, just a part of life. I don't think he ever took the time to look back and see that what he had done was wrong. I don't think that Jim ever really felt like he was doing something he shouldn't do to me. He did what he did and then he went on to the next task at hand.

There was talk about having a homecoming party for me when I was out of the women's shelter. I was not really up to that and though it was great to be back, celebrating was the furthest thing from my mind. My cousin had been speaking to the newspapers again. He had told them that there was concern as to what was going to happen to me from this point.

"We certainly are hoping that Jim will get the help that he so desperately needs. We also hope that Connie can pull her family back together and focus on getting back to a "normal" life." My cousin was so good about everything that was going on and I appreciated all that he had done throughout the difficult times..

My sister had been collecting some of the more than 100 clippings from the different newspaper articles that had been written. She wanted me to know for sure how much support I had while I was gone. The family had been good about keeping the writings about the abduction. Now, they were doing something they weren't always certain was going to be possible. They were collecting articles about my safe return to Minnesota. It was by grace that they were able to collect articles that told of me returning instead of coverage that I had been found dead. That was always a possibility and a true fear for my entire family.

I found myself falling back into the role of a reassuring mother to my children. I wanted them to know that I was alright and would be seeing them soon. It was important to me to try and put some of their fears to rest. Of course they were concerned with their father's well-being also. That was understandable and I tried to stay as neutral on him as

I could. He was after-all still their father and I had to respect that. I let them all know that I was fine and to not sit and worry.

The medical examination that I had in Arizona had revealed very little. I was going to see more doctors as soon as I could. I knew there were problems beyond a scrape or bruise that was causing the problem with my arm and hand. Whatever had happened to my arm and hand was not going to simply go away on its own. That much I was certain of already. It would not be until later that I would find that Jim had definitely caused the injury to my arm. It would be argued in court as to what had exactly happened to cause the arm to be so badly injured. The hospital in Arizona had said that the arm did not appear to be of any serious nature. They were very mistaken.

The family had spoken again to the media. They had vowed to make sure that Jim was punished for making my life a thirty year nightmare. There was one major difference between a nightmare and what had happened to me over the many years with Jim. In a nightmare, you are sleeping and have the chance to wake and have the nightmare dissipate into the air. Once awake, the nightmare becomes simply an element of your dreams. What I lived through was done with my eyes wide open. I felt every push and shove and kick and hair-pulling. I was very aware of what was happening to me and the pain was extremely real.

The family said that they were prepared for a long legal battle. I wasn't sure if I would be able to stay strong enough to face what was coming. I was going to need the support of all my family if I was to make it through the trial that was to come. Friends and family were busy collecting money from good-hearted people that wanted to help me. Offers to stay with cousins and friends were plentiful. I was appreciative for all that people were doing for me. It felt good to know that there was so much support. People were ready and more than willing to do whatever it took to make my return to the community as smooth as possible. I was not the only one that wanted to see all of it finished and behind us. The community and family knew however that there was still a trial to happen and the answer to everyone's question to be heard.

I remember when some questions were presented to me during the interview that I had a hard time focusing. I was still afraid that my answers might be heard by Jim and I didn't want to be hurt anymore. I told the interviewer that Jim and I did talk while I was in Mexico. There were definitely tense moments for me. Sometimes he would threaten my life and then right after that, he would become sweet and try to get me to reconcile.

The question, on more than one occasion, was asked as to whether I was actually kept against my will or if I had just gone along with Jim. The Sheriff kindly jump in and answered that question for me. He told them that I had done what was needed to survive.

I told the media that Jim had made sure that I was fed and clothed. I really didn't know what all to say. It had been Hell and I had no problems telling the media that it had been. I was worried about the kids and knew that they were living in fear of repercussions from other people because of what had happened. I just wanted to leave the last two weeks behind me. My only real thought was that I was hoping that it was all over for good. I didn't believe that so much but I wanted too.

My return to Minnesota was laced with fear and a yearning to find peace. There was a news conference scheduled on the 7th of March. I had a prepared statement that I read to the media and the public.

"First of all, I would like to thank all of the people that have kept me in their thoughts and prayers over the past few weeks. Our family has been through an ordeal that unfortunately happened and now we must move forward with our lives. My children and I had gathered together last evening {March 6, 2000} and shared and discussed the past happenings and our future. I told them I am willing to share my ordeal in hopes that it may never happen to another woman and to put to rest a lot of rumors."

My memory is unclear about some of the night that I was abducted. I know that he came to my apartment and I know that he forced me to go to Mexico. I do not have any idea why we went to Mexico or what his real plans were for us. During my time in Mexico, Jim was both threatening and trying to reconcile at the same time. I did what I felt I needed to do to survive long enough to be found. I felt very much like a captive and did not know where to turn for help. The ordeal can only be described as "Hell." He did provide me with food and clothing and shelter while we were in Mexico."

I felt totally stupid and humiliated after the news conference was finished. There were so many questions and the media was relentless in their pursuit of a good story. For me, all I wanted to do was to find a hole and crawl inside it to hide.

After a week or so of hearing what had actually happened at home the night of the abduction, I felt totally overwhelmed once again. The stories were horrifying and the fact that I remembered so little was discouraging to me. My cousin came and offered to help me remove the rest of my things from the apartment. I was not going to stay in the place that the incident had begun in. I also met with more of my family members for the first time since the abduction.

I needed help to get around because I was not allowed to drive for the first 30 days after my return home. There were more interviews and questions as well as doctor appointments that never seemed to end. I was experiencing dizzy spells and vision issues when I got back to Minnesota. The fact that I could not drive was more of an inconvenience than anything for me. I guess maybe it was more than that in a way. It was a freedom I had fought hard to win and another "privilege" that the abduction had stripped from me. It felt like a step backwards for me.

My family is still split today and I don't know that we will ever recuperate from all that came from the abduction, the stories and the laundering of our entire life. We had stood naked before the entire world and it hurt the family in so many ways. Having everything that had transpired over the 30+ years with Jim explode nationally was like leaving our front door wide open. None of us wanted that to happen and I certainly didn't ask for any of it to happen.

I think now about how many lives were affected because of one man's selfish desire to have what he wanted. Come Hell or the high waters and with no care or concern for the consequences that would follow, Jim stole me away from my home and ran. The suffering would be felt then as much as it is still felt today. Those that suffered then and now are the kids and grandkids and my mother and father and sister and friends. I wonder just how far out the sorrow and suffering reaches.

Chapter 17

"Talking with investigator Terry Bandemer"

James Sarff, accused of kidnapping his estranged wife from her apartment on February 19th, 2000 went before a U.S. District Court in Arizona. Arrested and held in Arizona since March 4th, 2000, James Sarff was charged with assaulting and kidnapping his wife, Connie Sarff. He was also charged with interstate domestic violence and causing severe bodily harm to another person or persons.

Jim waived his right to extraditing and returned to Minnesota to stand trial in a Federal court. Jim pleaded not guilty to all counts set forth against him. He stood by his statement that Connie had willingly gone with him to Mexico, where they planned to start a new life. He denied choking her and causing her to have a stroke. Jim claims that never, during their time in Mexico, did he inflict any type of injury on her.

Jim was returned to Minnesota shortly after the hearing in Tucson, Arizona. He was to face further charges in a Federal Court room. He held fast to his plea of not guilty, believing that he had done no wrong. The facts, stacked high with evidence that was un-deniable, clearly showed that Jim had gone into Connie's apartment in the early hours of February 19th, 2000 and dragged her, naked and unconscious to his vehicle. Witnesses and family would tell of the domestic violence that Connie endured throughout the couple's life together.

Their trek across state and country lines would be well documented and repeated over and over inside and outside of the court room. Hundreds of news articles would be written and people from Eagle Bend and Long Prairie, Minnesota would hear tales about a man they lived beside, sat beside in church and sometimes, even called friend. From Minnesota to Mexico; from Mexico to Arizona and finally, after 16 days in the desert, a return to Minnesota, where it all started 30+ years ago, the trial would open their lives up to the public.

"Skeletons" in a closet is something that every family has. Some of them are stories of secret romances while others are kept hidden for deeper, darker reasons. The "skeletons" that were inside the Sarff home were not always as hidden as the family may have thought or wished for. Stories came out, after the fact that leaves one wondering why Connie was made to live out her marriage in such a horribly abusive way. Things were seen by people passing by their farm that simply were ignored.

"I remember seeing her being chased though a field by Jim. He had something in his hand and was pursuing her. I continued to drive and hoped that she would be alright."

"My father would tell me not to speak with the lady on the farm. He would tell me to just go out there, do what I had to do and leave. He was concerned that I might have a confrontation with Jim Sarff. I did what I was told to do."

"Of course we talked about it… everyone talked about the things that were going on at their farm. We spoke about it in hushed places and lowered voices. We kept it inside of our homes or in small groups of people. No-one wanted to be on the bad side of Jim. I think sometimes, we spoke in private because we didn't want our words to cause issues for Connie. I guess… well, I know; we should have stood up for her and notified someone in a position to help her. In some ways, not only did the system fail Connie Sarff… we as a community also failed her."

Statements such as these give cause to sit and ponder why nothing was ever said. Why was this woman left to live in a survival mode, not unlike that of a prisoner in an unfriendly country? Connie was once referred to as exactly that by a judge, after walking into a court room during the trials. The judge, having viewed Connie's video interview described what Connie reminder her of as she looked down at the frail image of a broken woman. She spoke to Jim so that he understood where her thoughts were.

"On a certain level, I can relate to and try to understand the rage and the violence that went into the offense itself on the night that the abduction occurred. Much harder for me to try and fathom and analyze in sentencing is the ongoing and the prolonging of the pain and the humiliation that took place in the days following, when much to your surprise, I guess, you discovered that she was alive.

It certainly did not take a doctor or a medical professional to see that there was neurological damage to the victim. Clearly on the video tape, the inability to use an arm and the appearance of the victim from my viewing seemed all to similar to tapes that I have seen of prisoners of war coming out of difficult situations. I think that those are the sort of factors which mean that this sentence in this case must appropriately be a sentence in excess of the guideline factors."

The judge went on to tell of the sentencing and what Jim could expect. She saw the trauma that was in Connie's eyes and related to it. The justice system seemed to be, after a lifetime had gone by for Connie, on her side. It was a system that for Connie Sarff, held very little substance or trust for her. She had seen the system leave her alone to defend herself, while Jim was free to do whatever he took the notion to do to her. She was only alive to see the trial and to witness Jim being given a punishment for what he had done to her because she was a survivor. She took his violent rages and suffered in silence because she loved her children and wanted to give them love and a life. She stayed to be certain that their lives would be as near normal as was possible, given the Domestic violence that was alive and constant in their home.

Months went by waiting for a trial date to be set. Jim had appeared in court and was held over without bond. The judge felt that his leaving the U.S. and fleeing to Mexico made him a flight risk. There were delays and reschedules and appeals and of course, Jim asking for certain things to be omitted from the hearing.

The testimony given by Jim to the FBI and Sheriff in Arizona was ruled inadmissible because he did not have a lawyer present. He and his lawyers moved to have evidence found in the vehicle also tossed out. The judge ruled against that motion saying that none of Jim's rights had been violated during the search. Proper papers for the warrant search were presented and the judge found it to be a legal search. Hairs and semen and blood were collected during the search and used for identification later.

It was on April 11th that Jim was arraigned in a U.S. District Court in Minneapolis. He was then ordered to be held over for trial and his bond was again denied. Connie Sarff was not present at the arraignment however several of the couple's sons were present. There were also several other relatives and friends there. Jim's attorney told the media that they were there to support his client and to ask that he be released before the trial. That motion was denied without any further pleading by the family.

A federal grand jury indicted Jim on one count of kidnapping and one count of interstate domestic violence. Jim pleaded not guilty to both charges adding that he thought the entire trial would be a sham. His innocence and Connie's willingness to go to Mexico with him was what his plea was based on. He would wait until August, nearly five months after he was arrested and held in Arizona on a warrant for the trial to begin.

The jury was being selected just days before the trial was to begin. A pool of sixty-five people was brought in the first day. Twenty-four of them were excused for various reasons. Though the reasons for their dismissal wasn't all clear, fourteen of those sent home said they had personal knowledge of domestic violence, abuse or similar issues within families and/or close acquaintances. Four others that were excused reported knowledge of media coverage and two had watched the news and coverage of Jim and Connie and also were too familiar with abuse. More potential jurors were interviewed before the final selections were made.

Eight men and six women were seated as jurors on August 22nd in the federal trial against Jim. They would hear testimonies from doctors and friends and family, as well as from the FBI and Sheriff's department. Eye witnesses would tell their tale and lawyers would argue facts back and forth. It would be left to the jury of fourteen men and women from all walks of life, to determine what was true and what were lies. They would listen and ask questions and deliberate, in an effort to see that the guidelines were followed and whether James Sarff would spend the rest of his life in prison. Sorting the words of those that testified would be the first task at hand for the jurors.

~~~~~~~~~~~

Terry Bandemer, one of the main investigators in the Sarff saga, agreed to speak with me about the case. He was extremely involved in the case and came to become a friend of mine. He has since moved away and told me in the interview that he was quite happy being away from Long Prairie. He has always wondered if Jim would come back one day to make good on threats that were made.

As stated earlier in this story, no one was beyond Jim's threats or his intimidation. He felt he had the right to stare down, harass, strike or hurt anyone he chose. States attorneys, my attorney as well as law enforcement were open game to him. Terry said that his life was always in the "ready" mode. For Jim to suddenly show up and try to cause harm to those involved in the trial, including Terry, was not something that was inconceivable. Jim being released from prison was going to opened two doors. The door to his cell had been opened and the door to anyone that had ever caused Jim distress.

While speaking in an interview with Terry Bandemer, one of the main investigators involved in the abduction issues, he spoke of the first time I walked into the courtroom. He talked about many aspects of the case with me. He also had no objections to his name being used in this novel. I thank him for all of his support throughout the entire ordeal. Below is part of the interview with him.

"When you walked in to the courtroom, the judge was taken back a bit. Your appearance surprised her and she commented on it. She said that the video she saw of you reminded her of a refugee from a POW camp. I think the most noticeable reaction in the courtroom was Jim's. I remember seeing his face go ashen colored and he slumped in his chair a little. He suddenly appeared nervous and moved around in his seat. When the judge said to you "you poor, poor thing," I think that Jim knew he had problems now. I, myself, was thrilled to hear her say those words. I wanted justice for you and hoped that this would be your time.

In law enforcement, they teach us to not take any case personal. It makes it hard to be un-biased if you allow yourself to go to deeply in to a case. I will tell you that this one... I took very personal. I wanted to find you and I wanted to find you alive. I would not rest until we had you, one way or the other. Obviously I was praying for the outcome to be finding you alive. That of course did happen which made for a very nice celebration.

There was a problem within the family as the procedures were on-going. The siblings were split and I was a little astonished by that. Again, trying to remain not prejudiced in any way, I didn't speak my thoughts at that time. I will say that I wondered how and why any of the kids would lean towards Jim. It was in a sense, saying that your story didn't connect with some of them. I think there was still a great deal of denial going on with them. Those that did side with Jim did not like me at all. They might have rather seen me not exist at all.

I wasn't offended in any way as I understood what they were at least trying to do. Kids are going to protect their mom and they are going to protect their dad. This is seen even with children that have been physically abused by a parent. They will still try to protect the abuser and even lie concerning their being abusive. Your kids wanted to protect you both but a few weren't sure they could do that and so they chose sides.

It did make the case more difficult because there was conflict amongst the kids. There were disagreements and ill feelings in the family. We did work our way through it all but it was for certain… a struggle at times. It left us as investigators unsure if we were getting the right information. The questions being asked were very important and we needed as much cooperation as we could get. We did the best that we could with what we had to work with. We only wanted what was right and just for your sake.

Going back to the abduction, two days after Jim had taken you; another shake up for the town came. The call for me to David John's residence left the town in fear, more so than they already were. Many of the people thought Jim had already killed you and now, they had another death in the town. There was a panic that ran through the town and lasted until it was determined that David had committed suicide. People were scared that Jim was on a killing spree. There were many in the town that knew they had pissed Jim off in one way or another. They had the thought that maybe Jim was going to go down a list of persons that had angered him or disagreed with him.

When you take a little town and you toss in something as huge as a kidnapping with the chance that there was murder involved and then you add another sudden death, it sets the stage for a frightened town that sits on the edge of their seats. It was as if the town was just waiting for another body, another death to tell them that Jim was in fact out for revenge or vengeance. Finding a way to curb that fear and reassure a town that no one was on a hit list was not easy. Hell, we weren't even sure ourselves at that point. Tough to settle a crowd about something you yourself aren't even certain of.

Once the verdict came in as to how David had died, things calmed a bit. I don't know if the proper way to say it is, relief, because certainly no one was alright with David John's death. I only know that it did help to relax some of the fears in town. Your abduction was still top billing in the town and people wanted to know where you were.

I do remember our flight back to Minnesota from Arizona. We had some issues with the plane and were unable to take off. There were storms all around and the turbulence was horrible. We did arrive safely and I drove you to your daughters and we were still not sure what was happening with your family. It was very hard to let you go because I didn't want anything to happen to you. You had already seen enough, not just in Mexico but throughout your life with Jim. Trying to sort through all of the rumors and truths was a nightmare. All the while, my first priority was your safety and well-being.

Jim was arraigned in April and then during the Minnesota state fair, the trial was underway. The trial was five days but they had planned on it being two weeks long. It was good that the trial was a federal case because it left more options as far as testimony. In state court I would have been restricted as to how I spoke and answered questions. I testified for all of the officers and needed that freedom to be able to say "he said" or "she said" when telling about the investigation. I can't even tell you how many hours I testified but I do know I was called back in several times to verify other testimony.

Of course, some of the evidence was not allowed in the trial. The statement that Jim had given to me in Arizona was ruled inadmissible in court. He didn't have a lawyer present, even though he had agreed to speak to me. He had already asked for an attorney and therefore no statement should have been given or taken. Of course, we were willing to take his statement in hopes that later it would be allowed in court.

Trying to interview you was a little difficult. You had already had a stroke and it had affected some of your memory. You did speak of the coldness when you woke in the Jeep. You told me and the FBI agent that you were also thirsty and that Jim had given you a drink of something. You believed that there was something in the drink that made you go back to sleep. We did do a tox-screen but the results were negative for signs of any chemicals in your system. It was probably out of your system by that time.

You had asked Jim later where the clothes had come from that you were wearing. He had taken you completely naked from the apartment; that much we did know for sure. He told you that he had stopped at a Wal-Mart to get you some clothes. Jim did not have a lot of money with him at the time, but he could get you food and clothing. He fed you very little and I remember when we gave you some soup, you said that it was the best soup you had ever had. That did make me feel good.

When the call came in concerning you being found, I had a hundred thoughts run through my head. I had dealt with Jim and the family several times in their past. Jim did know me well and strangely, if Jim were capable of liking law enforcement officers, I believe that he liked me. We did have a fairly good relationship and often times, he would specifically ask for me during issues. I sometimes wondered if he wanted me there so he could put a bullet in my head. With Jim, you really did not know what to expect.

When Jim found out that I was in Arizona, he specifically asked to speak with me. Because he had made the request to see me, it gave me a foot in the door to interview him. I went in to speak with him but he did not want to talk about anything he had done. He spoke to me of things that were totally unrelated to the abduction. He kept control of the conversation and made certain that it was really all about him. I tried to get him to talk a bit about how he ended up in Mexico with you. He was extremely vague and continued to move the conversation to his liking.

Jim was very hard to talk with as he went from subject to subject. He would talk about him and you for a moment and then suddenly switch to the weather or some totally off the wall subject. He asked a lot of questions himself. He wanted to know when he would be able to leave or when he could go back to Minnesota. I tried to explain to him that he was not going to leave or be free to go anywhere.

As it would turn out, the information I did get from Jim was tossed out. We could not use it in any form. The judge ruled on it almost immediately and so my time talking to Jim was a wash. It wasn't as if he had told me any dark secrets or a plan that he had. The information would have done little to nothing to change the outcome of the trial. What I had gathered from him though was the admission that he was with you and that you two were together in Mexico. I did tell him that he needed his attorney but he was insistent that it was alright to talk to him.

As it turned out, his statement was something that was not needed and therefore, the loss was nothing we were too concerned with. It was a little bit of the judge tossing the defense attorney a little something as if to say "here, I did this for you." The simple fact that Jim had requested an attorney made everything from that point in Arizona, for Jim and me, at least, no good for anything.

I worked hand in hand with the FBI and we tried to do everything we could to make you comfortable. It was so important to me that you were treated well. I took a very personal interest in the case and in your safety. You had seen far too much violence and pain throughout your time with Jim. Knowing him and you personally automatically added to the "up close and personal" side of the entire case.

I think one of the things that bothered me as far as the case was Jim's brother. He was a pain to work with and he was totally scared to death of Jim. He was much less concerned with you than he was with where Jim was. The brother was certain that Jim was coming for him. He constantly tried to find out if we had any idea where Jim was or what we thought Jim might do. Anything that was added to our already very full plate made the investigation that much harder.

Once the family had been notified by Connie and Jim's son, sides were taken by the kids. The son that we had spoken to briefly was one hundred percent on Jim's side. Your two youngest daughters were all about you and stood by you. The choosing sides went on throughout the trial. The kids had a rough time because choosing sides was not something they might have wanted to do but found themselves doing that anyways. You had the two youngest daughters that were absolutely with you through it all.

The split made the investigation very difficult. There were some that wanted to help as much as possible and some of the kids did not like me in any way. There was an incident after Jim had been found guilty that occurred inside an elevator. One of the sons got right in my face and I tried to be decent about it. I understood they were frustrated and confused and that emotions were running high. The tension could have been cut with a knife. I wanted to be as kind as I could be and help them in any way that I could. This "in the face" was a bit more than I felt I needed to accept from any of them.

I told this particular son that he needed to step back. I explained to him that I was on the case to try and help his mother. I wanted him to know who the victim was in this case. I also told him that if he continued to push that he would end up exactly like his father; in jail. He did back off some but each time that something happened; the one would be back in my face. It was not a great time for us or for them. We did manage to work through the issues and get through the trial. That was really all of our thought s and desires at that time. I wanted to see this all end well for you. This kidnapping case was the biggest case of my career and I wanted things right. I remember losing so much sleep and I lost about 30 pounds during the ordeal.

There was some talk concerning David John's death but it was not totally brought out. I think that there was simply too much else going on at the time to really give it as much attention as it probably should have had. Two of the sons had supposedly gone to David's home and spoke with him. They told him that it was his fault that things were happening the way that they were. Whether or not the visit had actually taken place is still in question, but there had been talk about it. That David wrote in his note that he was responsible for the deaths of you and Jim made the talk more likely.

Sometimes, I think Jim lived in his own little world and truly believed that whatever he had done was alright. He had the thought too that he could one day get you to come home. His lawyer stated that Jim told her that you were thrilled to be in Mexico. It was somewhere that you and he always wanted to go. He told of you telling him how much you loved him and wanted to make things right. He said you talked about family and love and a new life together.

Walking back through the moments of the trial, there was little doubt that Jim was going to finally pay for the violence he made a huge part of your life. Numbers from 15 to 50 years and even a possibility of life in prison were tossed around the court room. It was no longer a question of if he would pay but more a question of how much it would cost him. I stayed with you throughout the trial and hoped that the sentence would match the years of pain you endured. In my mind, it did not. He paid far too little for the 30 years that he had hurt you. I am sorry that the sentence wasn't more equal to your pain and suffering. I am sorry that you have kids that still do not understand what it was that you gave for them."

Chapter 18

My Children

After talking with Bandemer and hearing him talk of all the trial brought to the family; I could not help but think of my children. The separation of family is very possibly the worst part of a family tragedy. During hard times, your family is the ones that you lean on and look to for support. I have six children and that should have been a huge, strong support team. Bandemer spoke the truth when he said that my children had chosen sides. Knowing that you have children that have turned their face away from you during a trying time is as painful as it gets.

Jim had already taken so much from me through his control and abuse. The kids were what I needed to get through all of the madness. Imagine my heart when I learned that there were some of my children that were not going to be supportive of me. That tore my heart out then and today, after so many years, it still is something that hurts much worse than any beatings Jim ever gave to me. More precious than I can convey in words, my children were my reason to fight back.

For those women out there that wonder how important it is to get out of an abusive relationship, there is so much more to lose than what sits in front of you. What you imagine to be just a given is not always going to be. Pain subsides and physical wounds will heal as much as they can. What won't heal are the scars that are inward. How much you can endure diminishes when you realize that precious gems have been taken from you. The longer you take the abuse without seeking help to find freedom, the more chance that you will lose something much more important to you than you could ever imagine.

I have said before that I tell you my story because I hope that someone will know that they do not stand alone. I want to show you that even though it seems hopeless at times, there is a place to go and be safe. You do not have to be someone's punching bag or stress reliever. You are better than that and you do have a brain and you can survive in the "other" world. I hope that you find that my words and my freedom inspire you to take that first baby step. And I want you to know… what is at stake if you stay.

Jim had not made any efforts to contact me after we were found in Mexico. I was surprised that he did not try to sway my words concerning him and me. I also think that in part, Jim still believed that he had a strong enough hold on me that I would not talk against him. What Jim didn't realize was that although he did still have somewhat of a hold on me, I wanted free from him forever. Those wants and needs to be my own person was stronger than any hold Jim could have on me.

Jim was talking with the kids while he was detained. I fully believed that he was slowing, methodically working on the kids. He was trying to put questions in their minds so that they would be unsure if I was telling them the truth. He wanted to destroy my character and take away some, if not all of my credibility so that the kids would side with him. It was something I was fairly confident about and thought I had full control over. What a terribly sad thing to discover how very wrong I was.

The fact that I was kidnapped and drug through Mexico and nearly choked to death, didn't either seem bad enough or believable enough for some of my children. There were some that simply had to have blocked out of their minds the violence and the abuse. I had two daughters that stood by me through everything. They were my strength and my confidants through it all. I had two that absolutely believed their father had done no wrong; they stood by him at the trial and after the trial.

One of my girls that had taken my side had spoken out and told the press that she believed what I was saying was truth. She remembers Jim treating me like I was a possession and that he owned me completely. He subjected them all too verbal abuse and had no issues with calling them stupid and worthless. She described her father as moody and easily angered. She was frequently frightened for me and my safety because of the abusehad seen him inflict on me. She does not believe that her father will ever say he is sorry, nor will he ever admit that he has done anything wrong. She didn't think that her father had any idea what damage he had done to the entire family. She also described her father as very manipulative and said she is still frightened of him today.

Another of my daughters totally sided with her father. She told people that she did not believe that I had ever been physically abused. She did not believe that I had suffered any injuries from Jim while I was abducted. She even went as far as to refer to the time I was in Mexico as a "vacation." She told reporters that the entire family was devastated by a guilty verdict. She was terribly upset that her father was going to prison for something she blamed on me.

A daughter that admitted she was her father's "number one fan" and denies that he was ever abusive in any way was not going to be someone that I could ever confide in. What I said would certainly be told to the very man that I feared. The daughter went on to say that her and her siblings grew up in a very normal home. They worked hard but had a lot of fun doing so. Her father taught her the importance of working till you dropped if you wanted to succeed. She was concerned that when our divorce was final that I might get part of the farm. She claimed that she had issues with me from the time that Jim and I separated in 1977. She had no issue in telling people that I had been abusive to her and her siblings. She believed that I had been unfaithful to her father but that Jim and I had an obsessive love for each other and simply needed some counseling.

She was very angry with the media for "dragging" her family name through the mud with lies about her father. She was angered by the law enforcement for not keeping the family apprised of the situation and the investigation. Finally, she felt that her father's lawyers were daft and that they had done a very poor job in defending Jim.

I sit and re-read those words, knowing they are very harsh. I struggle to understand what took her there and how she could have got her thoughts concerning me or the abuse. My heart aches at knowing that some of my children feel the way that they do. There are things that they may not have seen but the sounds of the abuse inside and outside had to have been heard by the children. I cannot and perhaps, do not know how to describe my pain at this. I think that when your children turn on you this way that a portion of you dies.

Chapter 19

The trial excerpts

August brought with it many long awaited events. It is the time of year that brings change with its season of fall. There are leaves that begin to change color and a chill in the night air now and then. It is the ending of one season and the beginning of a new season. The long awaited harvest of a hard summer's work and cooler days are a welcome happening. Summer slowly slips away, almost unnoticed, sneaking back in for a heat wave once in a while. There is a beauty in its change as well as a sadness that is all part of the changing seasons.

The event that was to finally begin involving Connie and Jim Sarff was not unlike summer becoming fall. There was a beauty in thinking that perhaps Connie's lifelong ordeal was going to end. The trial would mark a chance for her to live a life in peace and safety. Those two things alone were going to be new for her. Long, hard summers that had come and gone were finally yielding fruit. The sadness of how everything that happened had affected her life and the lives of her family and friends were evident. There would be a bitter/sweet feeling in the air.

The trial opened with two very different sides being told. Connie had her tale to tell and Jim presented a totally opposite story. Her reasons for not trying to escape while in Mexico were very clear. The fear that swallowed her whole could not be hidden any longer. She was now a free woman and Jim was where he belonged. Connie made a statement to the courts concerning the fact that she had not tried to escape.

"I had lived with my husband long enough to know if he wants something, you are going to know it without question. If he does not want you to do something, you will know that too. To try to escape and to fail in that attempt could mean death for me. I wasn't willing to risk my life. "

Her "consensual" sex that she had with Jim in Mexico was brought under fire by the defense. She had stated in an interview that Jim had "not" raped her. She said it was a gentle time. When questioned concerning her words, she said she had meant it reminded her of a time when they were first married. She added that she did not want to be with Jim, she did not want to be away from her loved ones and she for certain did not want to ever return to Mexico. Survival was still the first priority for her.

The video tape was shown in the court room. It was one hundred percent opposite of the calmness she was showing during the trial. In the video, she cried and shook as she spoke. The tape clearly showed that she had not been willing in any way.

"Why does he hate me so much? Why can't he just stop and let me go?" She sobbed while asking these questions. The video was extremely rent with sorrow and fear and deep emotions. What she had endured throughout her life was very important and people needed to know what had transpired.

The U.S. District judge felt differently about her past. She believed that Connie's past domestic violence at the hands of her husband had happened too far back to be admissible in court. She felt that the events were too long ago and that they could prejudice the jury members. She did add that if the defense pushed further the notion that Connie should have tried to escape, then the past abuse would be allowed.

A forensic scientist was brought in to testify, concerning blood found in the hall outside of Connie's apartment. She would also remark on the blood found inside of the Jeep. She testified that the blood from both places was an exact match to Connie's DNA. The findings left very little doubt that Connie had been taken from her apartment without her consent. The evidence also showed that there was in fact forced used to remove her from her home. The blood that was gathered from the drag marks in the snow also matched Connie's DNA. This was another indication that Connie had been abducted and not a willing participant.

There was an argument as to whether Connie had suffered a stroke during the ordeal in the hallway. The defense brought out a "paid" witness who testified that there was no proof of any sort that Connie had suffered a stroke as a result of being choked. The witness went on to say that without medical proof, there was little to back the "choking" issue. The witness told the jury that an MRI would not pinpoint when the stroke or damage had occurred. He said it was more likely that Connie had suffered from a blood clot at some time and that was the cause of her arm injury and memory loss.

"Choking is not a reasonable explanation for the medical issued suffered by the patient. I have no evidence that would lead me to believe she had a stroke at any time. The sources of damages showing on the MRI have not been adequately investigated, in my opinion. "

There were many factors that left the testimony of the doctor questioned by the defense as not based on his expertise of Connie herself. The validity of the witnesses statement was shredded by the prosecutors cross examination.

He was a paid consultant by the defense and therefore was going to be biased on the stand. He was not employed by any medical facility and so he was speaking without any backing from the medical field. The man never examined nor ever met Connie in person. He knew nothing of Connie's history and was really just a regular doctor. He needed the Board certified personnel to read and interpret the MRI scans. For these reasons, his testimony failed to reach the jurors thoughts concerning what he had said.

The prosecution also brought in two physicians that testified they believed that the stroke was caused by being choked for a period longer than a minute. They testified that the stroke may have also caused the memory loss and the confusion Connie suffered during the abduction. The stroke was most likely caused by severe choking according to neurologists testifying for the prosecution.

According to the expert witnesses, the level of brain damage suffered by Connie could only have occurred if she had been choked for at least six minutes. They told the courtroom that there was little to no doubt that Connie had been choked and that she had indeed suffered a stroke during the assault.

In the transcripts, my exam after my return to Minnesota showed that doctors had found extensive bruising and my arm was still not able to move as it should. There were bruises on my forehead and signs of trauma on my body. Some of this occurred just as routine from walking and sleeping in the jeep. I had contracted a bladder infection and the doctors were going to treat that issue also.

I was under so much stress during the trial and the doctors so noted it in my files. I was seeing some progress with the movement of my hand and arm. I saw the doctor again in April and his results would be very useful in the courtroom. He found that there was a very definite change in the signals of my right arm that were consistent with a stroke. He listed strangulation as the most probable cause of the stroke. Other testing was done to rule out any other medical issues that might have caused the changes in signal. None were revealed and the cause of the stroke was left at strangulation being the cause.

I was referred to physical therapy in the hopes that most of the usage of my arm would return. I could feel a change from the therapy and felt as if things were returning to near normal. My long term memory and short term memory was coming back and left me feeling nearly where I was before the abduction. That was helpful to me and I felt that I might make it through the court proceedings.

As I had before mentioned, there were many cancellations and reset dates for the trial. Jim seemed to always have another reason to postpone the inevitable and found an excuse to delay the proceedings time after time. He was either seeking to get something tossed out or looking for a new attorney. It took us from May until August to finally get into the courtroom. What Jim was doing was so in line with the person that he was. He still needed to feel as if he were in charge of the situation. He had that "something" inside of him that caused him to try and control every single thing that touched his life. Even inside a courtroom, Jim had to be the focus of everyone's attention. Truly, he did not know how to be any other way.

The charges were laid out for all to see when the trial opened. Jim was charged with Interstate domestic violence, kidnapping, serious bodily harm and life threatening injuries to a person. The charges should have carried twenty-five to life for Jim.

An FBI agent testified at the trial that he believed Jim always knew exactly what he was doing. "His actions were not that of an unthinking beast. He was very aware of all of his actions. He stalked Connie prior to abducting her and kept her in criminal confinement for their entire marriage. He kept her from her family and her friends and even chose the people that she could associate with. I believe that Connie was not only afraid of Jim Sarff but was possibly even a little afraid of a few of her own children. She has been reluctant to talk very much as she fears that whatever she says will eventually get back to Jim. She has very little trust in the judicial system and is not convinced that Jim will actually be locked up.

The things that Jim stole from this woman might never be recovered. Besides the "brain whacking", if you can call it that, that he did to her for 30 something years, Jim made Connie the fault of every failure he experienced. Anything bad that happened, she was going to be the scapegoat. The mistakes were never going to be Jims fault and he made that clear to everyone. She was more of an ownership deal than a partner to Jim. Nothing she was going to do would ever be right or good enough for Jim."

Interestingly enough, there were still those that saw Jim as someone to stand behind even after all had been revealed to the world. There were letters of character sent to the lawyers stating that Jim was to be considered a very good man. Some of those letters left me just staring and shaking my head. One such letter is below.

"To Whom It May Concern:

We have known Jim through the NFO for many years. We have been members since 1967. Jim served as National Director for over four years and was re-elected to that position more than once. Jim was exemplary in his work for the organization. He spoke at local organizations and was a great motivator for farmers and their need to organize. His wife Connie always accompanied him when he spoke to local farmers. They appeared to work wonderfully together as a team and Connie made many supportive gestures during and after Jim spoke.

Jim was a strong advocate and showed much integrity about his proposals and his vision for farm solutions. In our opinion, Jim was a very strong, good person. He treated his wife very well whenever we spent time together with them. He gave her public affirmation at our meetings. Jim seemed very caring and sincere and we feel he is a good man that loved his wife and children very much."

I find myself amazed at the perception of whom and what Jim was by those that did not feel the fury of Jim's fists or the repercussions of his anger. They saw what Jim wanted them to see and only that. He played the part of the loving, doting husband well. Even after hearing the horror stories of what he did to me, some people, including my own children, chose to not believe.

At one point during the trial, Jim and his lawyers tried to get copies of my psychiatric counseling. They felt that they needed them as part of Jim's defense. We were well into the trial by this point and I found it hard to understand how anything could take so long. The judge was wonderful and respected my right to privacy. She informed Jim and his lawyer that there would be no records handed over to them. She told them that my privacy needed to be respected.

Another letter that was sent to the judge came from the Todd County Attorney. It was a detailed writing of Jim and my issues and of the attorneys fear for my safety as well as others. I will write in part what he had written to show that there were those that did believe my words and did know the fear and danger I felt from Jim.

Dear Judge ************,

I write this letter to you on behalf of many of the citizens of Todd County who have concerns about James Sarff, whom I understand will be sentenced by you on December 8, 2000.

I have known Jim for almost as long as the twenty-five years that I have been a prosecutor in Todd County. My first involvement with him was when I prosecuted him for simple assault with his father –in-law being the victim that resulted in a misdemeanor conviction.

Next, I was involved in the drafting of the Felony Assault complaint charging him with assaulting his wife, Connie. I did not try this case but it did end up in a felony conviction. Over the years, I have had many dealings with Mr. Sarff, for the most part with people contacting me believing that they were intimidated and bullied by him. I did prosecute a case where Mr. Sarff was the victim of an assault that resulted in a misdemeanor conviction against the person that assaulted him.

When the kidnapping of Connie took place, there were many people in this area that felt Jim might feel he had nothing to lose and come back to cause harm to those that had run-ins with him in the past. I am concerned that should Jim get a light sentence, that when he does get out, he will present himself as a danger to the community. There are many people who are concerned that he will not be rehabilitated and that he will continue to act in his already proven violent ways when he is released from prison.

When Jim was found in Mexico, there was a universal sigh of relief, first for the fact that Connie is alive, and secondly that Jim has been taken into custody. I cannot begin to count the number of contacts or calls I have received from people in our area regarding this matter, most of whom are quite fearful of Jim Sarff.

I am concerned regarding the safety of Connie Sarff and I question whether there will be sufficient protection for her once Mr. Sarff is released. It is difficult for me to describe the degree of contempt and hatred that Jim has demonstrated to others in the community. He has his own set of values and seems to delight in acting like a bully to many individuals.

So many people are afraid to speak out for fear of retribution if and when he is released from prison. When I talked with the probation officer who is doing the PSI, she indicated that she was not going to address the community concern and suggested that I send a letter to the Court, addressing that concern myself.

Given the circumstances of this case, the cruel way in which he treated his wife and his complete disregard for her, I believe that the Court should require Mr. Sarff to serve a minimum of 20 years in prison. I understand there are guidelines but I also understand that kidnapping does allow for a life sentence.

I thank you for taking the time to read this letter and ask that you do consider the community concerns for the safety of Connie Sarff and others in making your determination."

The letter truly touched me inside as I read this. To know that there were people that cared beyond just Jim getting sentenced was amazing. The fears that more than just myself had, concerning Jim did not surprise me. I spent 30+ years watching him intimidate and bully his way through life. This letter was a plea for the safety of an entire community and showed the impact that Jim's ways had on anyone's life that he touched. Many felt the same way that the Todd County attorney felt.

There were many factors and legalities that needed to be considered during the trial and before the actual sentencing. Laws that at least somewhat protected me and the millions of women affected each year by domestic abusers like Jim. The question as to whether I had been "raped" by Jim was brought into the courtroom several times. The fact that in my statement I had told the investigators that Jim had not raped me gave the defense some leverage. In my favor was a law that sets "rape" into several categories. It allows for the "consensual" sex acts to be understood as "forced" without the physical harm needing to have happened.

In the actions that I took, out of fear for my life and/or physical abuse, the law leaned towards my side. I was still at that place that I could not to say that Jim had committed certain "acts' against me. The fear that I and so many other victims have inside that their abuser will return one day to cause more harm is very real. A huge part of the reason I have dug deep and found the courage to tell my story is because of those women. There has to be the knowledge that they can survive and that their abuser will be held accountable for what they have done. Stepping out into a scary world, often feeling abandoned and alone sometimes only is achieved by the knowing that you are not alone. Having the feeling inside that there are hands to reach out to and hold on to encourages victims to take that frightening first step.

I think that I might liken seeking help to a baby's first steps. They may walk along the side of a sofa or chair, holding on tight but not letting go to gain confidence. They need the security of something to hold on to in case they fall. That baby might even let go of their safety net now and then, a bit like testing the waters. To take the first step without the safety of something to hold on to often requires that baby seeing someone they trust reaching out to them. Slowly, and a bit wobbly at first, the baby will walk, arms out-stretched to the one waiting to catch them if they fall. Step by step, putting one foot in front of the other, the baby, knowing they are not alone, will walk. Once they know that there is someone there that loves them and cares for their safety, they will walk without the need to hold a hand.

All too often, women hold on to something to try and find comfort from it. They need to know that someone is there to catch them if they fall. Like that baby, once they know they are not alone they will step forward and walk on their own. It is so important to have a support team to feel safe with and allow them to come forward and escape the horrors that is domestic violence. I felt that safety with my family and now, I step forward, and one foot in front of the other so that the millions like me will know there is an out.

They can find a safe place and that their abuser will be prosecuted and locked away.

It was a law written that helped me in the "consensual" yet still forced by my fears sex that I engaged in with Jim in Mexico. According to documents from the trial, it was the belief of the judge that I was not only abused but exploited in its nature. The definition of aggravated sexual abuse is: {whoever knowingly causes another person to engage in sexual acts by threatening or placing that person in fear they will be subjected to death, serious bodily injury or kidnapping is guilty of sexual assault.}

The definition, according to the judge, fit me perfectly. She went on to speak of the assaults and of the fact that I felt threatened by Jim. She told the courtroom that after all that I had suffered in the past and in Mexico, it was clear that I consented only to save my life. The fact that Jim had hurt me physically to the degree of losing a kidney and the use of my arm was enough for her to call what we did in Mexico, domestic violence and sexual abuse. She went on to say that the fact that he took me against my will and left the country, he also had abused me mentally. He took me to a place that I could not communicate with the people due to an interpretation barrier. All of these elements were needed for Jim to be found guilty of the charges filed against him. They also went towards his sentencing and how many years he would be given to serve.

More evidence was introduced as the trial got on its way. Two certified doctors testified that the blood and semen found in the vehicle were mine and Jim's. They left absolutely no doubts that what I had described concerning our ordeal in Mexico had actually taken place. There were photographs and diagrams for the jury to view as well as medical proof that I was abused while in Jim's "care." The blood from the drag path at the apartment was matched without question.

Another doctor, an expert in the field of psychology, law and domestic abuse, would also testify. She spoke of the control dynamics in a abusive relationship and of how the abuser could control the victim through both physical and verbal, as well as unexpressed or unspoken means. She testified that just as I had done so many times over my life, the victim will quite often learn to control themselves and act in a certain matter as a way to appease and anticipate the needs and wants of the abuser. She would also state that even if a victim is in a severe abusive relationship, if that relationship stops and then resumes, the prior dynamics of the relationship resume. Victims, such as me, use lessons learned from the past to survive.

In closing, she would one more time state that the concept of "consent" is in no way the same concerning abusive relationships and the normal relationship. A victim's conduct that might appear unusual to others would not seem strange if the content of the prior abuse were shown. There is truly nothing to set a base of start for this as each individual case is different in far too many ways.

There were so many questions to be answered during the trial. Jim objected to a lot of what was being said. He still felt that the charges against him were bogus. I do think that he truly believed in his mind that he had done no wrong. He was certain that a little time alone together would bring me back to him. There was no dealing with a mindset like his and he would stand firm on his honor.

.

Chapter 20

The trial and verdict

After 30+ years of domestic violence, one would have thought that this trial would go on for weeks and maybe even months. I guess it is safe to say that it did and it didn't. If you consider that Jim and I were found in March of 2000 and the trial was the end of August of that same year, it did go on forever. It was like a nightmare that kept re-occurring every night for six months. Every time I closed my eyes I could feel his fists and hear his voice. My body and my mind grew tired of the constant reminder that came with the darkness.

Fear inside that, even though Jim was locked behind steel bars, came rushing back out at me, was almost too much at times. Day after day and week after week, life went on all around me. The only thing that did not seem to go forward was my mind. I wanted my life back and I wanted the years that Jim had stolen from me. I felt that I had a shot at one but to get back the years that had been taken from me, there was no chance of that ever happening.

From a "happening" standpoint, Jim was convicted in 1977 of domestic assault which resulted in two things for me. Jim received a stay of sentence and I... received the blunt end of a shovel. Jim walked away virtually unscathed and I was barely able to walk. There was little justice done and I had no trust in the judicial system left in me. By the time that March of 2000 had found its way in to my life, I was worn down to a distrusting, bitter woman that spent her every day looking over her shoulder.

February 2000 is not one of the great memories I carry with me. The 19th, Jim took me naked from my apartment in Minnesota to Mexico. The 21st saw the loss of my dear friend and lover, David John. The 22nd, Jim was charged with kidnapping me and later on would be charged with interstate domestic violence under the Violence Against Women Act. March 4th, Jim and I were found crossing the border between Mexico and Arizona. August brought with it the trial and Jim's conviction. And finally in December, Jim was sentenced and remained incarcerated until June of 2013, short of the years that he was given to serve.

Jim appealed again and again anything that he could think of to try and get tossed out of the trial. He tried to get the evidence obtained from the jeep tossed out. He tried to get most of my testimony thrown out as well as anything to do with crimes from our past. Most of what Jim asked for was denied and served only to prolong the end. He wanted the video tape of my statement after being found to be tossed out. He said that it would prejudice the jury because of my emotional state during the interview.

After reviewing each of Jim's allegations of an unfair trial, the judge said that he had shown no signs of actual innocence or remorse for any of his actions. His claim that no reasonable juror would have convicted him was also tossed out by the court. He wanted the court that had convicted him to vacate the sentencing and to correct the errors they displayed. None of his motions were granted except the interview in Arizona.

He needed no help in having most of our past to be not allowed based on the fact that the incidences were too far in the past. This trial was all about domestic abuse and the long term violation of me and yet, the words domestic violence was never used in sentencing. Strange that the very thing that had brought me to where I was at that time was considered "old news."

He fought to show the court that his counsel had been faulting and that it failed to defend him in what was the best manner for Jim. He felt they lacked in the knowledge and ability to give him a proper defense. He listed 25 errors that he claimed were made by his attorney, none of which were found to be true. It was decided that the 25 reasons given by Jim did not rise to the level of undermining confidence in the result of the jury trial.

His claim that he was denied the assistance of counsel is blocked by the facts. The records showed that his trial counsel work diligently in their representation of Jim. He had not demonstrated by his "laundry list" of should haves that his attorney was unreasonable in his decisions pertaining to representation of him. He had also not showed that the outcome of the trial would have been any different had the attorney pursued each of Jim's items. All of his requests were denied.

The defense called only one witness during the five day trial that was expected to last for more than a week. Only the paid doctor took the stand for the defense. It went much faster than was thought at first and the jury only deliberated for a day and a half. I was called to testify against Jim and although it was hard, I did my best to stay focused and strong.

The stories that rushed around the courtroom could not have been more opposite. Jim had a totally different version of what happened from the apartment assault to the Mexico stay. It was for certain not the wonderful "second honeymoon" that he described it as. The fact I didn't run; the issue of my fear and injuries were questioned and I told the story as well as I could remember.

My memory was put on the stand more times than I want to count. I was aware, as was the jury that I had sustained some memory loss during the abduction. I did not remember much of the abduction itself or a lot of the road trip. I did the best that I could and saw it through to the end. That was a challenge all by itself but I did it. My time on the stand had come way back in March and I was ready to be done.

I remember the questions asked of me then. They were personal and hard sometimes to answer. When asked if all of my children were aware of the past abuse, I answered yes. I even told them that their spouses knew of some it. The questions filled my mind with memories and I wanted it all to be over. I had no idea at that time that it would be December before Jim would be sentenced. Forever can be summed up in the waiting for it all to end.

I told my story one more time to the jury. They listened carefully and I recanted for them everything I could. There really wasn't a lot to add to what had already been said

1000 times. I filled in a few blank spots and let the jury figure it out for themselves. The ruling that the past could not be told made it harder to show how much abuse I had actually lived through. I told them that the abuse was constant and painful for a large part of our life together. I explained that the physical side of the abuse had lessened over the years. The verbal assaults on my character and my intelligence never, ever ended.

Jim's attorney did try to have any mention of physical violence thrown out. He said it had nothing to do with what Jim was being charged with. He got about half of what he wanted which hurt my attorney as far as any rebuttal. It was needed to show that there was very little, if any chance that I went to Mexico of my own free will.

Jim never did testify during the trial. I think that was a smart move on the attorney's side because I think that it might have hurt more than it helped. Jim needed to be in control and questions that he didn't want asked would not have set well with him. Somewhere along the way, he would have felt cornered and as with any one, cornered means to become defensive. Jim would surely have retaliated if he felt pressured or backed against a wall.

From the verdict, I guess they read between the lines and made a decision. One of the jurors said, after the trial that she had no idea of the violence I had endured prior to the abduction. She said they were still able to put two and two together and decide on how to vote. The jury found Jim guilty of one count of kidnapping and three counts of interstate domestic violence.

Under federal domestic violence laws, any person that causes a spouse or intimate partner to cross a state line by force and in doing so intentionally causes them life-threatening bodily injury, is guilty of interstate domestic violence. The Assistant United States Attorney stated that "violent crimes against women, whether done by a husband in the home or a stranger on the street will be aggressively prosecuted under the federal law."

The crimes that Jim was found guilty of carried very stiff penalties. The maximum potential penalty that Jim was looking at was life in prison and/or a $250,000.00 fine. He also faced an additional 20 years for the bodily harm count and another 10 years for the crossing of country borders. Each had a $250,000.00 tag on it. This was the type of sentencing I was looking for and that most of the people from the surrounding area were expecting. What a shock when the judge said "15 years." Even after seeing the video and hearing the full testimony, the sentencing still came out way too lax.

The attorney did call the sentence handed down an extended sentence. "The sentence reflects the unusually cruel and degrading conduct of Connie Sarff at the hands and mouth of James Sarff. The court does recognize the impact that Sarff's actions had on the victim and the family and resulted in the 15 year sentence. The judge added that the sentence was longer than normal because of the violent and rageful behavior Sarff showed towards his wife."

"On a certain level I can understand the violence and the rage on the night of the abduction; I don't need to see it to know that it existed for Ms. Sarff. It is however much harder for me to fathom the... prolonging of the pain and humiliation that took place during the abduction. I have done what I thought was legal and right for both parties involved."

The closing arguments were heard by the judge and jurors. The defense had submitted a request for acquittal. The judge answered the request by saying that after review, she was denying any idea of an acquittal.

My attorney spoke of the two levels of enhancement for a vulnerable victim. She told of the evidence that I was particularly vulnerable to the acts of Jim in two ways. Because of the abuse that I suffered during our marriage she said I was extremely vulnerable when Jim took me to Mexico. The fact that I suffered physical injury when I was abducted and the mental injury that affected my mental facilities made me totally vulnerable and incapable of helping myself.

The stroke was a main factor in my inability to escape from Jim. Because of all the factors, I was unable to run, hide, resist Jim or call for help. These were considered "normal" means that a kidnapping victim might have at their disposal. I had none of them and was further his victim because of the language barrier that was faced in Mexico.

The evidence on the sexual exploitation was that I had testified that prior to the assault; I had ceased all sexual relations with Jim. We communicated from time to time because of the kids but never touched one another. I had filed for divorce and was ending the marriage. Only because of my safety was there intercourse in Mexico. She had shown both levels and concluded that she hoped that the court would take it all into consideration. She asked for a sentencing of 18 years plus another 20 for the additional issues that had occurred during the abduction.

Jim's attorney was then given the opportunity to speak on behalf of Jim. It was as simple as arguing every issue that was presented by my attorney. He went on to say that the sex had been totally consensual and that only my word said differently. He said Jim believed that I truly wanted to have sex with him. He felt he had done nothing wrong by engaging in a relationship with the woman he loved.

He said that just because Jim had been violent in the past did not give reason to punish him for something that he might or might not do in the future. It was fundamentally wrong and unfair to his client. He didn't add much of anything except to say that he wanted Jim to speak and show the court what a good man he really was. He asked that the court be mindful of the goodness Jim had displayed over the years, while with me.

He told the court that Jim was a person who had provided for his large family for many years under extremely difficult times. He described our life as a "hardscrabble" farm existence. He told of the love that all of our kids had for their father and that the same love was shared for Jim by his daughter-in law and his nine grand-children. His part in the NFO was very well documented and he was liked by all that knew him.

"This is a man that is looking at going... losing all he loves including his family. This is a good man that is used to coming and going as he needed to. He has taken great pride in everything he has tried to accomplish. The fact that he is self-employed and has made his way in the world makes him proud of whom he is.

Yes, he is a person that has some issues as we have heard about, but I think we must remember that he tried to go to marriage counseling and individual counseling as well. Although not all of his issues have been resolved, Mr. Sarff made an effort to make things right. That is something important to remember during sentencing."

I remember sitting in the courtroom, crying while my sister and other family members comforted me. I was fine, I think, until Jim stood to give his final statement. As much bitterness and anger I had for him, he was still the father of our children and the man I called husband for 30 + years. His words were hard to fight off and the sadness for him that I felt was terrible. It was not sadness like one feels for someone that are endeared to. It was more of a feeling that somewhere inside of Jim, he truly didn't understand that he had done terrible things to me. He felt as if everything he had done was justified by something I had done first. I think that he truly believed that.

~~~~~~~~~~

"Good morning, your Honor and the courtroom.

I didn't take long to prepare my words. My duties as an officer in the NFO, my wife normally drove to meetings while I wrote. She would tell me to just say it and to say it from my heart. I wrote this at 4 o'clock in the morning. Just be patient with me."

The judge told him he was fine and to take his time. He complained about not being used to his new glasses before he went on with his statement.

"I wish to apologize to the people… I wish to apologize to the people that are the most innocent and will be hurt the longest for my mistakes. That's the little ones, my grandchildren. I do know what grand parenting is and what it has meant to me. My father's parents lived next door to us while I was growing up on the farm and through my youth they were always there. Whether we were raiding their garden or if they were taking me fishing or stuffing me with pancakes, they were always there. My grandmother passed away before Connie and I were married in 1968 and my grandfather before our first son was born. He lives in my grandparent's home that is 106 years old, with his wife and three children.

Talking about good grandparents, my mother's illness took her away from us long ago but not before she helped to deliver our last child, our sixth child, in our home. No matter how badly she hurt, she always had a smile for the grand kids.

This year, in February, we were told that my father's illness was terminal and he would live only a year. Six months later, during the trial, my father passed away. The trial, the media, my marriage and the loss of family farms all impacted his life. The police raid on his house, I believe shortened his life. Letters I received from my sisters, his wife and my children reflect the loss that they feel. It is an early loss that I do feel responsible for.

To my children, their husbands and wives, my heart goes out to them. In the community that they live in and the people they know and the comments they hear of what I've done, I ask God every day for their share of the pain.

To my family, my sisters who have stood beside me and encouraged me and my family and farming operations on the family farm, I apologize for my shortcomings. To my fellow farmers and their organizations, in which they asked me to lead as an officer and a trustee of millions of dollars, I feel that trust was destroyed in a matter of seconds. If I have embarrassed then in any way, I am truly sorry. I fought a good fight and I kept the faith. Excuse me.

And to David John's family and his friends who lost their person way to young, I feel very much sorrow for them. The law enforcement people, the prosecutors and the judges and jury, I realize all of the time the spent and the work they did while looking for Connie and I, I am sorry to all.

But truly, last but not ever least, to my wife; I say I am truly sorry. Connie, you are my first love and my only love. You bore the children of my youth. You are my lifetime companion, my friend and my life. Thank you for that. I ask you for your forgiveness. Through this world ordeal, I have not betrayed you but I have learned that I cannot make you love me. All I can do is be someone that you can love and the rest is up to you. Some people don't care back. I know it is time to let go. Thank you."

When he was finished, I realized that he had not once admitted to doing anything to me other than love me. He had turned things back on me as he had always done. He had made me the one that did not love him back and again, I was the fault of his situation. Jim was not ever going to change and he would always be my abuser.

There is very little to add here that has not already been said somewhere in this book. The trial lasting five days was then and still is a surprise to me. I truly expected it to be dragged out like everything leading up to the trial had been. Jim had done his very best to slow down or stop the trial from commencing. He had not accomplished what he had set out to do. All that was left now was to hear the sentencing.

The judge spoke to all of us now. She told us that this crime was a very complex series of human interactions. "The community has an interest in the relationships among people and clearly the effects of this crime and the sentence go beyond your life, Mr. Sarff and beyond that of the victims even. As you have alluded to in your letter or statement to me, people suffer from the effects of this offense beyond you and the victims: your grandchildren, as you mentioned, and others that have only a tangential effect, like Mr. John.

It is my decision that the sentencing factors and how they apply to you should be dealt with in focusing upon you and the offense. I am not trying to send any messages or make this a case that's symbolic in some way beyond the facts or issues of domestic abuse, but clearly the effects of this case have had a very divisive effect on your family and the trauma that not only the crime but the sentence will be felt for many years to come."

She went on to explain the points system she used to calculate the years for sentencing. She added years per crime and then put a monetary price to the crime as well including costs for imprisonment and his supervised release when it came time.

"In lieu of the crime and its impact, I believe that an upward departure from the normal guidelines is appropriate for three separate reasons. They are designated in all guidelines as per legal sentencing. I believe that the events of 1977 and the prior relationship in a most violent and rageful nature between you and the victim do serve as a backdrop for your offenses and are appropriately considered as grounds for additional years.

Perhaps, even more applicable is the guideline that instructs that: if the conduct was unusually heinous, cruel, brutal or degrading to the victim, the court may increase the sentence above the range to reflect the nature of the conduct. It gives me examples including torture of a victim, gratuitous infliction of injury and I think particularly appropriate in this case, the prolonging of pain and humiliation.

From the video tape I saw, I know of the prolonged pain of your victim. I could clearly see the pain and humiliation that she suffered at your hands. This takes me to a place that is far outside what is called the appropriate.

James Sarff, you have been charged with kidnapping, interstate domestic violence causing serious bodily injury that was in fact life-threatening. Based on the jury's verdict of guilty on all counts, it is so considered that you are guilty and adjudged of these offenses. Therefore, it is adjudged that you are committed to the custody of the Bureau of Prisons for imprisonment for a term of 180 months. This term consists of 180 months on count one, 60 months on count two, 120 months on count three and 180 months on count four. They will all be served concurrently with a five year supervised release following the terms of these conditions."

Jim was told of the no firearms rules and no breaking any laws. He was told that he had the right to appeal and that he was also entitled to set an appeal from his sentence. He was given the right to continued counsel of a lawyer in light of his finances. The judge stood and we were dismissed. Jim was taken away by the courts officers and began serving his sentence immediately.

A few spoke on the way out of the courthouse. One person said that the case had made an impact in the cities of Long Prairie and Eagle Bend. "It's forced us to say, up here, this is happening in our communities. Maybe, it will have some family members taking a look at what they have experienced. We can no longer deny that this stuff goes on all around us, every day."

Several of the kids, sitting on the opposite side of me in the courtroom, listened to the judge's ruling. There was crying and cursing heard across the courtroom. They were of course upset with the sentence. "Life" was what one of my daughters said and it could be heard clearly by all. I still sit astonished at the reactions from some of my own kids. Unwillingly to believe and refusing to say what they know to be truth.

Chapter 21

Done...but never gone.

I read back on the words written here and still feel as if it was just a nightmare. I wish that it had been exactly that. At least with a nightmare, you wake up and it is over. But, like some nightmares we have all had, there are those that may be done, but remain always alive somewhere in the back of our minds. They show up without warning or permission to eat away at our feeling of freedom. Some of the nightmare awakens me in a start from my sleep. Vivid remembrance of those terrifying years that left me little more than a shell still dance in my head.

I can hear myself saying to the interviewers, so many years ago now: "When is it going to be over? When will he leave me alone? Why, does he hate me so much?" Those questions still haunt my thoughts and I now, thirteen years later, find myself asking them again. The event that has come to light is now very alive and scares the Hell out of me. Once again, Jim has a place in my daily thoughts. Why is he so "up close and personal" again?

All of this came back only a month or so ago. That long feared day when my ex-husband was released from prison has come. His time served, though not in its fullness, he spent the last six months in a half-way house located somewhere in Minneapolis, Minnesota. Jim had been sentenced to fifteen years for the federal kidnapping and three other federal charges of interstate domestic violence.

He served 80% of his given sentence, with 20% of his time washed away for "good behavior" during his incarceration.

In the state of Minnesota, we have a state wide agency called the Bureau of Criminal Apprehension. I spoke of the BCA many times in this book. As I understand it, even though Jim was serving the last few days of his incarceration in a federal facility, Minnesota had no responsibility until he was moved to the half-way house in Minneapolis.

At some point, when he exited the federal prison, he was interviewed by state and federal authorities. It was then that a decision was made as to whether Jim qualified, by state law, as a "predatory offender." Because in Minnesota kidnapping is a crime that can place you on a "predatory offender" level, it depends mainly on where his level was when he was released. That was going to be huge as far as what he could or could not do with his freedom.

It was determined that Jim was a level 1 offender. That means that the public is most likely not in any danger from Jim, but the victim is. It means that he would likely come after me without involving or hurting anyone else. It leaves the possibility of Jim causing further harm to me likely in the eyes of the law. Seems strange to have that "tag" and still open the cell door for him. {Comforting thought for me, right?}

Any of you that are reading this and familiar with domestic violence will probably understand that in the mind of the abuser, their victim is very often thought to be the abusers possession for life. Whether they are still married or long ago divorced, it matters very little to the abuser. They far, far too often cannot get past their need to control the victim.

What that means to me is that here I am, reliving the sense of fear that consumed and stole from me 30+ years of my life. What, if anything, is he going to do now? When can I expect it to happen to me and where will it take place? I live each day of my life now with a feeling of certainty that there will be repercussions. He most certainly blames me for his imprisonment. He still, to this day has not admitted any guilt or responsibility for anything that he ever did to me or to anyone else. His time in prison is still someone else's fault. That will always be true in his mind and I will always be the one to blame.

How does one go about their life with a cloud following them everywhere that they go? I am not sure yet of the answer to that question. I try to make my life as normal as it can be. I work as a domestic violence advocate and I am thankful for that. It gives me some time to put my own concerns for safety and for the safety of my family on the back burner. It is a time for me to live life as it should be lived.

I am not blind nor am I stupid or foolish. I have no doubt who it is that controls my actions at certain times of my daily life. It is the same man that has been there for over 30 years. I am cautious and make sure that my "radar" is on high anytime I am alone.

I feel secure in my workplace but still, I am always on the alert. My co-workers and I are a little bit like the Meerkat colonies. We watch one another and will alert the rest of the group should something seem out of place or not quite right. That is great team work and it gives me at least a little sense of peace. The building that I work in is part of the government county center and that makes it a secured building which means that most of my day, I can feel safe.

When I go from building to building, I rarely walk alone. I turn up my personal observance of my surroundings to high alert. What is it I am expecting to happen? That is the trying element in my new survival because I don't know the answer to that question. I have always told my clients to "listen to your gut" and now here I am, trying to live that same advice. If I am going to talk the talk then I really must learn to walk the walk, as they say.

I will admit that for myself, I have very little trust in the federal government to keep me informed or make me aware of any changes in my ex-husbands activities. The couple of times that I have heard from the BCA, it has been to remind me of my "victim of a crime" rights. When I try to access those rights, I am told that I don't have the right to see a picture of Jim. This is a man that I have not seen in nearly fifteen years. They tell me I don't need to know how he is or where he is. When I ask questions about Jim, surprisingly and sadly, all I get is "we have to respect the offender's rights too, Maam."

I didn't choose to be a domestic violence victim or to be kidnapped and taken to another country. Jim chose to commit those crimes and his rights seem to supersede those of the person he made a victim. That is something that is twisted and needs to be corrected for the sake and the safety of the victim's well-being.

My current husband and I have added some safety measures to our home. I will not share those measures with you as they need to remain secret for obvious reasons. I am sure you understand. There are some updates to my "safety plan" that I practice faithfully every day. I want and need to be and feel as safe as I can feel.

When Jim was released in March from the half-way house, I was finally given a recent photograph of him. It was actually four days after his arrival that I received the photo. He is living only fifteen miles from my home and lives with one of our sons. I will not even comment on that situation or the feelings I have about it. You can use your imagination to figure that out.

Have I forgiven Jim for all the pain and suffering he put me through for so many years? Did I search my soul and gather the heart to forgive him? Yes, I did find it and I do forgive him for all that he put me and our family through. Does that mean that I can forgive and forget? I will absolutely *never, ever* forget what he did to us. I cannot forget because it has changed me and who I am or might have been. It altered how I think and feel and even the way that I act now.

In a letter he had written to the court system when I applied for the Order of Protection in the fall of 2012, he said that I had the "hands of hate"; a play on the name of the organization that I work for called the "Hands of Hope

Resource Center." I have given serious thought to his words.

I now stand up for people that have or are now experience some of what I dealt with. I have taken control of my life and by me doing this; I think it is sending Jim a message. The fact that I am showing him the safety boundaries and having it all concur with the signed papers from the judge may look like hatred to him. The ability to reapply for the same protection order when this 10 year order expires and knowing that I will reapply may seem to Jim as if I am saying "You no longer have control." Again, that may in fact transfer to his mind "hate." It is not hate at all. It is me doing what I can to continue to be a survivor of the harshest form of domestic violence. I will do whatever it takes to assure that I do remain a survivor.

I know that God is looking out for me as he has always done. My faith in him remains strong and that has taken me a long ways down the path of life. Though I suffered horribly for 30+ years Jim's inhumane treatment and the kidnapping, I am alive today because of God. He has stood with me and kept me alive; allowed me to have a new life with a wonderful husband and to reunite with family stolen away from me for over twenty years.

I do pray each and every single day that God will grant me one more gift. I yearn so deeply for a time that maybe I will enjoy a healthy relationship with *all* of my children and grandchildren. That would complete me and my life.

As for Jim, I do wish him well. I hope that sometime before it is totally too late, that he can accept responsibility for the things that he has done. I pray that he will make amends and finish his life with peace in his heart. I will never be a part of his life again; at least not by my choosing. I hope that he can accept that as fact and move on with his life.

As for me and where I am on this day in August of 2013... I am surviving and living a good life. I have been a very happily married woman of 12 beautiful years with a man that loves me unconditionally. He took me, baggage and all and has loved me tenderly. He treats me with respect, allows me to be me and to communicate without being yelled at or condemned. This blessing treats my children as if they were his own by loving them, listening to their thoughts, enjoying them and laughing with them. He hurts with them whenever they hurt and gives to them the best he has to give.

My family, in the course of the last fifteen years, has seen much pain and sadness over lost relationships in our immediate family. Three of my children are involved with my husband and myself and share our church. They come to family get-togethers and holidays and functions done as a family does. There are cookouts and campouts and I also have a wonderful relationship with my grandchildren.

My children and their children have a relationship with my parents now. They know and love the grandparents that they never knew existed until they were adults. This was of course because Jim did not allow my family to be a part of our life and so they never had the chance to meet one another. His isolation was deep and took away from us so many things that we are now enjoying and sharing. Mostly, we just love one another totally.

On a much sadder note for me and their siblings, three of my children have chosen not to have a relationship with my husband and I or their siblings. We have four grandchildren that we are not allowed to see ever. We have not been allowed near them since 2000. This is by choice of their parents and/or themselves. We have learned that there is nothing we can do at this time to make it different. We do pray that one day we will have a relationship with all of them. It does leave a hole in my heart and soul and in our daily lives. A day does not go by that I do not think of them and yearn for the chance to hug each one of them.

My love for God and the faith that I have in him has carried me through the fire. I am where I am today and who I am right now because of his love and grace. For that... I am forever thankful.

Made in the USA
Middletown, DE
02 September 2022